Small Business and Entrepreneurial Development in Africa

Robert E. Hinson
Doreen Anyamesem Odame
Eric Kwame Adae • Kwame Adom
Editors

Small Business and Entrepreneurial Development in Africa

A Route to Sustained Economic Development

palgrave
macmillan

Editors
Robert E. Hinson
Ghana Communication Technology University
Accra, Ghana

University of the Free State Business School
Bloemfontein, South Africa

Eric Kwame Adae
Drake University School of Journalism and Mass Communication
Des Moines, IA, USA

Doreen Anyamesem Odame
Ghana Communication Technology University
Tesano – Accra, Ghana

Kwame Adom
School of Business
Burman University
Accra, Ghana

ISBN 978-3-031-37674-0   ISBN 978-3-031-37675-7   (eBook)
https://doi.org/10.1007/978-3-031-37675-7

© The Editor(s) (if applicable) and The Author(s), under exclusive licence to Springer Nature Switzerland AG 2023

This work is subject to copyright. All rights are solely and exclusively licensed by the Publisher, whether the whole or part of the material is concerned, specifically the rights of translation, reprinting, reuse of illustrations, recitation, broadcasting, reproduction on microfilms or in any other physical way, and transmission or information storage and retrieval, electronic adaptation, computer software, or by similar or dissimilar methodology now known or hereafter developed.

The use of general descriptive names, registered names, trademarks, service marks, etc. in this publication does not imply, even in the absence of a specific statement, that such names are exempt from the relevant protective laws and regulations and therefore free for general use.

The publisher, the authors, and the editors are safe to assume that the advice and information in this book are believed to be true and accurate at the date of publication. Neither the publisher nor the authors or the editors give a warranty, expressed or implied, with respect to the material contained herein or for any errors or omissions that may have been made. The publisher remains neutral with regard to jurisdictional claims in published maps and institutional affiliations.

This Palgrave Macmillan imprint is published by the registered company Springer Nature Switzerland AG.
The registered company address is: Gewerbestrasse 11, 6330 Cham, Switzerland

Paper in this product is recyclable.

Contents

Part I Introduction　　1

1　Introduction　　3
Robert E. Hinson, Doreen Anyamesem Odame, Eric Kwame Adae, and Kwame Adom

Part II Entrepreneurial Intentions and Customer Management Issues　　17

2　Dynamics of Final Year Students' Entrepreneurial Inclination: Does Understanding of Entrepreneurship Matter?　　19
Gloria K. Q. Agyapong and Kojo Kakra Twum

3　Understanding Customer Service for Small and Entrepreneurial Firms　　53
Kwame Adom

Part III Local and International Perspectives 73

4 Enterprise Growth in the Informal Economy in Sub-Saharan Africa: An Empirical Qualitative Investigation 75
Kwame Adom, Melony Ankamafio, Golda Anambane, and Robert E. Hinson

5 Social Entrepreneurship in Focus: Evidence from Ghana 107
Atsu Nkukpornu, Kwame Adom, and Etse Nkukpornu

6 Exploring International Joint Ventures 125
Henry Boateng, Stanley Cofie, Robert E. Hinson, and John Paul Kosiba

Part IV Technology and Entrepreneurial Development 147

7 The Impact of 4IR Technologies on Venture Creation and Technology Commercialisation: Insights and Exemplars from an Emerging Economy Context 149
Patience Rambe and Ratakane Maime

8 The Impact of Digital Platforms on SMEs' Development and Performance 179
Judith Ochinanwata and Nonso Ochinanwata

Part V Conclusion 195

9 Theoretical, Policy, and Managerial Implications for Entrepreneurial Practice in Africa 197
Eric Kwame Adae, Patience Rambe, Kojo Kakra Twum, Doreen Anyamesem Odame, and Robert E. Hinson

Index 223

Notes on Contributors

Eric Kwame Adae is Assistant Professor of Public Relations at Drake University School of Journalism and Mass Communication, USA. He holds his Doctorate Degree in Media and Communication from the University of Oregon School of Journalism and Communication (SOJC). He is from Ghana in West Africa, where he received his undergraduate and master's degrees from the University of Ghana. He is an accredited public relations practitioner and was a communications consultant for over 15 years in Ghana. His research interests include Afrocentricity, responsible management, CEO activism, social justice, corporate social advocacy, and corporate social responsibility/sustainability.

Kwame Adom is Associate Professor of Business in the School of Business at Burman University, Lacombe, Alberta, Canada. He is the owner and senior consultant of Entrepreneur's Clinique, a business and Management Consulting firm based in Accra, Ghana. He holds a PhD in Management (entrepreneurship focus) from the University of Sheffield Management School, Sheffield, UK; an MBA in Finance from the University of Leicester; BSc in Planning from Kwame Nkrumah University of Science and Technology; and a Professional Diploma in Marketing from Chartered Institute of Marketing (CIM), UK. He is an associate member of Chartered Institute of Marketing (CIM, UK) and a member of the International Council for Small Business, Canada. His research interests draw on experiences from Africa, specifically Ghana, to inform theoretical developments in entrepreneurship dynamics, motives of Micro, Small, and Medium-sized Enterprises owners, the relationship between formal and the informal economy, social and immigrant entrepreneurship, gender and cultural issues in entrepreneurship, environmental factors, and socioeconomic development. He has over a decade's experience in teaching and researching in marketing, entrepreneurship, and human resource management. He has over 30 peer-reviewed published articles, book chapters, and edited books.

Gloria K. Q. Agyapong is the head of the Department for Marketing and Supply Chain Management at the University of Cape Coast, Ghana. She is a senior lecturer and a marketing scholar with many research articles in reputable journals. Her research is focused on public sector marketing, service marketing, and entrepreneurship.

Golda Anambane is a PhD candidate in Development Studies at the Institute of Statistical, Social, and Economic Research (ISSER), University of Ghana, Ghana. Her area of research interest includes female/women entrepreneurship, gender and entrepreneurship, women's unpaid care work, and socioeconomic development in Sub-Saharan Africa.

Melony Ankamafio holds both a Master of Philosophy (MPhil) in Marketing and a Bachelor of Science in Administration (marketing option) Degree from the University of Ghana Business School, Ghana. She also holds professional certificates, including French and secretaryship. Ankamafio has over fifteen years of experience in office administration at several corporate organisations, both local and international, including Nigeria High Commission, Accra, and Legislative Consult, Abuja. She also has about nine years of classroom facilitation and teaching experience at the higher education level, counting from the Department of Marketing and Entrepreneurship at the University of Ghana Business School, where she taught undergraduates marketing and entrepreneurship courses at all levels. She is an assistant lecturer in the Department of Management Studies at Heritage Christian College, School of Business and Leadership. Additionally, Melony is involved in voluntarily administering small-scale businesses. She loves administrative and coordinating roles. She has the flair to learn and speak several dialects.

Henry Boateng is the Director of Institutional Research at D'Youville College, USA. He holds a PhD in Knowledge Management and researches into information and knowledge management, social responsibility communications, tourism, and hospitality marketing. He is an active research consultant with special skills in qualitative, quantitative, and mixed method approaches. He has worked on several projects across the globe. Henry has consulted with several organisations, including the University of Technology Sydney (UTS), Australia; the Multicultural Health Communication Service (MHCS), NSW, Australia; and Health Education Training Institute, NSW Health.

Stanley Cofie is Associate Professor of Marketing at the Ghana Institute of Management and Public Administration (GIPMA), Ghana, where he has been since 2012. Cofie previously lectured at Birkbeck College, University of London, where he obtained his PhD. His research interests are in marketing strategies in emerging/developing economies, strategic positioning and branding in bottom of the pyramid markets, and services marketing. His recent publications are in academic journals and other outlets including *Industrial Marketing Management, Journal of strategic Marketing, Thunderbird International Business Review, Journal of Product and Brand Management, Journal of African Business, International Journal of Bank Marketing, The Routledge Companion to Contemporary Brand Management*, and *Branding and Positioning of the Pyramid Markets in Africa*.

Robert E. Hinson is Professor of Marketing and Pro Vice-Chancellor of the Ghana Communication Technology University, Ghana. He holds a DPhil in Marketing from the University of Ghana and a PhD in International Business from the Aalborg University Business School. He also holds several visiting and honorary professorships across some European and South African Universities.

John Paul Kosiba is a senior lecturer at the University of Professional Studies, Accra, Ghana. His research interests are in the areas of sales management, branding, consumer behaviour, and online communication. His work has been published in the *Journal of Business Research, International Journal of Contemporary Hospitality Management, Journal of Retailing and Consumer Service*, and *Journal of Product and Brand Management*, among others.

Ratakane Maime is a lecturer at the Central University of Technology, South Africa. He holds a Doctor of Business Administration (DBA). His teaching is focused on financial and management information systems. His research is on developing frameworks to enhance the financial benefits of implementing web technologies.

Atsu Nkukpornu is Lecturer in Entrepreneurship at Cape Coast Technical University, Ghana. He holds a PhD from the University of Ghana Business School. He is a serial entrepreneur. He has also worked with local and multinational companies. His research interest is in the area of entrepreneurship in Africa. He has written research articles and book chapters on entrepreneurial development in Ghana.

Etse Nkukpornu is Lecturer in Finance in the Department of Accounting and Finance at Christian Service University College, Ghana. He holds a Master of Science in Economics from Kwame Nkrumah University of Science and Technology, and a Master's Degree in Finance from Kwame Nkrumah University of Science and Technology. He has written papers on behavioural finance and drivers of business success in emerging markets.

Judith Ochinanwata is a researcher at African Development Institute of Research Methodology, Nigeria. She holds a Master's Degree in International Business from the University of Lincoln and a BSc in Estate Management from the University of Nigeria, Enugu campus. Her research interests are in the areas of entrepreneurship, platformisation, and small business.

Nonso Ochinanwata is an academic entrepreneur who applies his scholarship in commercial and non-commercial ventures to improve the world. He is director of research and innovation at African Development Institute of Research Methodology. He received B.Eng from Enugu State University of Science and Technology, Nigeria; MBA from Coventry University; and MRes in Business Economics and PhD in Strategic Management & International Business from Sheffield Hallam University, UK. His research interests are in the areas of digital internationalisation and digital entrepreneurship, platformisation, and business model innovation. Using primarily qualitative methods and mixed methods, he is particularly interested in how entrepreneurs establish digital firms that seek early international markets from inception and how firms innovate their business model.

Doreen Anyamesem Odame is a lecturer and the examination officer in the Department of General Studies at the Faculty of Computing and Information Systems, Ghana Communication Technology University, Accra, Ghana. She has written in prestigious outlets such as the *Journal of International Development* and completed her PhD in Development Studies at the Institute of Statistical, Social and Economic Research, University of Ghana, Legon, Accra, Ghana.

Patience Rambe is Research Professor of Entrepreneurship at the Faculty of Management Sciences, Central University of Technology, South Africa. He has written in high quality journals on innovation and competitiveness and the adoption of technology to promote business in Africa.

Kojo Kakra Twum is Senior Lecturer in Marketing. He is the head of Department of Business Administration at the Presbyterian University, Ghana. He has co-authored books on responsible management, social media marketing, and public sector marketing communications. He has written research articles in quality journals, focused on public sector marketing, services marketing, corporate social responsibility (CSR), marketing analytics, and innovative technologies.

Abbreviations

AU	African Union
IE1-IE30	Informal Entrepreneur 1 to Informal Entrepreneurs 30
AfDB	African Development Bank
ASEN	African Society Entrepreneurs Network
AI	Artificial Intelligence
AR	Augmented Reality
BDA	Big Data Analytics
B2B	Business-To-Business
B2C	Business-To-Customer
BOP	Base of the Pyramid
CV	Computer Vision
C2C	Customer-To-Customer
HERDIC	Higher Education Research Development in the Central Region
EDHE	Entrepreneurship Development in Higher Education
4IR	Fourth Industrial Revolution
GDPR	General Data Protection Regulation
GSS	Ghana Statistical Services
GEM	Global Entrepreneurship Monitor
GDP	Gross Domestic Product
HUDs	Head-Up Displays
HAR	Human Activity Recognition
SRMIS	Information Section
IT	Information Technology

Abbreviations

ILO	International Labour Organisation
IMF	International Monetary Fund
IoT	Internet of Things
NGOs	Non-governmental Organisations
OECD	Organisation for Economic Co-operation and Development
SMME	Small, Micro, and Medium Enterprises
SME	Small-Medium Enterprises
SEAA	Social Enterprise Academy Africa
SE	Social Entrepreneurs
SADC	Southern African Development Community
SDG	Sustainable Development Goals
SRMIS	Students' Records and Management Information Section
TVET	Technical and Vocational Education Training
TSV	Technology Social Venture
TPB	Theory of Planned Behaviour
UNCTAD	United Nations Conference on Trade and Development
VR	Virtual Reality

List of Tables

Table 2.1	Demographic variables	32
Table 2.2	Reliability results	32
Table 2.3	Descriptive statistics for entrepreneurial inclination	34
Table 2.4	Coefficients	35
Table 2.5	Coefficients	38
Table 2.6	Coefficients	40
Table 2.7	Peer association and entrepreneurial inclination	40
Table 2.8	Coefficients	43
Table 4.1	Demographics of entrepreneurs	88
Table 4.2	Marketing strategies commonly used by informal entrepreneurs	89
Table 4.3	Growth strategies commonly used by informal entrepreneurs	94
Table 5.1	Differences between social entrepreneurship, not-for-profit organisations, and commercial enterprises	111
Table 5.2	Similarities between social entrepreneurship and not-for-profit organisation	112

Part I

Introduction

1

Introduction

Robert E. Hinson, Doreen Anyamesem Odame, Eric Kwame Adae, and Kwame Adom

What Is Entrepreneurship?

Entrepreneurship has been defined and conceptualized in different ways due to the different positions of the different authors. Demirkan et al. (2008), for instance, conceptualize the term as a process of transforming a concept into an enterprise to create value. Casson (2003) on the other hand defines it as a process of making judgemental and subjective decisions about the usage and coordination of scarce resources. Dau and Cuervo-Cazurra (2014) offered a legal definition, describing it as the creation of new businesses made of stable collection of individuals who

---

R. E. Hinson (✉)
Ghana Communication Technology University, Accra, Ghana

University of the Free State Business School, Bloemfontein, South Africa
e-mail: rehinson@gctu.edu.gh

D. A. Odame
Ghana Communication Technology University, Tesano – Accra, Ghana
e-mail: dodame@gctu.edu.gh

coordinate their efforts to generate new value-added economic activities. Gries and Naudé (2011) on the other hand employ three basic elements to define entrepreneurship: resource coordination, enterprise creation, and innovation.

Entrepreneurship, by its description and definition, describes the ability to identify opportunities, and utilizing resources to attain these opportunities, to the benefit of the society. Entrepreneurship is seen as the 'engine' for economic growth, as well as the 'catalyst' for economic and promotion of income-generating activities in all sectors of the economy (Omoruyi et al., 2017:2). There is a common theme that runs through all the different definitions of entrepreneurship—*job creation, innovation, and coordination of scarce resources*. Apart from meeting policy goals, entrepreneurship remains a critical driver for sustainable economic development and poverty alleviation through the creation of jobs and income-generating activities. Entrepreneurial activities also guarantee productivity, welfare, and innovation in the end, contributing significantly to improved and resilient economic structures. In many developing countries, discussions around strategies for economic growth and development have received enormous attention due to the persistent high rates of unemployment, translating into poor lifestyles and low standards of living (Ndaguba & Hanyane, 2019). Entrepreneurship has therefore been referenced in several economic literature as a critical driver for job creation, with an expectant lead to economic growth and stability. It is also relied upon as an effective tool for improved welfare and innovation (Arimah, 2004; Hanjra et al., 2009; Khumalo, 2013). Various international organizations as well as successive governments have worked over the years to implement plans to lessen the scourge of poverty and advance Africa's

---

E. K. Adae
Drake University School of Journalism and Mass Communication,
Des Moines, IA, USA
e-mail: eric.adae@drake.edu

K. Adom
School of Business, Burman University, Lacombe, AB, Canada
e-mail: kwameaadom@burmanu.ca

economy. Majority of the Sub-Saharan African nations after obtaining independence in the 1960s, embarked on several state-led, centrally planned economic structures, with the aim of alleviating and improving wellbeing. However, evidence shows that most industrialized and emerging economies have followed a different approach for economic development, absolute poverty reduction, and job creation.

Countries have different developmental and economic growth levels, and at different pace. In view of this, countries are classified as developed, developing, or underdeveloped. A developed country is characterized by high economic and industrial activity, with high per capita income, well-structured and developed infrastructure, and a generally high human development index. A developing and underdeveloped economy, on the other hand, is characterized by low industrial activities, high unemployment rates, high dependence on the primary sector, and high dependence on exports of primary commodities (Luo et al., 2019; Male, 2011). The demand for poverty alleviation strategies such as job creation through industrial and entrepreneurial activities therefore can be relative and will depend greatly on existing societal pressures and patterns (economic position and population dynamics). The dynamics that pertain in a particular country at a given time, will determine the pace and the direction of these strategies. Establishing sustainable entrepreneurship, therefore, requires a multi-disciplinary approach, that employs different lenses to understand the different social patterns that exist.

Overall, entrepreneurship is influencing Africa's development in a significant way by generating new economic opportunities, fostering innovation, and enabling local communities to fight against poverty and inequality. Though Africa may not be there yet, entrepreneurship has opened up Africa's economy through the creation of jobs, establishments of industries, and generally stimulating economic growth in Africa. The urge for entrepreneurial advancement has stimulated innovative ideas, which have in turn contributed to economic growth within the African economy. Technology for instance is being used by entrepreneurs in Africa to innovate and address regional concerns. Technology has been adopted to increase financial inclusion as well as reducing the unbanked population in Africa through mobile banking and mobile money platforms. Entrepreneurs are also creating jobs while providing goods and services that meet the needs of the African population. Additionally, entrepreneurs are figuring out how to expand their companies across the continent and even internationally, which helps with regional integration and economic growth. Additionally, entrepreneurship in Africa has contributed to the reduction of poverty and inequality. Entrepreneurship helps individuals and communities to improve their living standards by generating jobs and opening doors for economic growth.

However, there are obstacles that African business owners must overcome, including lack of access to funding, poor infrastructure, and regulatory restrictions. This book is positioned to stimulate initiatives to address these challenges, such as the development of entrepreneurship-supportive policies and programmes and the formation of incubators andaccelerators.

Sustainable Entrepreneurship in Africa

Generally, entrepreneurial activities have different phases—idea creation, planning, execution, scaling, and hypergrowth. Each of the phases has peculiar dynamics that require tailored policies and strategies to ensure sustainability throughout the life cycle. There is evidence of several government policies targeted at promoting entrepreneurial activities. The question yet to be answered however is, are these policies designed to meet the specific dynamics of the different entrepreneurial phases (Akinyemi & Adejumo, 2018). In Africa particularly, several factors have impacted negatively on the trajectory of entrepreneurship advancement. These factors include colonization, political unrest, and inconsistent social reforms, which have all led to incidents like frequent collapse of businesses, seizures by governments, lack of access to capital and raw materials (Amankwah-Amoah et al., 2018). As a result, most African countries have only witnessed patchy Millennium Development Goal outcomes, with yet scanty outcomes of the Sustainable development Goals. Even though the zeal to start up a business may be self-motivated, it is essential for governments to enact policies that will create the conducive environment that businesses need to thrive because government policies and regulations have direct impact on competition and profitability, both of which are instrumental in business growth.

Several policies have been implemented to promote entrepreneurial growth in Africa. The state of entrepreneurship in Africa however confirms that these policies have not been successful in facilitating entrepreneurial advancements in Africa (Acs & Szerb, 1; Bygrave & Timmons, 2; Kreft & Sobel, 3). In Nigeria, for instance, there have been policies like the Small and Medium Enterprises Development Agency (SMEDAN), N-Power program, Government Enterprise and Empowerment Program (GEEP), and the You-win Program, which were all implemented to promote entrepreneurial activities by facilitating access to funds and resources for business growth (Oliyide, 4; Today.ng, 5). The state of entrepreneurship in Nigeria however confirms that these policies have not been effective in achieving this aim.

Africa is still confronted with persistent challenges that inhibit sustainable entrepreneurial growth and job creation. These challenges range from high environmental disruptions due to climate change, high fuel cost, documentation and formalization challenges, low agricultural productivity (leading to insufficient raw materials), and slow diffusion of technological strategies (Pattinson & Wanjiru, 2020). The prevalence of these challenges is not to say that Africa has alienated herself from global reforms and recommended strategies. Several African countries have undertaken political, market, and structural reforms, all in a bid to sustain the economy, improve overall standards of living, and promote economic and income-generation activities. Over the period, however, there have been inconsistencies in expected outcomes compared to the efforts and investments in reforms and strategies.

There are several factors that contribute to the entrepreneurial drive of a country. These are internal, entrepreneurial orientation of the population, managerial competence, technological capabilities, and external factors (finance, human resource, government policies, and regulations). According to Sallah & Ceasar (njn), lack of access to finance, lack of access to qualified personnel, access to credit facilities, domestic demand, competition from international markets, and management challenges are critical factors that inhibit entrepreneurial growth in Africa. Hagin and

Ceasar (2021) found, though all factors are important, managerial competence as the highest predictor for sustainable entrepreneurial growth in Africa.

Strategies to Address Entrepreneurial Challenges in Africa

Several scholars and policymakers have attested to the fact that a robust economy, made of manufacturing and entreprenuerial firms entrepreneurship remains the fundamental ingredient to sustainable development and improved wellbeing in Africa. It is argued that this strategy absorbs large numbers of the working population, mainly the youth and able-bodied, in effect providing them with decent sources of income which in turn improves their wellbeing. The strategy of leveraging on manufacturing, industrialization, and entrepreneurship as a factor for economic growth and sustainable development is cited to have been the success factor in places like the United Kingdom, the United States, France, and the Asian Tigers. It is well known that industrialization made the Chinese economy one of the fastest-growing economies in the world, with other Southeast Asian nations closely trailing behind. Industrialization facilitates rapid structural change and development by alleviating unemployment and poverty.

The same, however, cannot be said about Africa. Literature shows that, most African countries have not been able to tap into potentials for business growth and entrepreneurial development. This represents a missed opportunity for economic growth and transformation in Africa. Strategic realignment to tap into these existing potentials will open up huge development opportunities in the form of entrepreneurial opportunities for the regional outperformers (South Africa, Egypt, etc.) and the new players alike. In view of this, African leaders have stipulated strategies and frameworks to drive this agenda. The African Union (AU) Agenda 2063 (Agenda 63) framework puts entrepreneurship and business at the front and centre as it seeks innovative ways to nurture businesses.

The African Union's Agenda 2063

At the regional level, several strategies and framework have been embarked upon, with the aim of facilitating sustainable growth and development in Africa. Agenda 2063 (Agenda 63) is a development framework which was adopted by the African Union in 2013 to facilitate equitable and sustainable economic growth and development in Africa. Among other things, the agenda seeks to harness all factors and endowments to contribute to growth and development. These include human capital, history, cultural and natural resources, and geopolitical position.

Agenda 63 was adopted as part of efforts to envision Africa's growth and development agenda by leveraging on some emerging opportunities such as globalization, investment avenues, well-functioning regional institutions, and previous experience. The framework has seven aspirations, with the foremost seeking to achieve a prosperous Africa based on inclusive and sustainable development. The framework has outlined to achieve this through improving standards of living and wellbeing, improving science, technology, and innovation, and economic growth and development.

The potential for Agenda 63 to achieve the foremost objective of sustained economic growth depends on the ability of the framework to facilitate socioeconomic transformation of the African population, which will be manifested in improved wellbeing, education, human capital, and infrastructure. The many factors that remain a menace and hinder economic growth and development in many parts of Africa should be addressed by this framework: poor governance, corruption, inequalities, and conflicts. The framework has very detailed components that depict its ability to achieve the set target of inclusive prosperity and sustained development by 2063.

The question posed by many scholars however is, how feasible are the strategies in achieving this aim? Boldrin et al. (2012) argue that, inclusive development requires centralized political and economic institutions by providing basic public services and incentives to all members of the society. These incentives include education, access to finance, justice, and equity. Acemoglu et. al., (2012) adds that these incentives enable savings, investments, and innovation, which are critical for business startup and entrepreneurship. The challenge for Agenda 63 therefore revolves around how ordinary citizens can simultaneously tap into these incentives and also cope with the ingrained challenges on the continent which hinder business growth. DeGhetto et al. (2016) point out that presence of challenges to meet basic needs is negatively correlated to growth and development.

Sustainable Development Goals

Following from the Millennium Development Goals, one of the critical targets of the 2015 Sustainable Development Goals (SDG) is to alleviate poverty in all forms and standards. This agenda was particularly critical for the Sub-Saharan African region because, while the region recorded a poverty rate of about 67% in 2015, the rest of the world stood at about 36% (Page & Pande, 2018). Barne & Wadhwa advise that effective actions to alleviate the poverty situation in Africa should target creating more inclusive and sustainable business and entrepreneurial opportunities. In SDGs 1 and 8, the United Nations targets to improve livelihoods and wellbeing by alleviating poverty (SDG 1) and creating decent work and economic growth (SDG 8) (United Nations (UN), 2018). Further, at its 75th General Assembly in 2017, the United Nations highlighted the need for entrepreneurship and business growth as a critical driver for poverty alleviation in Africa specifically (UNCTAD, 2017).

The nexus between business creation and poverty alleviation has been well established in literature (Hoselitz, 1952; Schumpeter, 1934; Sergi et al., 2019). While distortions in the financial system hinder business and entrepreneurial activities, stability enables business start-ups and facilitates continuity (Khyareh & Rostami, 2018). Though the SSA region records the highest levels of global poverty, the region has exhibited high levels and potentials for entrepreneurial activities compared to other parts of the world. The population seems resilient with positive mindsets; however, the factors that necessitate business growth are nonexistent. In effect, though businesses are initiated, they remain at the subsistent level (Gosavi, 2018). Bate (2021) confirms that though records show South Africa as an entrepreneurial leader compared to Brazil and India, business growth is not sustained owing to issues surrounding a mismatch in tertiary education and low skills. It is therefore necessary to address support systems and opportunities that does not only facilitate business startup but also encourage growth and sustainability as a means to economic growth and development.

So far, the literature has pointed out that the challenges confronting entrepreneurship in Africa consist of several factors and at different degrees. This puts Africa in the position where infrastructural development alone for instance may not be adequate to curb the existing entrepreneurial challenges, nor ensure sustainability. Based on the peculiar characteristics and dynamics of the challenges, an ideal African-centred approach will require solutions and strategies that are multi-dimensional and having the capacity to tackle the different facets of the existing challenges.

Again, since the challenges are multi-faceted, it is crucial to have an improved understanding of the role of new agencies in entrepreneurial processes (Dencker et al., 2021; Lounsbury & Glynn, 2019). This book details multi-disciplinary dimensions to entrepreneurship and suggests innovative strategies to drive entrepreneurial activities in Africa. Such multi-disciplinary approaches can address challenges at social, environmental, traditional, public, private, and even not-for-profit sectors (Haigh & Hoffman, 2014). A multi-disciplinary approach will also offer an opportunity for a holistic view of the persistent challenges that exist.

Overview of the Book

Given the importance of entrepreneurship to the growth and development of the African economy, there is need for an understanding of factors that affect entrepreneurship in Africa, and how these factors interrelate with each other. This book sheds light on the current status of entrepreneurship in Africa and discusses the challenges that confront entrepreneurship by throwing light on factors that hinder business startup, sustainability, and continuity in Africa. In the various chapters of the book, the authors outline policy recommendations, and strategies to boost business start-ups' and sustainability in Africa. This book will serve as a practical tool to government, educators, students, and entrepreneurs by providing understanding of the dynamics that affect entrepreneurship in Africa, as well as facilitating the growth trajectory of entrepreneurship in Africa

This is a nine-chapter book structured under five main parts. Part I has the introductory chapter and gives a background to the issues of discussion in the book. Part II focuses on entrepreneurial intentions and customer management issues in Africa. We chose to explore entrepreneurial intentions and customer management because of the urgent need for customer-centric entrepreneurs to bolster Africa's economic growth. Student entrepreneurial intention could have an important bearing on creating the new pipeline of entrepreneurial talent in Africa, and in that regard, Agyapong and Twum, in Chap. 2, assessed the factors that drive entrepreneurial inclination of students in a public university in a developing country context. Drawing on the theories of planned behaviour, they explored the influence of academic curriculum, geographical distance, peer association, and parent views on the likelihood of being entrepreneurial. On issues of customer management, Adom argues in Chap. 3 that, customer service is more crucial for SMEs than it is for large corporations because it is a crucial prerequisite for organizational survival. He argues however that customer service research has only focused on larger organizations and proposes a remedy to this challenge through an exploration of the importance of customer service to organizational survival.

Chapters 4, 5, and 6 make up Part III of the book. This part discusses local and international perspectives of small businesses and entrepreneurship in Africa. Entrepreneurial activities are undertaken in both local and international contexts and Adom, Ankamafio, Anambane, and Hinson argue that although formal marketing is not inherent in the informal entrepreneurial space, developing key growth strategies such as diversification, ploughing back profit, business expansion, gaining financial support, and hiring the right number of employees are critical factors that necessitate enterprise growth in the informal economy. In respect of international joint ventures, Boateng, Cofie, Hinson, and Kosiba explored ways by which Ghanaian firms decide to enter joint ventures with foreign firms and the resources they obtain from their foreign partners. They find that although Ghanaian firms enter joint ventures with foreign firms in order to access financial resources and for foreign firms to reaffirm their credibility, local firms are also able to access knowledge and new markets once they enter into joint ventures.

Part IV of the book has two chapters (Chaps. 7 and 8) and discusses technology and entrepreneurial development in Africa. Our interest to contribute to the discussions on technology and entrepreneurial development issues in Africa is because new technologies are vital for SME's and business organizations for sustained survival. The 4th Industrial Revolution (4IR) does not really give small and medium enterprises an option of whether to adopt technology to survive or not. In Chap. 7, Rambe and Maime respond to the urgency of the 4IR, by drawing on the entrepreneurial ecosystems theory to challenge the monolithic, government-driven approach to 4IR. The authors propose a bottom-up approach in which serial technology entrepreneurs and their local entrepreneurial ecosystems become the main catalysts for effective venture creation and the commercialization of technology innovations. Chapter 8 examines the impact of digital platforms on SME development and performance. Judith Ochinanwata explores questions around how digital platforms facilitate SMEs development, how different social media platforms impact the creation of online small business, and the frameworks required for adopting digital platforms to create and foster online small businesses.

The fifth and the last part (Part V) of the book concludes our arguments by proffering theoretical, policy, and managerial implications for entrepreneurial practice in Africa.

How the Book Aligns with the SDGs

Looking through the literature, there remains a gap about how the specific entrepreneurial challenges in Africa can be churned to contribute to the achievements of the SDGs. The literature has emphasized the crucial role that entrepreneurship can play in achieving the SDG. The dynamics and the challenges present in Africa, on the other hand, have a unique potential of contributing to the attainment of the SDGs if they are addressed, and if appropriate strategies are adopted in addressing these challenges.

The SDGs outline 17 ambitious goals that seek to improve the lives and wellbeing of the world's population. Each of the 17 goals of the SDGs address critical issues that impact on humanity and societal wellbeing, aiming that by achieving them, living standards as well as wellbeing will be improved. In relation to entrepreneurship, there are various activities for almost all the SDGs that have either a direct or an indirect link to entrepreneurship. This book highlights the various strategies that entrepreneurship can use to facilitate the achievement of the SDGs.

Though each of the 17 goals speaks to various aspects of wellbeing, this book is directly linked to the SDG 8, which specifically aims to provide decent work and economic growth by 2030. Through the chapters of this book, we stand by the position that entrepreneurship remains a critical driver for development and cannot be exempted from the development agenda.

References

Acemoglu, D., Golosov, M., Tsyvinski, A., & Yared, P. (2012). A dynamic theory of resource wars. *The Quarterly Journal of Economics, 127*(1), 283–331.

Akinyemi, F. O., & Adejumo, O. O. (2018). Government policies and entrepreneurship phases in emerging economies: Nigeria and South Africa. *Journal of Global Entrepreneurship Research, 8*(1), 35.

Amankwah-Amoah, J., Osabutey, E. L., & Egbetokun, A. (2018). Contemporary challenges and opportunities of doing business in Africa: The emerging roles and effects of technologies. *Technological Forecasting and Social Change, 131*, 171–174.

Arimah, B. (2004). Poverty reduction and human development in Africa. *Journal of Human Development, 5*(3), 399–415.

Bate, A. F. (2021). A comparative analysis on the entrepreneurial ecosystem of BRICS club countries: Practical emphasis on South Africa. *SN Business & Economics, 1*(10), 121.

Boldrin, M., Levine, D. K., & Modica, S. (2012). A review of Acemoglu and Robinson's why nations fail. *Unpublished manuscript.* http://www.dklevine.com/general/aandrreview.pdf

Casson, M. (2003). Entrepreneurship, business culture and the theory of the firm. In *Handbook of entrepreneurship research* (pp. 223–246). Springer.
Dau, L. A., & Cuervo-Cazurra, A. (2014). To formalize or not to formalize: Entrepreneurship and pro-market institutions. *Journal of Business Venturing, 29*(5), 668–686.
DeGhetto, K., Gray, J. R., & Kiggundu, M. N. (2016). The African Union's Agenda 2063: Aspirations, challenges, and opportunities for management research. *Africa Journal of Management, 2*(1), 93–116.
Demirkan, H., Kauffman, R. J., Vayghan, J. A., Fill, H. G., Karagiannis, D., & Maglio, P. P. (2008). Service-oriented technology and management: Perspectives on research and practice for the coming decade. *Electronic Commerce Research and Applications, 7*(4), 356–376.
Dencker, J. C., Bacq, S., Gruber, M., & Haas, M. (2021). Reconceptualizing necessity entrepreneurship: A contextualized framework of entrepreneurial processes under the condition of basic needs. *Academy of Management Review, 46*(1), 60–79.
Gosavi, A. (2018). Can mobile money help firms mitigate the problem of access to finance in Eastern sub-Saharan Africa? *Journal of African Business, 19*(3), 343–360.
Gries, T., & Naudé, W. (2011). Entrepreneurship and human development: A capability approach. *Journal of Public Economics, 95*(3–4), 216–224.
Haigh, N., & Hoffman, A. J. (2014). The new heretics: Hybrid organizations and the challenges they present to corporate sustainability. *Organization & Environment, 27*(3), 223–241.
Hagin, C., and Caesar, L.D. (2021). The antecedents of success among small- and medium-sized enterprises: evidence from Ghana. *J Glob Entrepr Res 11*, 279–297. https://doi.org/10.1007/s40497-021-00285-y
Hanjra, M. A., Ferede, T., & Gutta, D. G. (2009). Reducing poverty in sub-Saharan Africa through investments in water and other priorities. *Agricultural Water Management, 96*(7), 1062–1070.
Hoselitz, B. F. (1952). Entrepreneurship and economic growth. *The American Journal of Economics and Sociology, 12*(1), 97–110.
Khumalo, P. (2013). The dynamics of poverty and poverty alleviation in South Africa. *Gender and Behaviour, 11*(2), 5643–5652.
Khyareh, M. M., & Rostami, N. (2018). Competitiveness and Entrepreneurship, and their Effects on Economic Growth. *International Journal of Management, Accounting & Economics, 5*(10).

Lounsbury, M., & Glynn, M. A. (2019). *Cultural entrepreneurship: A new agenda for the study of entrepreneurial processes and possibilities*. Cambridge University Press.

Luo, Y., Zhang, H., & Bu, J. (2019). Developed country MNEs investing in developing economies: Progress and prospect. *Journal of International Business Studies, 50*(4), 633–667.

Male, R. (2011). Developing country business cycles: Characterizing the cycle. *Emerging Markets Finance and Trade, 47*(sup2), 20–39.

Ndaguba, E. A., & Hanyane, B. (2019). Stakeholder model for community economic development in alleviating poverty in municipalities in South Africa. *Journal of Public Affairs, 19*(1), e1858.

Omoruyi, E. M. M., Olamide, K. S., Gomolemo, G., & Donath, O. A. (2017). Entrepreneurship and economic growth: Does entrepreneurship bolster economic expansion in Africa. *Journal of Socialomics, 6*(4), 1–11.

Page, L., & Pande, R. (2018). Ending global poverty: Why money isn't enough. *Journal of Economic Perspectives, 32*(4), 173–200.

Pattinson, S., & Wanjiru, R. (2020). Supporting sustainable, equitable growth in sub-Saharan Africa: A conceptual model for enabling social enterprise governance. *Research Handbook on Entrepreneurship in Emerging Economies*.

Schumpeter, J. A. (1934). The theory of economic development: An inquiry into profits, capital, credit, interest, and the business cycle.

Sergi, B. S., Popkova, E. G., Bogoviz, A. V., & Ragulina, J. V. (2019). Entrepreneurship and economic growth: The experience of developed and developing countries. In *Entrepreneurship and development in the 21st century* (pp. 3–32). Emerald publishing limited.

UNCTAD. (2017). Promoting entrepreneurship for sustainable development: A selection of business cases from the empretec network. Retrieved February 20, 2023, from https://unctad.org/system/files/official-document/diaeed2017d6_en.pdf

United Nations. (2018). *Ending poverty*. Retrieved February 20, 2023, from https://www.un.org/en/sections/issuesdepth/poverty/https://www.un.org/en/sections/issues-depth/poverty/

Part II

Entrepreneurial Intentions and Customer Management Issues

2

Dynamics of Final Year Students' Entrepreneurial Inclination: Does Understanding of Entrepreneurship Matter?

Gloria K. Q. Agyapong and Kojo Kakra Twum

Introduction

Employment and job creation have always been major factors in a country's development. Although most graduates from tertiary institutions in developing countries prefer to be employed in the public and private sectors of the economy after their education (Ng, Gosset, Chinyoka & Obasi, 2016), the unavailability of these jobs and the high rate of unemployment among the youth have led to the need for graduates to consider self-employment as a means of earning a living. This has resulted in the quest for graduates and students to embrace entrepreneurship. The

G. K. Q. Agyapong (✉)
Department of Marketing and Supply Chain Management,
Cape Coast, Ghana
e-mail: gagyapong@ucc.edu.gh

K. K. Twum
Presbyterian University, Abetifi-Kwahu, Ghana
e-mail: twumkojo@presbyuniversity.edu.gh

question as to what influences students to go into entrepreneurship had been on the mind of researchers (Misoska et al., 2016; Parker, 2018) as the issue of unemployment among graduates continues to worsen year after year (Ghafar, 2016).

Nonetheless, an appropriate starting point is a recognition that entrepreneurship is a complex process which takes place within the economic and social environments (Gedajlovic et al., 2013). While Dunn and Holtz-Eakin (2000) posited that economic factors such as human capital influence entrepreneurial inclination among students, Asamani and Opoku Mensah (2013) advanced social factors such as task performance attitude, leadership skills, achievement attributes and risk-taking attitude as critical for entrepreneurial inclination among students. Other economic factors identified in literature are factors that inform successful inclusion of entrepreneurship, such as unemployment rate, educational curriculum and geographical location (Vossenberg, 2013; Yeboah, Kumi & Awuah, 2013; Nabi et al., 2018), while peer influence, influence of relatives, religion and geographical location were suggested by Kacperczyk (2013) and Quagrainie (2018).

The 2016 Global Entrepreneurship Report shows that there has been little information as to factors that incline students' decision to engage in entrepreneurial venturing (Bergmann et al., 2016; Martin et al., 2013). Hence, questions remain about the determinants of students' entrepreneurial inclinations and how they should be understood among tertiary students in a developing economy. Understanding this angle of research is important as entrepreneurship is embedded in both economic and social systems (Welter, 2011). Consequently, this study is motivated by calls for research to be driven towards the workings of entrepreneurship among students (Bergmann et al., 2016). In paying attention to the environmental aspect of students' entrepreneurial inclination, we examine two research questions: (1) how do economic factors such as educational curriculum and geographical location work on students' entrepreneurial inclination? (2) How do social factors such as peer influence and parent view incline entrepreneurship among students?

The problem of unemployment among young people in the Ghanaian economy is of a major concern to inclusive development (Dadzie et. al.,

2020; World Bank Group, 2018). Despite the rapid economic growth in most developing economies in Sub-Saharan Africa, the growth has not been translated into employment avenues for their growing youth population. This has resulted in making youth unemployment one of the key challenges to economic development. According to the Worldbank Group, about 48% of the of the youth were unemployed. Disparities also exist in rural and urban employment rates. For instance, the proportion of unemployed youth in urban areas is higher (13.4%) than in rural areas (10.2%) (GSS, 2014). By 2019, as noted by Plecher (2020), the unemployment rate in Ghana was at approximately 4.33% of the total labour force. There is therefore the need to identify the factors that will influence graduates' inclination towards entrepreneurship and the necessary skill and knowledge graduates require to succeed in their quest to become entrepreneurs.

Our approach takes the view that entrepreneurial inclination among students are informed by social settings that prescribe norms, values and networks which inform entrepreneurial activities. Accordingly, we draw on sociological perspective of entrepreneurship (Schaper & Volery, 2004) and the Theory of Planned Behaviour (TPB) (Ajzen, 1991) to develop the theoretical framework for the study. We argue that combining these perspectives provides a conceptual framework to understand the conditioning of student entrepreneurial inclination. Whereas sociological perspective of entrepreneurship suggests that entrepreneurship is an aggregation of social interactions (Stam et al., 2014), theory of planned behaviour is found to be one of the best predictors of planned behaviours as behaviours are difficult to predict (Becker, 2013).

This chapter contributes to the understanding of student's entrepreneurial inclination among socially situated activity (Mueller & Goic, 2002). It reinforces context in entrepreneurial discourse, as well as strengthens the understanding of student entrepreneurship as a profoundly economic and non-economic practice. Our novel contribution demonstrates social determinants to be an enabler and basis for building student's interest to pursue a career in entrepreneurship. We try to demonstrate how in a developing economy setting entrepreneurial inclination exists, enables and sustains entrepreneurial careers among business students. Various studies have focused on the analysis of socioeconomic conditions and problems faced by youth, and women in the informal sector (AR Aharonovich, 2019; Peprah et al., 2019; Kabonga et al., 2021), but the studies on students' inclination to entrepreneurship is not well understood in Ghana. Thus, this study assesses determinants that predispose students to entrepreneurship for policymakers and entrepreneurship educators who are enthusiastic about developing youth entrepreneurship in Ghana. Additionally, an understanding of contextual influences of student's entrepreneurial inclination will help stakeholders in students' entrepreneurship in designing conditions that foster entrepreneurial activities of students.

Theoretical and Conceptual Review

Sociological Perspective of Entrepreneurship

Entrepreneurship recognition, exploitation and creating of products and service to meet economic opportunities are associated with economic development. This is made possible by the efforts of entrepreneurs who are engines that fast-track economic development (Vossenberg, 2013). The pivotal role of entrepreneurs in economic development include creating jobs, innovating, creating wealth, improving health and even in economic advancement. Until recently, entrepreneurship was viewed as a predominantly economic pursuit (O'Connor, 2013). However, as the field expanded its boundaries, researchers came to the conclusion that entrepreneurship is contextually based as they take place in real life (McKeever et al., 2014). Entrepreneurship, therefore, is situated within a social context where entrepreneurial inclination is embedded (Welter, 2011). As entrepreneurship is rooted in social systems, cultural context exerts a critical impact on competitive behaviour and performance (Yang, 2013).

The sociological perspective of entrepreneurship centres its explanation for entrepreneurship on the various social contexts that enable entrepreneurs to identify economic opportunities as well as having resources to leverage them. From this socialized perspective, entrepreneurship can be said to be the manifestation of the interaction among people who take risk by setting up or engaging in entrepreneurial venturing by taking of risks in the hope of profit and their social communities (Welter, 2011). The sociological perspective of entrepreneurship model approaches the question of entrepreneurship by placing it within the context and examining how social forces, such as social attitudes, norms, values and networks, shape the perception, emergence and the behaviours of entrepreneurs (McKeever et al., 2014). Therefore, sociological variables such as role expectation of children and parents, attitude towards wealth and innovation, migration and social class deviance are among the important factors that influence individuals' inclination towards entrepreneurship (Vesper, 1980). The sociological perspective entrepreneurship is a perspective on entrepreneurial behaviour as its connection to society as a whole. This suggests that society is not neutral as such and it affects attitudes and behaviours.

Theory of Planned Behaviour

Ajzen's theory of planned behaviour (TPB) assumes that human behaviours are planned and are therefore preceded by intention towards that behaviour. This links with the theory of planned behaviour that holds that attitudes towards behaviour are evaluated within the context of subjective norms. The subjective or social norms refer to the perceived social pressure to perform or not a behaviour, hence the desirability of the behaviour as well as the opinions of others about the behaviour (Ajzen, 1991). These people are part of the society that have set up norm that specifies how the people should behave. Thus, the attitude towards entrepreneurship refers to the degree to which a person has a favourable or unfavourable appraisal of it. Related to behaviour according to the theory is the perceived behavioural control which indicates the feasibility of the intention that is whether the person can easily realize his or her intention. Perceived behavioural control is assumed to reflect past experience as well as facilitating conditions. Additionally, the perceived behavioural control connotes perceived self-efficacy, which is the belief that one has the abilities such as physical mental, passion, finance and resources to personally control and execute a planned behaviour (Liñán & Chen, 2009). Using these assumptions to explain entrepreneurial inclination suggest that the final year tertiary students will undertake critical evaluations and dictate for themselves the extent to which the economic and social determinants that contribute to their entrepreneurial inclination.

University Student's Entrepreneurial Inclination

Entrepreneurship is a multifaceted and complex phenomenon which according to Krueger Jr et al. (2000) is better predicted by observing intentions towards a behaviour. Intentions are the single best predictor of planned behaviour (Bagozzi et al., 1989). While entrepreneurial inclination connotes a readiness to take advantage of business opportunity (Krueger & Brazeal, 1994), it is also referred to as the eagerness to undertake a new business venture (Piperopoulos & Dimov, 2015).

The unit of analysis of this study is students' entrepreneurship, which Bergmann et al. (2016) define as venture creation activities of people who are currently studying at a university. Ghanaian tertiary education is divided into university (academic education) covering a four years programme and Polytechnics (vocational) education is pursued for three years. University education is provided by both private and public institutions. The focus of this study is students in a public university. Entrepreneurship has become important in universities due to various reasons. Titus, House and Covin (2017) argued that universities are idyllic environment for experimenting entrepreneurial capabilities and ideas. This comes behind the observation that in recent times most universities have set out to exploit entrepreneurial opportunities to become 'entrepreneurial university' (Etzkowitz et al., 2000). Thus, Geissler and Zanger (2013) find a positive effect of perceived entrepreneurial climate at universities on students' entrepreneurial intentions. With this mindset, universities are able to 'provide thinking, leadership and activity to enhance entrepreneurship capital' (Audretsch, 2014, p. 320). With this approach they are able to transfer knowledge from the university to the market (Åstebro et al., 2012).

Mixed findings have been reported in empirical studies on student's entrepreneurial intention. In a study of the entrepreneurial perception of Puerto Rico students, Veciana et al. (2005) found that 90% of them showed high desirability for entrepreneurship. Similar findings were made among students from the United States, Korea, Fiji and China by Lee et al. (2006). They concluded that American students had low entrepreneurial intention due to the prosperous American economy that was able to provide more job opportunities. Another study by Guerrero et al. (2008) revealed that 70% of the students had high entrepreneurial intention. In addition, students' entrepreneurial inclination was higher in Ghana (Samuel et al., 2013) and South Africa (Shambare, 2013), while lower entrepreneurial inclination was identified among students in Spain (Sánchez, 2013). The higher level of Ghanaian students can be attributed to a core course in entrepreneurship, which most university students have to take and pass before they graduate.

Although university students are exposed to entrepreneurial training, Wennberg et al. (2010) observed that most students do not normally start their own businesses directly after completing their studies, but might be able to do some at a later stage in their career. As more universities equip their students with the entrepreneurial knowledge and skills for starting a business, gathering entrepreneurial experience during their studies can be assumed to facilitate subsequent start-up endeavours of students. This study thus agrees with Walter et al. (2013) that by offering entrepreneurship courses and training, the universities provide entrepreneurial context, thereby enhancing students' entrepreneurial inclination and abilities to engage in entrepreneurial venture. It can thus be said that since the students in this study have been exposed to entrepreneurship, they will have entrepreneurial inclination.

Empirical Review and Hypotheses

Economic Determinants of Students' Entrepreneurial Inclination

Economic factors affecting students' entrepreneurial intention include external factors such as educational curriculum and geographical location of the students. Entrepreneurial curriculum contains information on entrepreneurial activities which should be discussed in the classroom to provide students with another venue for examining entrepreneurial strategies and learning about the successes and failures of new ventures (OECD, 2010). Such education enhances students' entrepreneurial inclination by providing them with business management skills to integrate experience, skills and knowledge to start new ventures in the future (Hamidi, Wennberg and Berglund, 2008; Mazura & Norasmah, 2011), as well as learn from real life practical experiences (Hynes, Costin and Birdthistle, 2010). Thus, the focus of entrepreneurship education is to provide a basic knowledge of entrepreneurship (Hynes, Costin & Birdthistle, 2010). Students gain new and much-needed skills to interact with the marketplace as they are provided a chance to integrate creativity and skills during their course (Hamidi, Wennberg & Berglund, 2008). Hence, these programmes should increase their interest to become entrepreneurs (Mazura & Norasmah, 2011) because it increases their business knowledge such as human resource management, business failure signs and causes, general management, advantage on business planning and innovative problem solving (Fuller-Love, Lim and Akehurst, 2006).

The acquisition of such knowledge enables a student to have a high level of self-efficacy, risk tolerance, self-confidence, need for achievement and stress tolerance. Many studies have emphasized that persons with high self-efficacy have high intentions of becoming entrepreneurs. Furthermore, studies have shown that individuals who have positive perception of themselves and believe in their abilities have a high intention of starting their own entrepreneurial ventures. For example, Bullough et al. (2014) indicated that despite the conditions of war, individuals can develop their entrepreneurial inclinations if they believe in their entrepreneurial self-efficacy. Thus, it can be said that students who believe in themselves and are confident in their skills may be able to identify entrepreneurial ideas and turn them into business opportunities. Thus, we hypothesize that:

H_1: educational curriculum is positively related to the likelihood of students' entrepreneurial inclination.

The geographic location in which we live can either boost our zeal to become entrepreneurs or not. This is because a person is moulded by where he or she comes from or lives. A student found in an organizational advanced environment will not be too interested in entrepreneurship as compared to student from less developed areas. Verheul et al. (2001) indicate that decisions at individual levels are influenced by regional characteristics, including culture, but also other region-specific institutions as well as demand and supply factors generating differences in regional entrepreneurs. Further, Thornton and Flynn (2003) claimed that environments characterized by small firms result in more entrepreneurial activities in those areas.

Entrepreneurship is different in an urban environment when compared to a rural environment. Orford et al. (2004) describe entrepreneurship in the rural environment as being mostly necessity-based, whereas in the urban environment, entrepreneurship is more opportunity-driven. Furthermore, rural areas in Africa are characterized by lack of infrastructure and opportunities, high level of poverty and high levels of unemployment (Orford et al., 2004). The higher levels of development in an urban environment thus have a positive influence on entrepreneurship, as opportunities can be found much more easily, thereby creating an environment conducive to entrepreneurship, hence the increase in the number of entrepreneurs in the rural areas as compared to the urban areas. Obeng-Odoom (2011) describe the rapid urbanization in Africa as having caused a migration from rural areas to urban areas who engage in entrepreneurial activities in the informal sector. Thus, we believe that geographic location can be especially beneficial in facilitating students' inclination to entrepreneurship in developing countries, such as Ghana. We hypothesize that:

H_2: Geographic location is positively related to students' entrepreneurial inclination.

Social Determinants of Students' Entrepreneurial Inclination

Environmental factors which influence entrepreneurial intentions include social factors. Social factors look at the issues of peer association and parent influence. Human beings are social beings, according to Maslow's love and belongingness needs theory. This posits that humans need social feelings of belongingness. Examples are friendship, acceptance, receiving and giving affection and love from friends. The effect of peer influence on student's entrepreneurial inclination was studied by Biddle et al. (1980). They conducted a study to examine peer influence on adolescents and found that peer behaviours are more likely to affect the adolescent behaviours. The observation supports the claim of social capital theory which posited that social network of entrepreneurs based on associations, interdependences and trust allows entrepreneurs to identify opportunities (Batjargal et al., 2013) and mobilize resources (Stam et al., 2014). In a related study, Robson and Bennett (2000) posited that friends act as the preferred source of advice for small-medium enterprise owners. Basically, new graduate entrepreneurs rely on informal sources such as family members, colleagues and social networks as well as universities (Greene & Saridakis, 2007) for support and guidance in business. Furthermore, peer businesses are also known to inspire fresh graduates by providing a supportive environment which gives them information and resources to start a business after they graduate (Bagheri & Pihie, 2010). Kacperczyk (2013) examines the social transmission of entrepreneurial behaviour across university peers. The analyses show that social influence has a stronger effect on the transition to entrepreneurship when exerted by university peers who share gender with the focal individuals. Therefore, we hypothesize:

H_3: Peer association may be positively associated with students' entrepreneurial inclination

The idea of family members including parents being a source of social capital is based on the conclusion that family is 'a key institution through which social capital is transmitted' (Wright et al., 2001; Buang & Yusof, 2006; León et al., 2007; Mustikawati & Bachtiar, 2008). This capital that according to social theory is embedded and inherent in family relations. In associating with social theory in which networking and embeddedness relate, the family is perceived as an asset that exists in family relations and networks. Thus, social setting with lower levels of social capital considers family capital to be a pivotal resource for professional life and career development (Kovacheva, 2004). Studies carried out by researchers have revealed mixed findings on the importance of family capital provided by parents in facilitating career path. BarNir et al. (2011) discussed how role model contributes to entrepreneurship as a career choice. The results indicate that role models have a significant and positive impact on entrepreneurial career intention. Polin et al. (2016) obtained mixed findings on the determination of the degree to which self-employed parents increase or decrease the desire of children to be self-employed. They found that self-employed mothers have a greater positive impact on the entrepreneurial inclination of their children than self-employed fathers. Additionally, the result revealed that sons have the highest entrepreneurial inclination when both parents are self-employed. However, daughters, have a low entrepreneurial inclination when both parents are self-employed than when only one parent is self-employed. Thus, we hypothesize that:

H_4: Parents views are positively related to students' entrepreneurial inclination in Ghana.

Methodology

Research Design

The study was guided by quantitative research approach. This helped to analyse the hypotheses formulated for the study. The researchers are in agreement with Aliaga and Gunderson (2002) that an explanation of a phenomenon can be done by collecting numerical data that are analysed using mathematical methods. Additionally, the objectives of the study sought to find out the factors that can be used to predict students' entrepreneurial inclinations. The research design used for this study was explanatory research design. The primary drive for explanatory research is to elucidate why things happen and predict what will happen next (Viotti & Kauppi, 2019). Given that the study examines factors that influence students' entrepreneurial inclination, an explanatory research design with a cross-sectional survey approach was employed.

Survey is commonly applied to a research designed to collect data from a specific population, or a sample from that population, and typically utilizes a questionnaire or an interview as the survey instrument (Robson et al., 1993). Surveys are used to obtain data from individuals about themselves, their households, or about larger social institutions. The survey design was therefore appropriate for this study since it entailed the process of collecting data in order to answer questions concerning the factors that influence entrepreneurial inclination among tertiary students.

The study was carried out at the University of Cape Coast and it focused on final year undergraduate management students. According to the Students Records and Management Information Section (SRMIS, 2018), the number of management students were 295. The researchers used a census—complete enumeration, which means a complete count of every unit in the target population. It was deemed appropriate for the study as every unit was known and accessible. Using such technique enabled the researchers to increase statistical confidence of the results as well as giving every unit in the population an opportunity to provide feedback.

Measurement of Variables

These were the key variables for the study—peer association, parents influence, academic curriculum and geographical location. They were measured using 26 items. The next section is a breakdown of how each of the variables was measured.

Entrepreneurial Inclination

Entrepreneurial inclination was measured using the scale provided by Yusof et al. (2008) from 1 strongly disagree to 5 strongly agree.

Economic Factors

Economic factors comprised academic curriculum and geographical location. These were measured using the scale developed by Walter and Block

(2016) and Belas et al. (2017). Academic curriculum had six items and geographical location also had six items. The constructs were measured using a five-point Likert scale from 1 strongly disagree to 5 strongly agree.

Social Factors

Social factors, comprising peer association and family influence were measured using the instrument developed by Sahban et al. (2015). Peer association had five items; while parents influence had nine items. The constructs were also measured using a five-point Likert scale ranging from 1 strongly disagree to 5 strongly agree.

Data Collection Procedures

Instrument

Structured questionnaire was used as the instrument of data collection. As Kothari (2004) observed, questionnaires are more objective than interviews because they gather responses in a standardized way. They are also easy to use when collecting information. The closed items captured personal details and attitude scales. The questionnaire had four sections—demographic profile of students, students' entrepreneurial inclination and determinants of students' entrepreneurial inclination.

Data Collection and Analysis

The data collection involved administration of the questionnaires to the students with the assistance of some teaching assistants during free periods of the students. The self-administration method allowed students to answer the questions at their convenience and also to avoid the injection of the biases of the researcher into the responses. Using the free periods for data collections was based on these factors. First, it is a time where students are relaxed, thus, reducing the level of anxiety and stress associated with research. Second, the method provided an opportunity for the researchers to first explain the research topic and objectives and thus motivate respondents to participate in the survey. Third, it allowed the students to clarify doubts and ask questions on the spot. After a month, 180 out of 295 questionnaires were returned, representing 61% response rate. The rate was acceptable for the study based on the recommendation of Mugenda and Mugenda (2003), that a response rate of 50% is sufficient for scrutiny and exposure, 60% is good and a response rate of 70% and over is excellent. All the 180 questionnaires were completely filled and, thus, were used for further analysis. Questionnaires filled by the respondents were edited for completeness and consistency. The data was checked for coding errors and omissions. Reliability analysis was performed using the Cronbach's alpha and all the values exceeded the 0.7 benchmark. The data was then analysed using descriptive statistics such as means and standard deviations, and inferential statistics such as multiple regression.

Results and Discussions

This section presents the results and discusses the findings. Tables 2.1 and 2.2 present results on demographic characteristics and reliability analysis, respectively. This is then followed by regression analysis of the determinants of entrepreneurial inclination.

Table 2.1 Demographic variables

Description	Frequency	Percentage (%)
Male	118	65.6
Female	62	34.4
Total	180	100.00

Table 2.2 Reliability results

Constructs	Cronbach's alpha	No. of items
Peer association	0.730	4
Parent influence	0.790	6
Academic curriculum and excellence	0.826	6
Geographical location	0.747	5
Entrepreneurial inclination	0.798	12

Table 2.1 shows gender distribution among the respondents who took part in the survey. 65.6% were male while their female counterparts were 34.4%. The findings suggest a gender imparity between the two sexes which can be attributed purely to more boys joining the university than girls.

Factors that Influence Student Entrepreneurial Inclination

This section presents results of regression analysis on the economic and social factors that influence students' entrepreneurial inclination. The first section discusses the economic factors of academic curriculum and geographical distance and how they influence students' entrepreneurial inclination. The second section discusses the social factors of peer association and parental views and their influence on students' entrepreneurial inclination. The reliability analysis is first presented in Table 2.2.

Reliability results presented in Table 2.2 show that all the constructs reliably measured the internal consistency (Cronbach's alpha values >0.7).

Descriptive analysis was performed to measure the state of entrepreneurial inclination through the use of means and standard deviations. On a 5-point scale, a mean score of 0–2.5 is considered low, between 2.51 and 3.5 is considered moderate (average) and above 3.51 is considered high (Okorley & Addai, 2010). The results show that the students have high level of inclination in respect of a strong desire to be the owner of their businesses. The scores of the remaining indicators of entrepreneurial inclination show the respondents have moderate levels of such measure such as the belief that there are many businesses/entrepreneurial opportunities in the Ghanaian society, having the propensity to drop out of school if some good opportunity comes their way, they are always inclined towards entrepreneurship and that they are interested in starting their own businesses (Table 2.3).

Table 2.3 Descriptive statistics for entrepreneurial inclination

	Mean	Std. deviation
I have strong desire to be the owner of my business	3.5390	3.17369
There are many businesses/entrepreneurial opportunities in Ghanaian society	3.3174	2.83735
I will not mind dropping out of my studies if some good business opportunity comes my way	3.2846	1.12461
I am always inclined towards entrepreneurship	3.2695	1.21039
Entrepreneurs are highly respected in our society	3.2569	1.22453
I am interested in starting my own business	3.2267	2.18674
Five to seven years from now, I see myself doing a job in some company	3.2191	1.16984
I see myself becoming some type of entrepreneur one day	3.2040	1.46893
I have strong plans to venture into business once I complete my studies	3.1965	1.20884
Present economic conditions in the wake of globalization are favourable for entrepreneurs	3.0806	1.08876
Planning for some kind of business has been, is, or will be an important part of my college career	3.0277	1.17281
Ghanaian social and economic environment is highly supportive of entrepreneurship	2.9295	1.24724

Effect of Academic Curriculum on Entrepreneurial Inclination

Preliminary results show there was no autocorrelation between the predictor (academic curriculum) and entrepreneurial inclination (Durbin-Watson = 1.828). However, there was a strong correlation between academic curriculum and entrepreneurial inclination ($r = 0.704$). There were no multi-collinearity problems in the measures of the predictors given the VIF scores obtained in respect of academic curriculum and excellence construct. An examination of the predictive capacity of the model shows changes in academic curriculum accounts for 48.7% change in entrepreneurial inclination ($r^2 = 0.495$; $p = 0.0001$; $p < 0.05$). Thus, academic curriculum accounts for a statistically significant positive moderate variance in entrepreneurial inclination (Table 2.4).

Regarding the contributions of the predictors (measures of academic curriculum and excellence) to causing significant positive moderate change

Table 2.4 Coefficients

Model	Unstandardized coefficients B	Std. error	Standardized coefficients Beta	t	Sig.	Tolerance	VIF
1 (Constant)	0.767	0.141		5.458	0.000		
My programme exposes me to entrepreneurial knowledge and skills	0.248	0.036	0.318	6.875	0.000	0.605	1.653
I am likely to start a venture because of what I have studied at school	0.088	0.036	0.107	2.424	0.016	0.665	1.504
My programme of study prepares me to become an entrepreneur	0.072	0.040	0.083	1.792	0.074	0.599	1.668
My Venture will be based on the programme I have studied	0.090	0.036	0.116	2.471	0.014	0.590	1.695
Entrepreneurship is for student with high academic performance	0.162	0.040	0.190	4.094	0.000	0.599	1.670
Entrepreneurship is for student with low academic performance	0.118	0.048	0.120	2.475	0.014	0.555	1.802

$R = 0.704$; R-square $= 0.495$; R-square adjusted $= 0.487$; Durbin-Watson $= 1.828$; $p = 0.0001$

in entrepreneurial inclination, it was found that the assertion that academic programme exposes students to entrepreneurial knowledge and skills makes the strongest statistically significant positive unique contribution to predicting the variance in entrepreneurial inclination among students (Beta = 0.318; t = 6.875; p = 0.0001; p < 0.05). Similarly, the assertion that entrepreneurship is for students with high academic performance also causes a statistically significant positive variance in entrepreneurship inclination (Beta = 0.190; t = 4.094; p = 0.0001; p < 0.05). Furthermore, the claim that students' venture will be based on the programme they have studied also causes a statistically significant positive variance in entrepreneurship inclination (Beta = 0.116; t = 2.471; p = 0.014; p < 0.05). Again, the assertion that students are likely to start a venture because of what they have studied at school causes a statistically significant positive contribution to predicting the positive variance in entrepreneurial inclination (Beta = 0.107; t = 2.424; p = 0.016; p < 0.05). However, the assertion that the programme of study prepares students to become entrepreneurs was not a significant positive predictor of entrepreneurial inclination (Beta = 0.072; t = 1.792; p = 0.074; p > 0.05). The results provide support for the studies of Trivedi (2016) and Mustafa et al. (2016), who found that academic curriculum provided the basis for students to develop their entrepreneurial abilities. However, the results contradict the studies of Anne-Støren (2014) and Barba-Sánchez and Atienza-Sahuquillo (2018) who concluded that Norwegian students who study entrepreneurship-related courses did not have the desire to become entrepreneurs.

Effect of Geographical Location on Entrepreneurship Inclination

Preliminary results show there was no autocorrelation between the predictors and entrepreneurial inclination (Durbin-Watson = 1.803), though there was a strong positive joint correlation between geographical location and entrepreneurial inclination (r = 0.769). The VIF scores show there is no multi-collinearity problem in respect of the measures of the geographical location construct. An examination of the predictive capacity of the model shows changes in geographical location accounts for 59.2%

significant change in entrepreneurial inclination (r^2 = 0.592; p = 0.0001; $p < 0.05$). Thus, geographical location accounts for a statistically significant positive moderate variance in entrepreneurial inclination. The results support the studies of Verheul et al. (2001), and Thornton and Flynn (2003) who claimed that environment surrounded by small business can influence students' decision to be entrepreneurial. Regarding the contributions of the predictors (measures of geographical location) to causing significant positive moderate change in entrepreneurial inclination, it was found that the assertion that the existence of a large number of companies in my community prevents me from entering into entrepreneurship makes the strongest statistically significant positive unique contribution to predicting the variance in entrepreneurial inclination among students (Beta = 0.445; t = 12.278; p = 0.0001; $p < 0.05$). Similarly, the assertion that my community is highly industrialized causes a statistically significant positive variance in entrepreneurship inclination (Beta = 0.297; t = 6.932; p = 0.0001; $p < 0.05$). Furthermore, the claim that students' community is highly populated also causes a statistically significant positive variance in entrepreneurship inclination (Beta = 0.248; t = 6.892; p = 0.0001; $p < 0.05$) (Table 2.5).

On the contrary, it is seen that the assertions that the community in which I live influences my decision to become an entrepreneur (Beta = 0.042; t = 1.227; p = 0.220; $p > 0.05$) and the size of my town influences my decision to become an entrepreneur (Beta = 0.034; t = 0.816; p = 0.415; $p > 0.05$) were insignificant positive predictors of entrepreneurial inclination.

Holistic Regression Model

In the holistic multiple regression analysis, the results proved that there was no autocorrelation between the predictors (determinants of entrepreneurial inclination) and entrepreneurial inclination (Durbin-Watson = 1.755). There was a strong positive correlation between the predictors and entrepreneurial inclination (r = 0.737). The VIF values indicate there were no multi-collinearity problems with the measures of the predictors considered in the study. The predictive capacity of the model however shows that the predictors account for a statistically

Table 2.5 Coefficients

Model	Unstandardized coefficients B	Std. error	Standardized coefficients Beta	T	Sig.	Collinearity statistics Tolerance	VIF
1 (Constant)	0.321	0.135		2.369	0.018		
My community is highly populated	0.215	0.031	0.248	6.892	0.000	0.808	1.238
My community is highly industrialized	0.252	0.036	0.297	6.932	0.000	0.567	1.763
The community in which I live influences my decision to become an entrepreneur	0.021	0.017	0.042	1.227	0.220	0.912	1.096
The size of my town influences my decision to become an entrepreneur	0.030	0.037	0.034	0.816	0.415	0.605	1.653
The existence of large number of companies in my community prevents me from entering into entrepreneurship	0.382	0.031	0.445	12.278	0.000	0.796	1.257

$R = 0.769$; R-square $= 0.592$; R-square adjusted $= 0.587$; Durbin-Watson $= 1.803$; $p = 0.0001$

Table 2.6 Coefficients

Model	Unstandardized coefficients B	Std. error	Standardized coefficients Beta	t	Sig.	Collinearity statistics Tolerance	VIF
1 (Constant)	0.168	0.147		1.145	0.253		
Peer association	0.081	0.050	0.081	1.615	0.107	0.460	2.175
Academic curriculum and excellence	0.264	0.081	0.230	3.274	0.001	0.236	4.235
Geographical location	0.393	0.075	0.327	5.216	0.000	0.296	3.377
Parental influence	0.202	0.058	0.183	3.498	0.001	0.427	2.339

$R = 0.737$; R-square = 0.543; R-square adjusted = 0.538; Durbin-Watson = 1.755; $p = 0.0001$

significant positive 54.3% variance in entrepreneurial inclination. With respect to the contributions of the predictors, it was found that geographical location is the strongest unique positive significant predictor of entrepreneurial inclination (Beta = 0.327; $t = 5.216$; $p = 0.0001$; $p < 0.05$). Again, academic curriculum and excellence also made a statistically significant positive contribution to predicting the positive variance in entrepreneurial inclination (Beta = 0.230; $t = 3.274$; $p = 0.001$; $p < 0.05$). Similarly, parental influence is adjudged a significant positive predictor of entrepreneurial inclination among final year students in University of Cape Coast (Beta = 0.183; $t = 3.498$; $p = 0.001$; $p < 0.05$). However, peer association was not significant positive predictor of entrepreneurial inclination (Beta = 0.081; $t = 1.615$; $p = 0.107$; $p < 0.05$) (Table 2.6).

Effect of Peer Association on Entrepreneurial Inclination

The assessment of the predictive model included assessment of autocorrelation, correlation, multi-collinearity, the predictive capacity, the path coefficients and the estimated regression model. The classification of the correlation results depends on the following cut-off points suggested by

Cohen (1988) in that respect: r = 0.10 to 0.29 or r = -0.10 to -0.29 (Very weak); r = 0.30 to 0.49 or r = -0.30 to -0.49 (Weak); r = 0.50 to 0.69 or r = -0.50 to -0.69 (Moderate); r = 0.70 to 0.99 or r = -0.70 to -0.99 (Large). There is a strong positive correlation between the predictors and entrepreneurial inclination (r = 0.716). There was no autocorrelation (Durbin-Watson = 1.700). The predictive capacity of the model was measured with the R-square value. The R-square is the most common effect size measure in path models (Garson, 2016). Hock and Ringle (2006) further prescribed some tentative cut-off points for describing R-square as follows: R-square results above 0.67 (Substantial), 0.33 (Moderate) and 0.19 (Weak). The R-square value includes the unique variance explained by each variable and also that shared (Pallant, 2005). VIF needs to have a score of 5 or lower to avoid multi-collinearity problem (Kock & Lynn, 2012) (Table 2.7).

Table 2.7 Peer association and entrepreneurial inclination

Model	Unstandardized coefficients B	Std. error	Standardized coefficients Beta	T	Sig.	Tolerance	VIF
1 (Constant)	0.582	0.138		4.211	0.000		
I care what close friends think about my employment decision	0.075	0.036	0.084	2.094	0.037	0.779	1.283
I believe what close friends think about entrepreneurship	0.292	0.040	0.333	7.225	0.000	0.587	1.705
Friends are main source of business-related information	0.207	0.037	0.227	5.545	0.000	0.743	1.346
I will pursue entrepreneurship because my friends are into it	0.230	0.034	0.281	6.717	0.000	0.711	1.407

R = 0.716; R-square = 0.512; R-square adjusted = 0.507; Durbin-Watson = 1.700; p = 0.0001

Variations in peer association accounts for 51.2% significant change in entrepreneurial inclination (r^2 = 0.512; p = 0.0001; $p < 0.05$). Thus, peer association accounts for a statistically significant positive moderate variance in entrepreneurial inclination. Regarding the contributions of the predictors to causing significant positive moderate change in entrepreneurial inclination, it was found that students believe what their close friends think about entrepreneurship makes a statistically significant positive unique contribution to predicting the variance in entrepreneurial inclination among students (Beta = 0.333; t = 7.225; p = 0.0001; $p < 0.05$). Similarly, the assertion that students will pursue entrepreneurship because their friends are into it also causes a statistically significant positive variance in entrepreneurship inclination (Beta = 0.281; t = 6.717; p = 0.0001; $p < 0.05$). Furthermore, the claim that friends are the main source of business-related information also causes a statistically significant positive variance in entrepreneurship inclination (Beta = 0.227; t = 5.545; p = 0.0001; $p < 0.05$). Finally, the assertion that students care what close friends think about their employment decisions (Beta = 0.084; t = 2.094; p = 0.037; $p < 0.05$) makes a statistically significant positive contribution to predicting the positive significant variance in entrepreneurial inclination among the students. The results provide support for the studies of Batjargal et al. (2013); Stam et al. (2014); and Lingappa et al. (2020), who found that parent and peer had significant influence on students' entrepreneurial inclination.

Effect of Parent Influence and Entrepreneurial Inclination

There was strong positive correlation between the predictors and entrepreneurial inclination (r = 0.732), although there was no autocorrelation between the predictors and entrepreneurial inclination (Durbin-Watson = 1.824). The VIF scores show there were no multi-collinearity problems in respect of the measures of parental influence. The predictive capacity of the multiple regression model shows variations in parent influence accounts for 53.6% significant change in entrepreneurial inclination (r^2 = 0.536; p = 0.0001; $p < 0.05$). Thus, parent influence accounts for a statistically significant positive moderate variance in entrepreneurial inclination (Table 2.8).

Regarding the contributions of the predictors to causing significant positive moderate change in entrepreneurial inclination, it was found that the assertion that other family members' occupation influences students' entrepreneurial decision makes a statistically significant positive unique contribution to predicting the variance in entrepreneurial inclination among students (Beta = 0.347; t = 7.899; p = 0.0001; $p < 0.05$). Similarly, the assertion that parents' opinions affect students' entrepreneurial decision also causes a statistically significant positive variance in entrepreneurship inclination (Beta = 0.186; t = 4.215; p = 0.0001; $p < 0.05$). Furthermore, the claim that siblings' opinions affect my entrepreneurial decision also causes a statistically significant positive variance in entrepreneurship inclination (Beta = 0.167; t = 3.828; p = 0.0001; $p < 0.05$).

Also, the assertion that students would be entrepreneurs if their parents could support them with the start-up capital causes a statistically significant positive contribution to predicting the positive variance in entrepreneurial inclination (Beta = 0.158; t = 3.819; p = 0.001; $p < 0.05$). The results provide support for the studies of Buang and Yusof (2006); León et al. (2007); and Sahban et al. (2016) that found a positive association between parents' influence and students' entrepreneurial inclination. Similarly, the assertion that siblings' occupation influences students' entrepreneurial decision also causes a statistically significant positive variance in entrepreneurship inclination (Beta = 0.099; t = 2.146; p = 0.033; $p < 0.05$). Parents' occupation failed to predict significant change in entrepreneurial inclination (Beta = 0.051; t = 1.215; p = 0.225; $p > 0.05$).

Conclusion and Implications

This study sought to determine whether academic curriculum and excellence, geographical location, peers, parents, had an influence on the entrepreneurial inclination of final year Management students at a public

Table 2.8 Coefficients

Model	Unstandardized coefficients B	Std. error	Standardized coefficients Beta	T	Sig.	Collinearity statistics Tolerance	VIF
1 (Constant)	0.538	0.139		3.861	0.000		
Parents' opinions affect my entrepreneurial decision	0.156	0.037	0.186	4.215	0.000	0.611	1.636
Parents' occupation influences my entrepreneurial decision	0.040	0.033	0.051	1.215	0.225	0.682	1.466
I would be an entrepreneur if my parents could support me with the start-up capital	0.155	0.041	0.158	3.819	0.000	0.697	1.436
Siblings' opinions affect my entrepreneurial decision	0.136	0.036	0.167	3.828	0.000	0.624	1.602
Siblings' occupation influences my entrepreneurial decision	0.080	0.037	0.099	2.146	0.033	0.565	1.771
Other family members' occupation influences my entrepreneurial decision	0.293	0.037	0.347	7.899	0.000	0.617	1.622

$R = 0.732$; R-square $= 0.536$; R-square adjusted $= 0.528$; Durbin-Watson $= 1.824$; $p = 0.0001$

university. The results supported the fact that academic curriculum has a strong influence on entrepreneurship intentions. Thus, courses pursued by the students exposed them to entrepreneurial knowledge and skills. The implication is that a student can be entrepreneurial whether the student has high or low academic performance. Hence, academic programmes should have in them entrepreneurship to create the mindset and also help students who are future entrepreneurs to cultivate the habit of working for themselves. There should also be robust career guidance during open days and orientation of fresh students. By doing so, students would have the advantage to understand specific courses and future career prospects. With regard to geographical location and entrepreneurial inclination, the results also showed a positive outcome. This means that if communities in which students live have entrepreneurs, they are likely to develop interests or be inclined to entrepreneurship. The results on the effect of peers on entrepreneurial inclination were positive, which implies that if students have friends who thought of being entrepreneurs, they were likely to think likewise. The length of time one stays unemployed influences entrepreneurship decisions of students. The results further revealed that parents' opinion had a significant influence on students' entrepreneurial inclination. This means that parents had a significant influence on their entrepreneurship inclination. Implication is that students will venture into entrepreneurship if parents, siblings and other relatives could provide them with the support and important resources needed to undertake entrepreneurship ventures.

Limitations and Directions for Future Research

The chapter assesses determinants for students' entrepreneurial inclination in a public university. Four factors were examined, including academic curricular and excellence, geographic distance, peer and parent influence. The results reveal that all these factors significantly influence students' entrepreneurial inclination. In as much as this study contributes to the debate on students' entrepreneurial inclination, we believe other factors such as demographic characteristics, religion and support for entrepreneurs could influence their perception and hence, the need to be entrepreneurs. Again, since the study was conducted in one public university, there is a need to compare public and private universities to determine if there are differences in their students' entrepreneurial inclination.

References

Aharonovich, A. R. (2019). Socio-economic importance of state support for youth innovative entrepreneurship in the economic development of the state. *Academy of Entrepreneurship Journal, 25*(Special Issue 1), 1–6.

Ajzen, I. (1991). The theory of planned behavior. *Organizational Behavior and Human Decision Processes, 50*(2), 179–211.

Aliaga, M., & Gunderson, B. (2002). *Interactive statistics*. Virginia, America: Pearson Education.

Anne-Støren, L. (2014). Entrepreneurship in higher education: Impacts on graduates' entrepreneurial intentions, activity and learning outcome. *Education & Training, 56*(8/9), 795–813.

Asamani, L., & Mensah, A. O. (2013). Entrepreneurial inclination among Ghanaian university students: The case of University of Cape Coast, Ghana. *European Journal of Business and Management, 5*(19), 113–125.

Åstebro, T., Bazzazian, N., & Braguinsky, S. (2012). Startups by recent university graduates and their faculty: Implications for university entrepreneurship policy. *Research Policy, 41*(4), 663–677.

Audretsch, D. B. (2014). From the entrepreneurial university to the university for the entrepreneurial society. *The Journal of Technology Transfer, 39*(3), 313–321.

Bagheri, A., & Pihie, Z. A. L. (2010). Entrepreneurial leadership learning: In search of missing links. *Procedia-Social and Behavioural Sciences, 7*, 470–479.

Bagozzi, R. P., Baumgartner, J., & Yi, Y. (1989). An investigation into the role of intentions as mediators of the attitude-behaviour relationship. *Journal of Economic Psychology, 10*(1), 35–62.

Barba-Sánchez, V., & Atienza-Sahuquillo, C. (2018). Entrepreneurial intention among engineering students: The role of entrepreneurship education. *European Research on Management and Business Economics, 24*(1), 53–61.

BarNir, A., Watson, W. E., & Hutchins, H. M. (2011). Mediation and moderated mediation in the relationship among role models, self-efficacy, entrepreneurial career intention, and gender. *Journal of Applied Social Psychology, 41*(2), 270–297.

Batjargal, B., Hitt, M. A., Tsui, A. S., Arregle, J. L., Webb, J. W., & Miller, T. L. (2013). Institutional polycentrism, entrepreneurs' social networks, and new venture growth. *Academy of Management Journal, 56*(4), 1024–1049.

Becker, A. O. (2013). Effects of similarity of life goals, values, and personality on relationship satisfaction and stability: Findings from a two-wave panel study. *Personal Relationships, 20*(3), 443–461.

Belas, J., Gavurova, B., Schonfeld, J., Zvarikova, K., & Kacerauskas, T. (2017). Social and economic factors affecting the entrepreneurial intention of university students. *Transformations in Business & Economics, 16*(42), 220–239.

Bergmann, H., Hundt, C., & Sternberg, R. (2016). What makes student entrepreneurs? On the relevance (and irrelevance) of the university and the regional context for student start-ups. *Small Business Economics, 47*(1), 53–76.

Biddle, B. J., Bank, B. J., & Marlin, M. M. (1980). Parental and peer influence on adolescents. *Social Forces, 58*, 1057–1079.

Buang, N. A., & Yusof, Y. M. (2006). Motivating factors that influence class of contractors to become entrepreneurs. *Jurnal Pendidikan, 31*, 107–121.

Bullough, A., Renko, M., & Myatt, T. (2014). Danger zone entrepreneurs: The importance of resilience and self-efficacy for entrepreneurial intentions. *Entrepreneurship Theory and Practice, 38*(3), 473–499.

Cohen, J. (1988). Set correlation and contingency tables. *Applied Psychological Measurement, 12*(4), 425–434.

Dadzie, C., Fumey, M., & Namara, S. (2020). *Youth employment programs in Ghana: Options for effective policy making and implementation*. World Bank Publications.

Dunn, T., & Holtz-Eakin, D. (2000). Financial capital, human capital, and the transition to self-employment: Evidence from intergenerational links. *Journal of Labor Economics, 18*(2), 282–305.

Etzkowitz, H., Webster, A., Gebhardt, C., & Terra, B. R. C. (2000). The future of the university and the university of the future: Evolution of ivory tower to entrepreneurial paradigm. *Research Policy, 29*(2), 313–330.

Fuller-Love, N., Lim, L., & Akehurst, G. (2006). Guest editorial: Female and ethnic minority entrepreneurship. *International Entrepreneurship and Management Journal, 2*, 429–39.

Garson, G. D. (2016). *Partial least squares: Regression and structural equation models*. Statistical Associates Publishers.

Gedajlovic, E., Honig, B., Moore, C. B., Payne, G. T., & Wright, M. (2013). Social capital and entrepreneurship: A schema and research agenda. *Entrepreneurship Theory and Practice, 37*(3), 455–478.

Geissler, M., & Zanger, C. (2013). Entrepreneurial role models and their impact on the entrepreneurial pre-founding process. http://www.sbaer.uca.edu/research/ICSB/2013/58.pdf

Ghafar, A. A. (2016). Educated but unemployed: The challenge facing Egypt's youth. *Brookings Doha Center*, 1–16.

Greene, F. J., & Saridakis, G. (2007). Understanding the factors influencing graduate entrepreneurship. *National Council for Graduate Entrepreneurship Research Report, 1*.

GSS. (2014). Ghana living standard survey round 6: labour force report. available at: http://www.statsghana.gov.gh/gsspublications. (accessed 22 March 2022).

Guerrero, M., Rialp, J., & Urbano, D. (2008). The impact of desirability and feasibility on entrepreneurial intentions: A structural equation model. *International Entrepreneurship and Management Journal, 4*(1), 35–50.

Hamidi, D. Y., Wennberg, K., & Berglund, H. (2008). Creativity in entrepreneurship education. *Journal of Small Business and Enterprise Development, 15*(2), 304–320.

Höck, M., & Ringle, C. M. (2006). Strategic networks in the software industry: An empirical analysis of the value continuum. IFSAM VIIIth World Congress, Berlin 2006.

Hynes, B., Costin, Y., & Birdthistle, N. (2010). Practice-based learning in entrepreneurship education: A means of connecting knowledge producers and users. *Higher Education, Skills and Work-based Learning, 1*(1), 16–28.

Kabonga, I., Zvokuomba, K., & Nyagadza, B. (2021). The challenges faced by young entrepreneurs in informal trading in Bindura, Zimbabwe. *Journal of Asian and African Studies*.

Kacperczyk, A. J. (2013). Social influence and entrepreneurship: The effect of university peers on entrepreneurial entry. *Organization Science, 24*(3), 664–683.

Kock, N., & Lynn, G. (2012). Lateral collinearity and misleading results in variance-based SEM: An illustration and recommendations. *Journal of the Association for Information Systems, 13*(7), 546–580.

Kothari, C. (2004). *Research methodology, methods and techniques*. New Delhi: Wiley Easton.

Kovacheva, S. (2004). The role of family social capital in young people's transition from school to work in Bulgaria. *Sociologija, 46*(3), 211–226.

Krueger, N. F., & Brazeal, D. V. (1994). Entrepreneurial potential and potential entrepreneurs. *Entrepreneurshihp, Theory and Practice, 18*(3), 91–104.

Krueger, N. F., Jr., Reilly, M. D., & Carsrud, A. L. (2000). Competing models of entrepreneurial intentions. *Journal of Business Venturing, 15*(5-6), 411–432.

Lee, S. M., Lim, S. B., Pathak, R. D., Chang, D., & Li, W. (2006). Influences on students' attitudes toward entrepreneurship: A multi-country study. *The International Entrepreneurship and Management Journal, 2*(3), 351–366.

León, J. A. M., Descals, F. J. P., & Domínguez, J. F. M. (2007). The psychosocial profile of the university entrepreneur. *Psychology in Spain, 11*(1), 72–84.

Liñán, F., & Chen, Y. W. (2009). Development and cross-cultural application of a specific instrument to measure entrepreneurial intentions. *Entrepreneurship Theory and Practice, 33*(3), 593–617.

Lingappa, A. K., Shah, A., & Mathew, A. O. (2020). Academic, family, and peer influence on entrepreneurial intention of engineering students. https://us.sagepub.com/en-us/nam/open-access-at-sage

Martin, B. C., McNally, J. J., & Kay, M. J. (2013). Examining the formation of human capital in entrepreneurship: A meta-analysis of entrepreneurship education outcomes. *Journal of Business Venturing, 28*(2), 211–224.

Mazura, M., & Norasmah O. (2011). Consulting-based entrepreneurship education in Malaysian higher education institutions. *International Conference on Social Science and Humanity, 5*, 163–167.

McKeever, E., Anderson, A., & Jack, S. (2014). Entrepreneurship and mutuality: Social capital in processes and practices. *Entrepreneurship & Regional Development, 26*(5–6), 53–477.

Misoska, A. T., Dimitrova, M., & Mrsik, J. (2016). Drivers of entrepreneurial intentions among business students in Macedonia. *Economic Research-Ekonomska istraživanja, 29*(1), 1062–1074.

Mueller, S. L., & Goic, S. (2002). Entrepreneurial potential in transition economies: A view from tomorrow's leaders. *Journal of Developmental Entrepreneurship, 7*(4), 399.

Mugenda, O. M., & Mugenda, G. A. (2003). *Research methods: Quantitative and qualitative approaches*. Acts Press.

Mustafa, M. J., Hernandez, E., Mahon, C., & Chee, L. K. (2016). Entrepreneurial intentions of university students in an emerging economy: The influence of university support and proactive personality on students' entrepreneurial intention. *Journal of Entrepreneurship in Emerging Economies, 8*(2), 162–179.

Mustikawati, I., & Bachtiar, M. (2008). Hubungan Antar social welfare (Orang Tua) with Minat Berwirausaha At Siswa Sekolah Menengah Kejuruan. Faculty of Psychology and Social Sciences Budaya, Islamic Universities Indonesia. Yogyakarta.

Nabi, G., Walmsley, A., Liñán, F., Akhtar, I., & Neame, C. (2018). Does entrepreneurship education in the first year of higher education develop entrepreneurial intentions? The role of learning and inspiration. *Studies in Higher Education, 43*(3), 452–467.

Ng, E. S., Gossett, W. C., Chinyoka, S., & Obassi, I. (2016). Public vs private sector employment: An exploratory study of career choice among graduate management student in Botswana. *Personnel Review, 45*(6), 1367–1385. https://doi.org/10.1108/PR 10 2014 0241

Obeng-Odoom, F. (2011). The informal sector in Ghana under siege. *Journal of Developing Societies, 27*(3–4), 355–392.

O'Connor, A. (2013). A conceptual framework for entrepreneurship education policy: Meeting government and economic purposes. *Journal of Business Venturing, 28*(4), 546–563.

Okorley, E. L., & Addai, E. O. (2010). Factors influencing the accessibility of yam planting materials in the Techiman District of Ghana. *Journal of Development Studies, 7*(2).

Orford, J., Herrington, M., & Wood, E. (2004). Global entrepreneurship monitor: South African report. *Graduate Schools of Business, University of Cape Town, Cape Town.*

Organisation for Economic Co-operation and Development (OECD). (2010). *Education at a glance 2010: OECD indicators*. Paris: OECD.

Pallant, J. (2005). *SPSS: A survival manual*. New York: McGraw-Hill.

Parker, S. C. (2018). *The economics of entrepreneurship*. Cambridge University Press.

Peprah, V., Buor, D., & Forkuor, D. (2019). Characteristics of informal sector activities and challenges faced by women in Kumasi metropolis, Ghana. *Cogent Social Sciences, 5*(1), 1656383. https://doi.org/10.1080/23311886.2019.1656383

Piperopoulos, P., & Dimov, D. (2015). Burst bubbles or build steam? Entrepreneurship education, entrepreneurial self-efficacy, and entrepreneurial intentions. *Journal of Small Business Management, 53*(4), 970–985.

Plecher, H. (2020). Youth unemployment rate in Ghana in 2019. Retrieved February 24, 2023 from https://www.statista.com/statistics/812039/youth-unemployment-ratein-ghana/

Polin, B. A., Ehrman, C. M., & Kay, A. (2016). Understanding parental and gender impact on entrepreneurial intentions. *Journal of Small Business and Entrepreneurship, 28*(4), 267–283.

Quagrainie, F. A. (2018). Family values and practices promoting entrepreneurial competencies among Ghanaian women. *International Journal of Entrepreneurship and Small Business, 33*(2), 202–219.

Robson, P., & Bennett. R. (2000). SME growth: The relationship with business advice and external collaboration. *Small Business Economics, 15*(3), 193–208.

Robson, D., Hague, J., Newman, G., Jeronomidis, G., & Ansell, M. (1993). *Survey of natural materials for use in structural composites as reinforcement and matrices*. Biocomposites Centre, University of Wales.

Sahban, A.M., Ramalu, S.S. And Syahputra, R. (2016). The influence of social support on entrepreneurial inclination among business students in Indonesia. *Information Management and Business Review, 8*(3), 32–46.

Sahban, M. A., Kumar, D., & Ramalu, S. S. (2015). Instrument development: Entrepreneurial social support assessment instrument (IESSA). *Research Journal of Economic & Business Studies, 4*(3), 21–36.

Samuel, Y. A., Ernest, K., & Awuah, J. B. (2013). An assessment of entrepreneurship intention among Sunyani Polytechnic Marketing students. *International Review of Management and Marketing, 3*(1), 37.

Sánchez, J. C. (2013). The impact of an entrepreneurship education program on entrepreneurial competencies and intention. *Journal of Small Business Management, 51*(3), 447–465.

Schaper, A., & Volery, M. V. (2004). Tracking student entrepreneurial potentials. *Problems and Perspective in Management, 6*(4), 45–53.

Shambare, R. (2013). Barriers to student entrepreneurship in South Africa. *Journal of Economics and Behavioural Studies, 5*(7), 449–459.

SRMIS. (2018). *Students records and management systems*. University of Cape Coast.

Stam, W., Arzlanian, S., & Elfring, T. (2014). Social capital of entrepreneurs and small firm performance: A meta-analysis of contextual and methodological moderators. *Journal of Business Venturing, 29*(1), 152–173.

Thornton, P. H., & Flynn, K. H. (2003). Entrepreneurship, networks and geographies. In Z. J. Acs & D. B. Audretsch (Eds.), *Handbook of entrepreneurship Research* (pp. 401–433). Springer.

Titus Jr, V., House, J. M., & Covin, J. G. (2017). The influence of exploration on external corporate venturing activity. *Journal of Management, 43*(5), 1609–1630.

Trivedi, R. (2016). Does university play significant role in shaping entrepreneurial intention? A cross-country comparative analysis. *Journal of Small Business and Enterprise Development, 23*(3), 790–811.

Veciana, J. M., Aponte, M., & Urbano, D. (2005). University students' attitudes towards entrepreneurship: A two countries comparison. *The International Entrepreneurship and Management Journal, 1*(2), 165–182.

Verheul, I., Wennekers, S., Audretsch, D., & Thurik, R. (2001). *An eclectic theory of entrepreneurship: policies, institutions and culture* (No. 01-030/3). Tinbergen Institute Discussion Paper.

Vesper, K. H. (1980). New venture planning. *Journal of Business Strategy, 1*(2), 73–75.

Viotti, P. R., & Kauppi, M. V. (2019). *International relations theory*. Rowman & Littlefield.

Vossenberg, S. (2013). Women entrepreneurship promotion in developing countries: What explains the gender gap in entrepreneurship and how to close it? *Maastricht School of Management Working Paper Series, 8*(1), 1–27.

Walter, S. G., & Block, J. H. (2016). Outcomes of entrepreneurship education: An institutional perspective. *Journal of Business Venturing, 31*(2), 216–233.

Walter, S. G., Parboteeah, K. P., & Walter, A. (2013). University departments and self-employment intentions of business students: A cross-level analysis. *Entrepreneurship Theory and Practice, 37*(2), 175–200.

Welter, F. (2011). Contextualizing entrepreneurship-conceptual challenges and ways forward. *Entrepreneurship Theory and Practice, 35*(1), 165–184.

Wennberg, K., Wiklund, J., De Tienne, D. R., & Cardon, M. S. (2010). Reconceptualizing entrepreneurial exit: Divergent exit routes and their drivers. *Journal of Business Venturing, 25*(4), 361–375.

World Bank. (2018). Unemployment, youth total (% of total labor force ages 15–24) (modeled ILO estimate). Available at: https://data.worldbank.org/indicator/SL.UEM.1524.ZS?locations=GH (accessed 18th July 2023).

Wright, J. P., Cullen, F. T., & Miller, J. T. (2001). Family social capital and delinquent involvement. *Journal of Criminal Justice, 29*(1), 1–9.

Yang, J. (2013). The theory of planned behaviour and prediction of entrepreneurial intention among Chinese undergraduates. *Social Behaviour and Personality: An International Journal, 41*(3), 367–376.

Yeboah, A.S., K.umi, E., & Awuah, J. B. (2013). An assessment of entrepreneurship intention among Sunyani Polytechnic Marketing students. *International Review of Management and Marketing, 3*(1), 37–49.

Yusof, M., Sandhu, M. S., & Jain, K. K. (2008). Entrepreneurial inclination of university students: A case study of students at Tun Abdul Razak University. *UNITAR e-Journal, 4*(1), 1–14.

3

Understanding Customer Service for Small and Entrepreneurial Firms

Kwame Adom

Introduction

The survival or otherwise of the business rests on the customer. The old phrase "the customer is the King/Queen" is still relevant to enterprises' creation and growth. The customer is still always "BOSS" and, thus, customer service remains a topic for debate. Consequently, excellent customer service delivery remains one of the several elements that enterprises worldwide use to attract, satisfy, and win the life customers' lifetime loyalty and a competitive edge. Zeithaml et al. (1996) opine that customer service, which results in customer satisfaction, is central to firm performance and revenue. However, excellent customer service is anchored on service quality delivery, influencing loyalty (Meesala & Paul, 2018). When entrepreneurs deliver service quality that meets or exceed customers' expectations, the outcome will be customer satisfaction and loyalty

---

K. Adom (✉)
School of Business, Burman University, Lacombe, AB, Canada
e-mail: kwameaadom@burmanu.ca

(Izogo & Ogba, 2015). Based on customer service's phenomenal contribution to the bottom lines, most firms apply several customer service activities to meet customer expectations (Mahmoud et al., 2018). The concept and practice of customer service, particularly in well-developed and large businesses, have been well researched (Cook, 2010; Mahmoud et al., 2018; Meesala & Paul, 2018), but there is little attention paid to the practice of customer service within the context of the Micro-, Small-, and Medium-Scale Enterprises—MSMEs (Naatu et al., 2016). The size and unique business processes of MSMEs differ from large enterprises or corporations in their formation, functionality, and strategy formulation. Therefore, customer service approaches and their associated managerial connotations vary from one business to another (Abosede et al., 2016). The need has consequently arisen for a study on customer service practices in MSMEs within the Ghanaian context.

In recent times, the concept of MSMEs has gained attention in the literature and long-held notions formed at the end of the nineteenth century that large firms offer the most outstanding support for the economy has been challenged since the 1950s (Wang, 2016). The reason is that the contributions of MSMEs across the world cannot be overlooked. In several developed and developing countries, MSMEs form a large part of the private sector (Beck & Demirguc-Kunt, 2006). They are drivers of economic growth and job creation in developing countries (Ayandibu & Houghton, 2017; Wang, 2016). Ayyagari et al. (2007), in examining the role of MSMEs in job creation, indicated that MSMEs with less than 250 employees are the engines of growth in several countries. Beck et al. (2005) add that MSMEs constitute over 60% of total employment in manufacturing in most developing countries. Bello et al. (2018) reveal that a significant relationship exists between MSMEs' operation and economic growth in developing nations. In Ghana, MSMEs contribute about 70% to Ghana's GDP and account for about 92% of businesses in Ghana (Abor & Quartey, 2010).

The concept of MSMEs, like many concepts, has generated much debate in the development discourse, and it remains a contested sphere in terms of agreed definition (Abor & Quartey, 2010; Akorsu & Agyapong, 2012; Gibson & Van der Vaart, 2008). As such, different scholars, institutions, and even governments have offered various definitions for

MSMEs. Some definitions tend to focus on the number of employees, amount of capital invested, and production volume (Jordan et al., 1998; Osei et al., 1993). According to Gibson and van der Vaart (2008), taking into account the country-specific economic context in which the SME operates, for example, an SME in Ghana would be defined as having an annual turnover of between US $23,700 and US $2,370,000. As highlighted by Akorsu and Agyapong (2012, p. 137)

> According to Akorsu and Agyapong (2012), NBSSI in 1998 provided an operational definition of small business. According to this body, a small business is any business that employs up to 29 people. They are divided into micro, small, and medium enterprises: micro-enterprises, employing up to 5 employees with fixed assets (excluding land and building) not exceeding the value of $10,000; small enterprises employ between 6 and 29 employees or having fixed assets (excluding land and building) not exceeding $100,000; and medium enterprises employ between 30 and 99 employees with fixed assets of up to $1m. This chapter uses this definition of MSMEs cited by Akorsu and Agyapong (2012) as a working definition.

However, the chapter focuses on micro and small firms because interest in such firms' research is low. As such, there is little knowledge regarding the customer service practices of MSMEs.

The rest of the chapter presents a literature review on some key areas that create an understanding of the research phenomenon. In conducting the literature review internet search engine like Google Scholar and other databases such as Emerald, Science Direct, Inderscience, Elsevier, and so on just to mention but a few were utilised. Attention is then turned to a customer service analysis of micro and small enterprises and, hence, entrepreneurial ventures.

Understanding the Concept of MSMEs in Ghana

Ghanaian scholars and organisations have, over the years, carved various definitions or descriptions of MSMEs. One of the earliest definitions of MSMEs in Ghana was proposed by Osei et al. (1993). According to the authors, the term MSME refers to businesses that employ less than 30 employees. They go further to categorise MSMEs into micro (less than six employees), tiny (6–9 employees), and small (10–29 employees). The National Board for Small Scale Industries—NBSSI (2009) uses the criteria of the number of employees and the value of fixed assets to provide an operational definition of MSMEs. NBSSI (2009) opine that an SME is a business that employs a maximum of up to 29 employees. The board also divides MSMEs into micro enterprises, small enterprises, and medium enterprises. Per the NBSSI, a micro-business employs up to 5 employees with fixed assets (excluding land and building) not exceeding the value of $10,000—using the 1994 exchange rate; and a small enterprise employs between 6 and 29 employees and having fixed assets (excluding land and building) not exceeding $100,000.

There appears to be a consensus with regards to what constitute MSMEs in Ghana. The cut-off point in terms of the number of employees that an MSME should have is 29, as indicated by Osei et al. (1993) and NBSSI (2009). No definition of MSME in the Ghanaian context pegs the number of employees to more than 29. There are still deliberations in Ghana for finding a more unified definition for MSMEs. Currently, there is a final draft of the MSME policy waiting for Parliamentary approval. This chapter, however, sees the adoption of number of employees only as an indicator for the classification of business as problematic, especially in this it is problematic with the use of the number of employees only as an indicator of the size or contemporary times where the use of technology is used to augment human efforts. The study suggests that the volume of activity carried out by a business should be part of the boundary of businesses in Ghana.

Overview of the MSME Sector in Ghana

Abor and Quartey (2010) and Kayanula and Quartey (2000) observe that Ghana's MSMEs can be grouped into urban enterprises and rural enterprises. Urban enterprises can further be divided into organised and unorganised enterprises, otherwise known as informal enterprises (See Adom, 2016). Organised enterprises in Ghana often have a registered office for business activities and have paid employees, whilst the unorganised or informal enterprise mainly operates in open spaces, wooden structures/kiosks/containers or at home (Adom, 2016, 2017). Most of them also rely on unpaid workforces, such as family members and apprentices (Kayanula & Quartey, 2000; Osei et al., 1993). The MSME sector of Ghana comprises businesses of different categories. These include retailing, wholesaling, manufacturing, services, among several others. Most MSMEs in Ghana are owned and operated by women (Abor & Quartey, 2010). This could be explained by the flexibility and independence working MSMEs offer, which most women desire considering their positions in society as wives, mothers, caretakers, and the likes.

Scholars agree that the existence of MSMEs contributes significantly to national economic development in developing countries (Ahiawodzi & Adade, 2012; Akugri et al., 2015). Abor and Quartey (2010) report that 92% of businesses in Ghana are MSMEs. It presupposes therefore that, the Ghanaian economy, to a more considerable extent, is dependent on MSMEs. Unfortunately, as a country, Ghana does not fully realise the benefits of the dominance of MSMEs in the economy. The majority of these MSMEs operate in the informal sector and are mainly necessity-driven entrepreneurs (Adom & Williams, 2014; Buame, 1996), where they are not well traced for tax purposes. Irrespective of this, the significant contributions of MSMEs in Ghana cannot be overlooked. MSMEs in Ghana play a role in reducing unemployment and ensuring income stability (Abor & Quartey, 2010). However, Akugri et al. (2015) contend that MSMEs in rural regions play minimal roles in employing since most of them rely on unpaid labour (family members). Kayanula and Quartey (2000) maintain that MSMEs play a key role in making domestic markets efficient, and they make use of scarce resources, thereby triggering economic growth. Though they are providers of goods and services, MSMEs are also consumers of raw materials and other services needed in the production. The purchasing power they exhibit positively influences the Ghanaian economy (Abor & Quartey, 2010).

By nature of their size and location, micro-firms have direct contact with consumers better than larger firms. Large firms tend to focus on business-to-business (B to B) markets instead of the Business-to-Consumer (B to C). Most micro-firms bridge the gap between the producers of some products and consumers by making the goods or services conveniently accessible to consumers. In other words, they are retailers. For instance, although Nestle Ghana is the producer of milo, ideal milk, and so on, micro and/or small firms in the form of provision shops, supermarkets, among others, make these goods available at various locations convenient. In the service context, a large energy firm like the Electricity Company of Ghana sells its services to consumers heavily through micro/small vendors. Most micro/small firms in Ghana engage in businesses that involve the sale of larger organisations' products. For this reason, the survival and growth of such firms are of importance not just to their owners but to the large businesses as well. The benefits of being derived from excellent customer delivery by these firms could also impact larger organisations. For example, a supermarket that has been able to capture a larger share of the local market due to excellent customer service is likely to buy more inventory, thus promoting the growth of medium and large enterprises. Therefore, the impact of excellent customer service delivery by these enterprises is multifaceted.

Over time, there have been concerns regarding the quality of customer service rendered by MSMEs, especially micro/small enterprises. It may, in part, be due to limited financial resources inhibiting the firms' ability to hire people with the required skills and experiences needed for a specific role, especially in customer service or customer care. Aside from this, they are unable to invest in customer service training for their employees. Customer service in these enterprises is not properly cultured and may not have a standard for handling customer service. Therefore, these employees rely on their knowledge regarding delivering excellent customer service and how a customer should be handled to ensure there is always a repeat purchase. The outcome is that customers are unhappy, unsatisfied, and may not wish to transact business with the firm again unless they have no alternatives.

Assessing the Notion of Customer Service

In the views of Munusamy et al. (2010), research on customer service delivery has gained maximum attention in line with the concern for quality goods and services in contemporary times. Hinson et al. (2006) note that firms that aspire to be successful need more than a competitive advantage in customer service to build customer loyalty within the service sector. Over time, customer service has been identified as a strategic tool critical for firm differentiation (Piccoli et al., 2017). Customer service is seen as a marketing strategy (Zeithaml et al., 1993) and a competitive advantage source. It can also lead to customer loyalty (Parasuraman et al., 1991). As a result of customer service's importance, Wong et al. (2015) emphasise that firms are increasingly relying on customer service personnel or employees to offer quality service that aid repeat purchases and profitability. Xue et al. (2013) indicate that customer service is the extent to which a firm can identify, understand, and satisfy customers' needs and expectations through the delivery of high-quality products. Wagenheim and Reurink (1991, p. 3) define customer service as "an organisational perspective and process that focuses on meeting customer expectations by doing the right things right the first time." The authors further state that customer service is a management strategy that is premised on meeting customer expectations. These definitions show that customer service is drawn from or is in line with the marketing concept.

According to Kotler and Keller (1988, p. 17), "the marketing concept holds that the key to achieving organisational goals consists of determining the needs and wants of target markets and delivering the desired satisfactions more effectively and efficiently than competitors." Thus, customer service is a philosophy as well as an attitude. On the one hand, the customer service philosophy believes that firms can operate better when they cooperate with the customer to offer what the customer wants rather than dictate and control what the customer receives. On the other hand, customer service is an attitude when an organisation's culture reflects that the customer is the focus and reason for the firm's existence.

Effective customer service aims to achieve customer satisfaction, higher customer retention, and reduce customer complaints (Díaz, 2017). The enterprise must not perceive customer complaints as a nuisance, in that, those complaints are needed to signal that the business is not meeting the customer's needs adequately. Parasuraman et al. (1991) stress that the key to providing excellent service is understanding and responding to customer expectations. The prevalent ideology about customer service is that it satisfies only external customers and increases costs. Wagenheim and

Reurink (1991), however, consider this notion to be a misconception because they believe that customer service targets both internal and external customers and reduces costs. Misopoulos et al. (2014) pinpoint that, within the airline sector, customer service is exhibited in online and mobile check-in services, memorable flight experiences, and favourable prices. According to the authors, an airline firm fails to demonstrate good customer service when there are delays in scheduled flights, difficulty using the firm's website and lost luggage issues.

In Dooley and Dooley (2003) view, a business spends 15 times more to attract a new customer than retain an existing one, hence the need for excellent customer service delivery. The author then proposes seven steps that firms that are concerned about customer service should follow:

a. Conduct research on the customer to provide tailored goods and services.
b. Greet the customer by name or title when necessary.
c. Demonstrate through gestures that the customer is valued.
d. Find out how the customer can be helped by asking.
e. Provide a listening ear to the customer to help identify needs.
f. Help the customer by fulfilling their needs and wants.
g. Add an extra touch that invites customers back for business.

The selection of these steps was influenced by lived experiences of the researcher and anecdotal evidence through observation.

Levy et al. (2012) also indicate that sustainable customer service is achievable through a combination of standardised and personalised services. The authors, therefore, emphasise that providing customer service entails: having knowledge about customers through research or interactions with customers; creating service standards based on the perception of customers and not internal operations; meeting and exceeding the set service standard through motivating and empowering employees; communicating the promised service via the effective customer expectations management and making realistic commitments.

Some Customer Service Research in Ghana: A Critical Analysis

Discourse on customer service in Ghana is receiving the attention of scholars. However, a more significant portion of these researches have focused on the banking industry and other large firms (see Hinson et al., 2006; Nimako et al., 2013). For Nimako et al. (2013), customers of two Ghanaian banks, Merchant Bank Ghana (MBG) and Ghana Commercial Bank, were dissatisfied with the banks' customer service through internet banking. Specifically, the customers were dissatisfied with the timeliness of response to customer request, the capability to be directed online to resolve problems, and the transaction fee for online banking transactions. Narteh and Owusu-Frimpong (2011) add that, within the banking industry, the attitude and behaviour of bank staff, which reflects the customer service rendered, influences customers' decision to start a business with a bank or maintain a bank account.

Owusu-Frimpong (2008) indicates that Ghanaian banks' customers view the bank staff attitude and behaviour in customer service delivery in the banking industry as unacceptable to say the least. To ascertain the gender differences of bank customers' customer service expectations, the author finds no gender differences and concludes that there is no significant gender difference in the expectations of bank customer services. Atinga et al. (2011), in examining the relevance of excellent customer service in Ghana's healthcare sector, highlight that excellent customer service delivery plays a significant role in patient satisfaction and recovery.

It can be deduced from these extant studies on customer service done in the Ghanaian context that Ghanaians desire excellent customer service delivery from businesses. However, most of the service providers, especially in the banking sector, which has been extensively researched, do not receive good customer service as desired. Research on customer service in the Ghanaian context has primarily focused on large organisations. Attention now is turned on customer service in the micro/small enterprises.

The Relevance of Customer Service in the Ghanaian MSME Sector

Customer service is at the core of a successful business enterprise (Kumar, 2017). Customers often prefer large businesses because they are assured of a higher degree of dependability concerning customer service than MSMEs. However, unless a large organisation implements an in-depth customer service process, it will be more prone to losing customer focus. Mostly, large organisations have the option of serving several other customers. Hence, the loss of a few customers may insignificantly affect finances. This is, however, not the same for MSMEs. To MSMEs, especially micro-firms, every customer or every business transaction is of importance. This can be linked to the difficulty these firms encounter in getting new customers due to their size and resources availability Cooper (2021). Consequently, in contrast to popular notion, MSMEs should have an advantage in customer service due to the personal contact they have with customers.

However, customers' closeness should present an opportunity to render better customer service to meet and exceed customer expectations. The irony is that firms in Ghana often have a narrow perspective regarding the customer service notion. They think customer service only occurs during the product or service exchange period. Due to the limited view of customer service, micro/small enterprises fail to research the consumer needs and want to provide goods and services that meet the customer's expectations. As a result, consumers end up being delivered services that are at variance with their expectations.

Given the rising competition in the MSME landscape in Ghana, there is a need for firms in the sector to effectively use customer service to sustain their positions in the marketplace or to survive. One issue affecting the micro/small enterprise sector is that innovative goods and services rolled onto the market do not take time to be imitated. Hence, these firms must rely on innovation for sustainability and add extra value through customer service. For instance, in 2008, a revolution occurred in the Ghanaian indigenous porridge meal industry, (which I call Entreprevolution) when a small enterprise ('Koko King') brought innovativeness in this industry through packaging. This innovation was not inimitable in that it did not take long for other businesses that provide the same services as 'Koko King' to copy the idea. Presently, there are countless such businesses in Accra, especially, rendering 'Koko King' to lose such competitive advantage gained through innovation. Today, even the traditional micro/small porridge business under a shed serves porridge using disposable cups which, customers can opt for. The use of disposable cups for local packaging beverages has since become the norm in that business sector.

For this reason, 'Koko' King, the originator of the idea, must rely on other elements such as excellent customer service to distinguish itself again from competitors. Thus, some innovation forms are not enough to sustain MSMEs in industry, except the innovation is inimitable. Presently, 'Koko' King faces stiff competition from 'Starterpack'. Although their products differ, they appeal to the same breakfast consumers or customers. To enhance customer service, 'Koko' King has implemented a customer ordering service where consumers order meals via a Website, WhatsApp, or phone call. The use of technology-aided equipment or creating a website is not common in the industry in which 'Koko' King operates. Hence, the website has become a platform for enhancing customer experience, which gives the consumer a favourable perception of the business's customer service.

Another business that has distinguished itself in the Ghanaian MSME sector through customer service is "Cook House Ghana" with its "Waakye (rice and pea) on Wheels" food delivery service. This business has broken through the traditional food vending business by providing prompt delivery services. "Waakye" is a local delicacy enjoyed by many. Rooted in the Ghanaian traditions and culture is the ideology that food should not be transported to the final consumer through a third party. Therefore, the idea of delivering a traditional meal like "waakye" was interesting to consumers who value time and convenience. With the "Waakye on Wheels" concept, no longer do consumers have to queue to buy "waakye," rather, they place an order for it online in the comfort of their homes and offices, among others. "Cook House" Ghana has been able to gain customer trust by its prompt delivery of service.

The above discourse shows that customer service is essential for the SMEs context. Through it, MSMEs can build a competitive advantage, gain consumer trust, and influence repeat purchases.

Customer Service for the Ghanaian MSME Sector in the Spotlight

There have been concerns regarding the level of customer service delivered by MSMEs in Ghana. Whereas some MSMEs are making significant efforts to satisfy customers through excellent customer service, others are reluctant, leaving their survival and growth to chances. For some businesses, growth and sustainability rest on some mystical powers, such as anointing oils, juju, prayers, and leap of faith, among others. To the owners of these businesses, the belief is that human element alone cannot alter the misfortunes of the firm. Traditionally, MSMEs have viewed customer service as "a smile" during a business transaction. However, in times past, delivery services have been popularly pursued to enhance customer service in the sector. Yet, customer service management has been tagged as a preserve for large organisations instead of the MSMEs sector.

A large number of MSMEs are providing delivery services to their customers at their convenience. These customers order their items through WhatsApp, phone call, Facebook, or others. For example, "Bathers" is a micro-enterprise that sells ladies footwear and bags, advertises heavily on Facebook, and consumers can place orders via the same platform or WhatsApp. The business also promotes on WhatsApp via status updates. Customers view these statuses and select a preferred item for delivery to be made by the company. This act minimises the time and effort the customer would spend to visit the business premises to select an item, thereby enhancing the business's customer service.

However, as indicated earlier, customer relationship management or database marketing is ignored mainly by micro/small enterprises in the Ghanaian context. Several of these firms perceive that creating a customer database, which enhances customer service, is the preserve of large and well-established firms due to the cost implications. As a result, the idea of customer relationship management is new within the micro-enterprise context. Customer relationship management must not necessarily be applied in the same way larger organisations use it. Micro-firms have always thought that they do not have enough funds to implement customer relationship management systems to keep customer data, but this could be done in cost-effective ways or manually. A business that has purchased a computer can keep customer records by creating a customer database using Microsoft excel. However, in the absence of a computer, a customer database can be created manually using books, diaries, receipt books, and others. One unique identifier of Ghanaians is the mobile phone number. No two people have the same phone number. Therefore, an MSME interested in reaching out to customers after a business transaction can, instead of writing only the customer's name on the receipt book, also request the customer's phone number. Using these phone numbers, MSMEs can always inform customers about the arrival of new stock, sales promotions, extension of branches, among other relevant information that is likely to improve revenue. The carbon copy of the receipt book then becomes a database for the business.

Customer service is an art and must be acted or performed. To do this, the entrepreneur must have adequate knowledge and understanding of who his/her customer(s) is/are. This has led the author of this paper to propose this new way of perceiving the customer, which will facilitate the implementation of an effective customer service delivery programme. In a bid to achieve this, entrepreneurs must compare customers to the modern-day smartphone (e.g., iPhone). iPhone is indeed one of the most expensive phones in the market. It is also true that users of costly phones such as an iPhone pay particular attention to its handling.

In comparing customers to iPhone, customers, like the iPhone, have options. There are often close substitutes to your product or service, and thus, the customer can use any option at any given time. Therefore, it is incumbent on the entrepreneur to realise this, especially at the initial stages of the firm's growth, so that all effort will gravitate towards the customer who is fluid in terms of available options at his/her disposal.

Customers are also like the smartphone in that they depend on being charged up (motivated/encouraged) to function. It means customers will seldom act if the service provider does not motivate them to act. Through effective customer service, the customer is always ready to act. Flowing from this is that they need to be updated through information sharing either through the traditional marketing communication platforms or through the modern social media platforms. Like the smartphone, lack of updates will render some of the applications inactive. Excellent customer service is where the customer gets informed about the changes around the firm and its products and services.

Again, if entrepreneurs were to protect their customers the same way an iPhone user would do for his/her phone, businesses will thrive better. For instance, an iPhone user has a phone case/cover, screen protector and some liquid to clean it as and when it is dirty. The question is, how often do entrepreneurs protect their customers by building artificial walls—through customer service to ensure that the customer is happy? The answer may not be farfetched. If the entrepreneur is interested in sustaining the business's growth, then the customer must be protected. Some of the ways to protect the customer is knowing the customer touchpoints (Halm, 2014). Do things that will make the customer stick by you, which differs from one firm to another.

More so, customers like the iPhone are developed to perform the same function, but they are different in what and how they interact with their surroundings. Remember, customers are not born equal, and that requires deliberate effort to treat customers as individuals with a peculiar need that requires the entrepreneur's attention. In doing this, every customer is treated like the last one. For example, some customers like chilled beer, others, warm beer, and for this reason, excellent customer services mean each of their needs is met. It is important also to realise that businesses that grow and sustain the enterprise's growth are those who strictly adhere to the customers' requirement.

Customers like the iPhone have more capacity than what can be imagined. However, the entrepreneur must ensure that their capacity utilisation transcends the core functions by exploring new roles.

Above all, the entrepreneur must be aware that customer service inextricably interrelates with trust-building and focuses on building trust to retain customers. Trust is one party's willingness to be vulnerable to another party based on the belief that the latter party is:

(a) **Reliable**: doing what you say you are going to do (most straightforward place to start)
(b) **Open**: not lying to another person (being honest is another easy entry point)
(c) **Competent**: a person's ability or skill level to perform a specific task (setting clear expectations)
(d) **Concerned**: requires empathy (passion about someone's needs and concerns)

These four key elements, when present, define the level of trust in the business relationship (Kramer et al., 1996). For some, excellent customer service, more often than not, is a function of the relationship that may exist between the service provider and the customer. If, for example, a customer happens to be a critical account, such a customer is more likely to receive a better service than those who add little value to the business in terms of their purchases.

Service Quality Delivery for the Ghanaian MSME Sector

Service quality (SQ) has been regarded as an antecedent of customer satisfaction (Ardakani et al., 2015; Hinson et al., 2011; Izogo & Ogba, 2015). Scholars have argued that a high level of quality is the company's key to success and a point-of-difference in today's competitive business environment (Ardakani et al., 2015; Chen & Hu, 2010). This has made it very difficult to decouple service quality from the success trajectory of businesses. Therefore, it is incumbent on companies, mainly, MSMEs to adopt Service Quality Management (SQM). Ghotbabadi et al. (2015) explain SQM as "matching the perceived quality with expected quality and keeping this distance as small as possible to reach customers satisfaction."

Service quality, in general, is subjective. SQ in the MSME sector differs in respect of the industry in which the MSMEs are operating. For instance, SQ among MSMEs in the manufacturing industry is different from those working in a dominant service industry (Latif et al., 2019).

One of the most important and widely applied quality measurement models is SERVQUAL (Parasuraman et al., 1988).

SERVQUAL determines the level of service quality by comparing the customer perception of the service received with customer expectation in five dimensions as the following:

Reliability: the ability to perform the promised service both dependably and accurately;

Responsiveness: the willingness to help customers and to provide prompt service;

Assurance: the knowledge and courtesy of provider employees, as well as their ability to convey trust and confidence to the customer;

Empathy: the provision of caring and individualised attention to customers; and

Tangibles: the appearance of physical facilities, equipment, personnel, and communication materials (Parasuraman et al., 1988).

Though the SERVQUAL dimensions proposed by Parasuraman et al. (1988) has been widely applied, some scholars (Izogo & Ogba, 2015) cautioned that basing service quality assessment on the original SERVQUAL dimensions can be misleading. As a result, context and industry-specific service quality dimensions are needed to assist companies in their service quality improvement programmes.

Conclusion

The chapter discusses customer service practices in MSMEs and recognises SMEs' contributions to the Ghanaian economy. It discusses the contextual differences in the definition and description of SMEs. The chapter emphasises a need for a paradigm shift in customer service in the SME sector. SMEs should begin to move away from the idea that customer service occurs during the business transaction to database marketing and building relationships beyond the period when the business and the customer meet face-to-face. The chapter trusts that, in an ever-increasing competitive business environment in the MSME sector, the application of excellent customer service suggestions can enable firms to reposition themselves and offer unique selling propositions. The chapter also shed light on the relevance of service quality as a conduit for the success of MSME. The chapter has also outlined some ideas to help entrepreneurs in their customer service implementation become more profitable and sustainable.

References

Abor, J., & Quartey, P. (2010). Issues in SME development in Ghana and South Africa. *International Research Journal of Finance and Economics, 39*(6), 215–228.

Abosede, A. J., Obasan, K. A., & Alese, O. J. (2016). Strategic management and Small and Medium Enterprises (SMEs) development: A review of the literature. *International Review of Management and Business Research, 5*(1), 315.

Adom, K. (2016). Tackling informal entrepreneurship in Ghana: A critical analysis of the dualist/modernist policy approach, some evidence from Accra. *International Journal of Entrepreneurship and Small Business, 28*(2-3), 216–233.

Adom, K. (2017). Formalisation of entrepreneurship in the informal economy in Sub-Saharan Africa and the role of formal institutions: An analysis of Ghana's experience. In *The informal economy in global perspective* (pp. 277–291). Palgrave Macmillan.

Adom, K., & Williams, C. C. (2014). Evaluating the explanations for the informal economy in third world cities: Some evidence from Koforidua in the eastern region of Ghana. *International Entrepreneurship and Management Journal, 10*(2), 427–445.

Ahiawodzi, A. K., & Adade, T. C. (2012). Access to credit and growth of small and medium scale enterprises in the Ho municipality of Ghana. *British Journal of Economics, Finance and Management Sciences, 6*(2), 34–51.

Akorsu, P. K., & Agyapong, D. (2012). Alternative model for financing SMEs in Ghana. *International Journal of Arts and Commerce, 1*(5), 136–148.

Akugri, M. S., Bagah, D. A., & Wulifan, J. K. (2015). The contributions of small and medium scale enterprises to economic growth: A cross-sectional study of Zebilla in the Bawku west district of northern Ghana. *European Journal of Business and Management, 7*(9), 262–274.

Ardakani, S. S., Nejatian, M., Farhangnejad, M. A., & Nejati, M. (2015). A fuzzy approach to service quality diagnosis. *Marketing Intelligence & Planning, 33*, 103–119.

Atinga, R. A., Abekah-Nkrumah, G., & Ameyaw Domfeh, K. (2011). Managing healthcare quality in Ghana: A necessity of patient satisfaction. *International Journal of Health Care Quality Assurance, 24*(7), 548–563.

Ayandibu, A. O., & Houghton, J. (2017). The role of Small and Medium Scale Enterprise in local economic development (LED). *Journal of Business and Retail Management Research, 11*(2).

Ayyagari, M., Beck, T., & Demirguc-Kunt, A. (2007). Small and medium enterprises across the globe. *Small Business Economics, 29*, 415–434.

Buame, S. (1996). *Entrepreneurship: A contextual perspective, discourses and praxis of entrepreneurial activities within the institutional context of Ghana* (Vol. 28). Lund University Press.

Beck, T., & Demirguc-Kunt, A. (2006). Small and medium-sized enterprises: Access to finance as a growth constraint. *Journal of Banking & Finance, 30*(11), 2931–2943.

Beck, T., Demirguc-Kunt, A., & Levine, R. (2005). SMEs, growth, and poverty: Cross-country evidence. *Journal of Economic Growth, 10*(3), 199–229.

Bello, A., Jibir, A., & Ahmed, I. (2018). Impact of small and medium scale enterprises on economic growth: Evidence from Nigeria. *Global Journal of Economics and Business, 4*(2), 236–244.

Chen, P. T., & Hu, H. H. (2010). How determinant attributes of service quality influence customer-perceived value: An empirical investigation of the Australian coffee outlet industry. *International Journal of Contemporary Hospitality Management, 22*, 535–551.

Cook, S. (2010). *Customer care excellence: How to create an effective customer focus*. Kogan Page Publishers.

Cooper, R. G. (2021). Accelerating innovation: Some lessons from the pandemic. *Journal of Product Innovation Management, 38*(2), 221–232.

Díaz, G. R. (2017). The influence of satisfaction on customer retention in mobile phone market. *Journal of Retailing and Consumer Services, 36*, 75–85.

Dooley III, J. F., & Dooley Jr, J. F. (2003). Convincing a venture capitalist to invest in your idea. *Bioentrepreneur*, 1–3.

Ghotbabadi, A. R., Feiz, S., & Baharun, R. (2015). Service quality measurements: A review. *International Journal of Academic Research in business and social sciences, 5*(2), 267.

Gibson, T., & Van der Vaart, H. J. (2008). *Defining SMEs: A less imperfect way of defining small and medium enterprises in developing countries*. Brookings Global Economy and Development.

Halm, J. A. (2014). *Customer romance; A new feel of customer service*. JN Halm Books.

Hinson, R., Mohammed, A., & Mensah, R. (2006). Determinants of Ghanaian bank service quality in a universal banking dispensation. *Banks and Bank Systems, 1*(2), 69–81.

Hinson, R., Owusu-Frimpong, N., & Dasah, J. (2011). Brands and service-quality perception. *Marketing Intelligence & Planning, 29*, 264–283.

Izogo, E. E., & Ogba, I. E. (2015). Service quality, customer satisfaction and loyalty in the automobile repair services sector. *International Journal of Quality & Reliability Management, 32*, 250–269.

Jordan, J., Lowe, J., & Taylor, P. (1998). Strategy and financial policy in UK small firms. *Journal of Business Finance & Accounting, 25*(1-2), 1–27.

Kayanula, D., & Quartey, P. (2000). *Paper on the policy environment for prompting small and medium-sized enterprise in Ghana and Malawi* (Working Paper Series, Paper No 15). IDPM, University of Manchester.

Kotler, P., & Keller, K. (1988). *Marketing management*. Pearson, Education. NY.

Kramer, Roderick M., & Tom R. Tyler. (1996). *Trust in organizations: Frontiers of theory and research*. Sage.

Kumar, A. (2017). Why superior customer service should be the key for SMEs. https://economictimes.indiatimes.com/small-biz/sme-sector/why-superior-customer-service-should-be-the-key-for-smes/articleshow/56773042.cms?from=mdr

Latif, K. F., Latif, I., Farooq Sahibzada, U., & Ullah, M. (2019). In search of quality: Measuring higher education service quality (HiEduQual). *Total Quality Management & Business Excellence, 30*(7–8), 768–791.

Levy, M., Weitz, B. A., & Grewal, D. (2012). *Retailing management* (Vol. 6). McGraw-Hill/Irwin.

Mahmoud, M. A., Hinson, R. E., & Adika, M. K. (2018). The effect of trust, commitment, and conflict handling on customer retention: The mediating role of customer satisfaction. *Journal of Relationship Marketing, 17*(4), 257–276.

Meesala, A., & Paul, J. (2018). Service quality, consumer satisfaction and loyalty in hospitals: Thinking for the future. *Journal of Retailing and Consumer Services, 40*, 261–269.

Misopoulos, F., Mitic, M., Kapoulas, A., & Karapiperis, C. (2014). Uncovering customer service experiences with Twitter: The case of airline industry. *Management Decision, 52*(4), 705–723.

Munusamy, J., Chelliah, S., & Mun, H. W. (2010). Service quality delivery and its impact on customer satisfaction in the banking sector in Malaysia. *International Journal of Innovation Management and Technology, 1*(4), 398–404.

Naatu, F., Anafo, S. A., & Nsubugah, L. F. (2016). An assessment of the application of customer service in small and medium scale enterprises in the WA municipality, Ghana. *European Journal of Business and Management, 8*(18), 200–209.

Narteh, B., & Owusu-Frimpong, N. (2011). An analysis of students' knowledge and choice criteria in retail bank selection in sub-Saharan Africa: The case of Ghana. *International Journal of Bank Marketing, 29*(5), 373–397.

The NBSSI News. (2009). The growth of small scale enterprises through credit. *National Board for Small Scale Industries, 1*(15), 10–12.

Nimako, S. G., Gyamfi, N. K., & Wandaogou, A. M. M. (2013). Customer satisfaction with internet banking service quality in the Ghanaian banking industry. *International Journal of Scientific & Technology Research, 2*(7), 165–175.

Osei, B., Baah-Nuakoh, A., Tutu, K. A., & Sowa, N. K. (1993). Impact of structural adjustment on small-scale enterprises in Ghana. In *Small Enterprises and Changing Policies: Structural Adjustment, Financial Policy and Assistance Programmes in Africa*. IT Publications.

Owusu-Frimpong, N. (2008). An evaluation of customers' perception and usage of rural community banks (RCBs) in Ghana. *International Journal of Emerging Markets, 3*(2), 181–196.

Parasuraman, A., Berry, L. L., & Zeithaml, V. A. (1991). Understanding customer expectations of service. *Sloan Management Review, 32*(3), 39–48.

Parasuraman, A., Zeithaml, V. A., & Berry, L. (1988). SERVQUAL: A multiple-item scale for measuring consumer perceptions of service quality. *Journal of Retailing, 64*(1), 12–40.

Piccoli, G., Lui, T. W., & Grün, B. (2017). The impact of IT-enabled customer service systems on service personalisation, customer service perceptions, and hotel performance. *Tourism Management, 59*, 349–362.

Wagenheim, G. D., & Reurink, J. H. (1991). Customer service in public administration. *Public Administration Review*, 263–270.

Wang, Y. (2016). What are the biggest obstacles to the growth of SMEs in developing countries? – An empirical evidence from an enterprise survey. *Borsa Istanbul Review, 16*(3), 167–176.

Wong, A., Liu, Y., & Tjosvold, D. (2015). Service leadership for adaptive selling and effective customer service teams. *Industrial Marketing Management, 46*, 122–131.

Xue, L., Ray, G., & Sambamurthy, V. (2013). The impact of supply-side electronic integration on customer service performance. *Journal of Operations Management, 31*(6), 363–375.

Zeithaml, V. A., Berry, L. L., & Parasuraman, A. (1993). The nature and determinants of customer expectations of service. *Journal of the Academy of Marketing Science, 21*(1), 1–12.

Zeithaml, V. A., Bitner, M. J., & Dremler, D. (1996). *Services marketing, international edition*. McGraw Hill.

Part III

Local and International Perspectives

4

Enterprise Growth in the Informal Economy in Sub-Saharan Africa: An Empirical Qualitative Investigation

Kwame Adom, Melony Ankamafio, Golda Anambane, and Robert E. Hinson

Background of the Study

The relevance of enterprises in the informal economy to most developing economies is infinite (Adom, 2017; Stanculescu, 2017) as the informal economy is highly regarded as the second economy—complementary to the deficits of the planned economy (formal sector), which enables economies and societies to function well (Welter & Smallbone, 2011). Morris

K. Adom (✉)
School of Business, Burman University, Lacombe, AB, Canada
e-mail: kwameaadom@burmanu.ca

M. Ankamafio
Department of Marketing & Entrepreneurship, University of Ghana Business School, Accra, Ghana

G. Anambane
Institute of Social & Economic Research, University of Ghana, Accra, Ghana
e-mail: ganambane001@st.ug.edu.gh

et al. (1996) described the informal economy in developing countries as the answer to issues regarding economic development. It is due to the comprehension that most people in the Sub-Saharan African region rely on the informal economy for livelihood (Aryeetey, 2015). Furthermore, the informal economy embodies a global characteristic of entrepreneurial activity, except that it operates outside the law but is acceptable by society (Welter et al., 2015). The expanded or varied economic activities, such as enterprises, jobs, and workers, are primarily unregulated or protected by the state. Initially, the idea was connected to independent work or self-employment in small, unregistered undertakings but has been extended to incorporate wage work in unprotected or precarious occupations.

The International Labour Organization (ILO) points out that the informal economy acts as "an incubator for business potential and transitional base for accessibility and graduation to the formal economy," and many informal workers show "real business acumen, creativity, dynamism, and innovation" (ILO, 2002, p. 54). Discourse on enterprise growth has recently heightened because growth concerns improvement and value addition to businesses; hence, necessary for either formal or informal enterprises depending on their economic situations, business environment, and management strategy (Morris et al., 2006). Although characteristically, informal enterprises are small, it allows a business to compete effectively in domestic and international markets (Kumar, 2016). They can grow large in countries with weak regulatory enforcement (Benjamin & Mbaye, 2014). However, Aryeetey (2015) describes the growth of informal enterprises as procyclical and toughly linked to the economy's growth. It downgrades the individual efforts of the enterprise owners.

In contrast, the belief is that the growth of informal enterprises is highly linked to the individual efforts of players in the sector than the economy. It explains why all informal enterprises are on different levels regarding growth. Regardless, entrepreneurs need to reinvest their

---

R. E. Hinson
Ghana Communication Technology University, Accra, Ghana

University of the Free State Business School, Bloemfontein, South Africa
e-mail: rehinson@gctu.edu.gh

expertise, money, and time to achieve the desired growth rather than simply creating poor supportive framework conditions. Thus, growth is an indispensable phenomenon to every enterprise, irrespective of its form of operationalization.

By careful observation, Meagher (2010) identifies an intellectual marginalization of Africa in the theorization of present-day economic Informality. The author expresses that although the African continent was the foundation of the informal sector/economy, scholars of informal organizations in contemporary eras perceive African communities as culturally inadequate and structurally irrelevant to the new ongoing global advances. Aryeetey (2015) asserts that several issues regarding the informal economy in Sub-Saharan Africa still need to be discovered. Aryeetey (2015) indicates that the structure of the informal economy is drawn by the sociocultural norms influenced by several years of social engagement. It presupposes that the structure of firms in the informal economy, which determines the achievement of goals, differs among nations and regions. Hence, the growth strategies of informal entrepreneurs could be contextual.

Empirically research in the informal economy spans areas such as characteristics of informal entrepreneurs (Mróz, 2012; Williams, 2007), motives for Informality of enterprises (Adom & Williams, 2012; Williams, 2009; Williams & Lansky, 2013), formalization of informal firms (Adom, 2017; Williams & Nadin, 2011), and so on. Presently, a dearth of research on enterprise growth in the informal economy has been discovered. Again, the research identifies a productivity gap between formal and informal firms. Informal firms have been found to show low productivity (Benjamin & Mbaye, 2012; Benjamin & Mbaye, 2014; Gelb et al., 2009). Therefore, it is necessary to study how these informal enterprises grow despite their size and low productivity, since productivity is a critical growth dynamic. This study aims to fill these gaps by exploring the growth strategies of informal entrepreneurs in Sub-Saharan Africa, particularly in a transition nation such as Ghana. The rest of the study is structured as follows: a conceptual background that discusses extant literature and the theory that grounds the study follows this section; research methodology; analysis of the data collected; and a discussion of the findings. The study ends with a conclusion and suggestions for future research.

Conceptual Background

Explaining the Informal Economy

The term "informal sector" became popular in the 1970s as a tag for economic activities undertaken outside the framework of certified institutions (Hart, 1973). The coining of the term initially arose in response to the proliferation of self-employment and casual labour in Third World economies (Hart, 1985). This informal sector has, over the year, metamorphosed into an informal economy (ILO, 2002). Webb et al. (2013) iterate that the informal economy entails the economic activities that occur outside the jurisdiction of formal institutional boundaries. From the perspective of the ILO (2015), the "informal economy" refers to all economic activities conducted by workers and economic units that are in law or practice not covered or inadequately covered by formal arrangements. Informal economic activities are legal, except that they occur in non-formal or improperly regulated institutions. In a Sub-Saharan African country like Ghana, the informal economy consists of businesses in different sectors. Some are required to register with the Registrar-General's Department and maintain proper financial accounts (Ghana Statistical Service, 2016). A popular explanation for the existence of the informal economy posits the neoliberal perspective, which promotes and encourages private sector investment and indifference to creating more public sector jobs. As a result of the neoliberal perspective, businesses spring up. The proportion of entrepreneurs who participate fully or partially in the informal economy is well noted across developed and emerging regions with big working-age populations (Antonopoulos & Mitra, 2009; Swamy & Singh, 2018; Williams, 2015).

The informal economy is difficult to describe because there are still patchy differences in research regarding definitions and operationalization of informal entrepreneurship (Lubell, 1991; Welter et al., 2015). The sector is referred to as a grey economy, which unlicensed and illegal businesses consist of tolerated entrepreneurial activities at the state and personal levels, and other illegal activities that may vary (Welter et al., 2015). However, Williams (2015) contends that the informal economy includes businesses that are legal that undertake economic activities not declared to the state for tax, benefit, and/or labour purposes. The informal economy has been studied in several dimensions. Prior to the 2010s, the informal economy was viewed as a residual sector created either out of necessity or as a supplement to the formal economy (Adom & Williams, 2014). Beyond its identification and positioning, the concept has been linked to the leading steam economy and theoretical paradigms in strategic management (Godfrey, 2015; Madichie et al., 2020). As it merged into the management literature, the need to operationalize its practice arose, hence its investigation in the Base of the Pyramid (BOP). Examining the informal economy in the BOP provided a new and different context for testing the institutional framework in developed and transition countries (Godfrey, 2015; Kistruck et al., 2015). Consequently, the concept has been studied in the areas of family, child labour, and pensions (Altındağ et al., 2020). The causes, consequences, and actions of the informal economy have also been studied to better show the advantages and disadvantages of its development (Elgin, 2020). Thus, the socioeconomic and political factors influencing the informal economy and their link to institutional quality, tax burden, and tax enforcement are duly outlined (Elgin, 2020; Nobert et al., 2020). The informal sector employs about 60% of the global population. Low- and middle-income economies account for an average of 35% of GDP, compared to 15% in developed countries. Although the informal economy is a worldwide phenomenon, there are significant differences between and within nations. The regions with the lowest informality rates are East Asia and Europe. In contrast, the regions with the highest rates are Latin America (51%), North Africa (62%), Asia (65%)—[AfDB, 2013]; Africa (83%) and Sub-Saharan Africa (85%). It is estimated that Ghana's informal economy accounts for 35.6% of the country's GDP, or about US $63 billion. (https://www.worldeconomics.com).

Assessing the Determinants of Business Growth

Enterprise growth has become of the utmost importance to several governments because of the contributions of these businesses to economic development (Nnamseh & Akpan, 2015). The impact of enterprise growth transcends governments to individuals seeking meaningful employment. In the view of Ghosh (2016), all firms, irrespective of their nature and size, aim to follow a course of uninterrupted growth. Nevertheless, the growth path is more complex (ibid.).

Consequently, competitive growth strategies are necessary for enterprises (Machado, 2016). Again, enterprise growth varies in speed and size (Penrose & Penrose, 2009). Business growth is phenomenal for smaller businesses because it reduces the chance of ceasing business operations (Machado, 2016). Studies have shown that small businesses grow faster than larger ones (Simbaña-Taipe et al., 2019). Inversely, Rizea (2015) finds that larger firms achieve economies of scale, resulting in production and marketing strategies. Higher growth levels allow firms to access more resources.

Extant studies illustrate that enterprises embrace different strategies for survival and growth based on different business sectors (Damayanti et al., 2017). One determinant of enterprise growth is disruptive innovation, as Ghosh (2016) opined. The author contends that disruptive innovation leads to higher levels of growth. Enterprise growth is also influenced by internal finance, past year's growth and sales, and management efficiency (Oke, 2018). Bravo-Biosca et al. (2016) state that a well-functioning financial system catalyses dynamic firm growth in finance-dependent sectors. However, rigid employment protection regulation in labour and research-concentrated sectors bans firm growth and leads to less dynamic enterprise growth dissemination. In the Thai context, Suehiro (2017) finds that the determinants of growth of leading family businesses cover niche products and markets instead of new product development and technology. Shibia and Barako (2017), however, emphasized the entrepreneur's attributes as a determinant of business growth factor. The entrepreneur's level of education and experience is significant in ensuring enterprise growth (ibid.). Other factors such as access to formal credit, lower crime occurrences, and the entrepreneur's mindset about the justice and affordability of the courts influence the growth of medium and small businesses. Further, Baporikar et al. (2016) find access to finance, suitable marketing strategies, excellent customer service, and skilled human resources or labour as the bedrock of the growth of enterprises.

From the preceding discourse, enterprise growth factors heavily rely on the type and size of the business, and business growth is intentional. Growth factors for micro and small enterprises rely heavily on the personal characteristics and strengths of the entrepreneur. On the contrary, larger enterprises tend to be dependent on economic and policy issues in the broader business environment. However, factors limiting enterprises' growth include employee pilfering, security issues, and customer misunderstandings. Even if enterprises, especially small and medium-sized ones, understand the essence of technology in improving business growth, they need to meet the changing technological environment that negatively impacts the business (Baporikar et al., 2016).

Theoretical Underpinnings: Theory of Critical Success Factors

Different authors have defined CSF inversely. To begin with, Rockart (1979), based on the ideas of Daniel, defines it as "the limited number of areas in which results, if they are satisfactory, will ensure successful competitive performance for the organization" (p. 85). The author emphasizes that a firm should constantly and prudently manage these areas. Also, Leidecker and Bruno (1984) describe CSF as the features, elements, and conditions that could significantly impact a firm competing in a stated industry if they are appropriately sustained, maintained, or managed. In the words of Boynton and Zmud (1984), CSF refers to "those few things that must go well to ensure success." In 1987, Pinto and Slevin viewed CSF as "factors which, if addressed, significantly improve project implementation chances" (p. 22). There seems to be a unification of thought regarding the definitions given by these authors; hence, the definition of the term in academic discourse is clear.

Over the years, the CSF theory has been used in studies in different fields. Studies such as Li et al. (2014); Koh et al. (2011); Richey et al. (2009); and Routroy and Pradhan (2013) apply the CSF theory in the area of supply chain management. Also, Luthra et al. (2015) use the theory of CSF to analyse the interactions of critical success factors to implement green sustainability management. In the study by Kim and Rhee (2012), the theory of CSF is used in examining the impact of critical success factors on the balanced scorecard performance in Korean green supply chain management enterprises.

The marketing field has also witnessed some studies underpinned by the theory of CSF. For instance, Cherubini et al. (2015) examine the critical success factors in the marketing of electronic cars. This study applies the theory of CSF to explore the critical success factors that are key to enterprise growth within the informal economy of Ghana. It explores crucial activities informal entrepreneurs perform that are crucial to the growth of their enterprises. In so doing, the growth strategies pursued by the informal entrepreneurs and the marketing activities performed are examined or explored. The Ghanaian informal economy is large but has minimal government support since the majority are operating "off the books," and the government may not be aware of their existence in official government records. Most informal entrepreneurs also operate mainly for survival. As such, business survival and growth have become of the utmost importance to them. To this effect, several informal firm operators do not leave growth to chance, but formulate some growth strategies to help achieve growth goals. Enterprise growth is not an accident but is achieved through hard work and strategic thinking.

The Informal Economy in Sub-Saharan Africa

As scholars postulate, the relevance and scope of the informal economy in contemporary Sub-Saharan Africa must be considered (Adom, 2014; Adom, 2017; Aryeetey, 2015). The ILO notes that at least eight out of ten young workers in Sub-Saharan Africa fall in the classification of informal employment. The informal economy also contributes significantly to the Gross Domestic Product (GDP) of countries in the Sub-Saharan

Africa sub-region (Benjamin & Mbaye, 2014). It gives the impression that the informal economy in Sub-Saharan Africa is larger than the sub-regions' formal sector. There is a need to pay attention to the sector regarding research and policy directions.

Stuart et al. (2018) emphasize that the informal economy in Sub-Saharan Africa is a challenge, and governments of various nations in the region have been battling with how to react to this challenge. It is because it frequently adds to congestion in cities and contributes little to revenue mobilization. Additionally, it is traditionally characterized by low productivity, the production of non-exportable products, and low wages (Sutter et al., 2017). Irrespective of these challenges, the informal economy remains a crucial sector that provides sources of livelihood to the most vulnerable or marginalized in Sub-Saharan Africa (Adom, 2014, 2017). The survival and performance of firms depend on their ability to balance internal needs and adapt to environmental circumstances. The capability of an informal firm to adapt to environmental changes is primarily linked to how the firm is structured (Aryeetey, 2015).

Additionally, the informal economy is large and significant in Ghana. A percentage of about four scores of the Ghanaian labour force is engaged in the informal economy (Hormeku, 1998; Osei-Boateng & Ampratwum, 2011). Nyamekye et al. (2009) render that the size or span of the informal economy of work during the 1980s was twice that of the formal economy. Be that as it may, by the 1990s, the informal business had expanded by five and a half (5½) times that of the formal sector (ibid.). The upward Informality is partly explained by low educational accomplishment. For example 34% of Ghanaians aged 15 or older have never toast in the classroom (GSS, 2012). Thirty-four per cent of Ghanaians have achieved basic training, and 13.7% have achieved secondary education or higher (Adom, 2014; GSS, 2012).

Methodology

Based on the belief that reality is socially constructed and fluid, the interpretive research paradigm is adopted to obtain subjective views that explain how informal entrepreneurs manage and grow enterprises (Angen,

2000). Further, based on the six qualitative research approaches Yin proposed, we follow an intrinsic case study approach to find answers to the overarching research question. We consider the intrinsic case study approach to be the most suitable since we attempted to explore a rare research issue (Yin, 2014). This research's case study is Ghana's informal enterprises. We used a multiple case study design involving 30 founders and owners of informal enterprises within Accra (the capital of Ghana). The study trusts that a sample size of 30 is enough to answer the research questions because the depth of data acquired is essential to a qualitative study rather than frequencies (Marshall, 1996). Accra was chosen because it is a hub for a large informal economy in Ghana. Within Accra (the capital of Ghana), a maximum variation sample was selected from three contrasting neighbourhood types, ranging from disadvantaged to affluent suburbs. They are Nima, Madina, and East Legon. Whereas Nima is a disadvantaged area, East Legon is an affluent area. The suburbs were deliberately chosen (Creswell & Creswell, 2017). Research attempts to use these differences in the economic condition of the suburbs to explain the research phenomenon in its entirety. A convenience sampling technique was implemented within these suburbs to select respondents for the study (Kitchen & Tate, 2001). Thirty (30) owners of informal business participated in in-depth personal interviews. Interview sessions were conducted at the business premises of the respondents. It allows them to express their views in their environment and language, which encourages openness (Symon & Cassell, 2012).

An interview guide was designed as the data collection tool for the study. It used a mixture of closed and open-ended questions to collect data on informal ventures' growth and marketing practices. Aside from questions on the profile of the respondents, such as age, gender, education, and employment status, among others, questions were asked on the growth strategies these informal entrepreneurs formulate to stimulate business growth. Interview sessions are recorded after participants' permission is sought. The recordings were later transcribed. The respondents spoke three main languages: English, Twi, and Ga. The responses of respondents who spoke in the English language were transcribed verbatim. However, the views of those who answered in Twi and Ga (Local

Ghanaian dialects) were translated while ensuring that the meaning of the conversations was preserved. The collected data were then analysed qualitatively in line with the three-stage iterative methodology developed by Miles et al. (1994); data reduction, data display, and drawing and verifying conclusions. The data were following identified themes. To preserve the identities of the participants, codes were developed; IE1-IE30 (i.e., Informal Entrepreneur 1 to Informal Entrepreneurs 30). For ethical issues, the respondents were briefed about the research's essence and their free will to participate. In this regard, participants were made to sign an informed consent form to show that no respondent was coerced to participate in the study. Data were validated by transcripts sent to all respondents to verify if they matched their thoughts and expressions during the interview. They all agreed that the transcripts matched their thoughts and what they said during the interview. The data for this study was collected in 2019, before the Covid-19 pandemic.

Data Reporting/Presentation

Demographic Characteristics of the Respondents

The gender disparity in this study is not so great, yet over one-half of the respondents (56.7%) are males, while female entrepreneurs represent approximately 43.3%. Thus, the reflection on the number of female entrepreneurs and the viability of their activities in venture creation cannot be overemphasized, especially where the masculinity of entrepreneurship has been well documented. Note that informal female entrepreneurs are well represented in this study.

The profile of the respondents also indicates that some of these business enthusiasts have engaged in their activities as early as the age of 15. As such, participants are between the age range of 15 and 65 years. Four respondents, forming 13.3%, fall between the ages of 15 and 24. The 17 (56.7%) participants make up most of these entrepreneurs and are between the ages of 25 and 35, while 8 (26.6%) of these respondents are the second majority between the ages of 40 and 65. Nonetheless, a paltry

3.3% (1) of the respondents were over 65 years. This data reveals that people are agile and active in business while still relatively young.

Arguably, it is understandable that some jobs/businesses require some relative amount of energy to be exerted for efficiency and subsequent growth; hence, this makes it necessary to reveal the sectors in which these business owners operate to help paint a better picture of some of the businesses that are likely to be still viable regarding the owners' ages or the age (existing period) of the business venture. Business operators were found in many sectors, including retail, manufacturing, and service, such as hotel and catering. Most respondents (21–70%) are engaged in the retail business, while 4 (13.3%) of respondents provide services in various forms (e.g., auto mechanic, hairdressing, printing). However, most (13.3%) of these service providers are in the hotel and catering business.

Further, regarding employment status, almost two-thirds of participants (63.3%), who form a majority, are employers with at least one employee to work with, while a little above one-fourth (36.7%) are job creators who work all alone or on their account. Nonetheless, the employment status data reiterates the benefits of entrepreneurship: first, by creating a job for oneself, and second, by offering jobs to others, thereby creating employment for society. It also communicates the essence of enterprise growth in the informal economy.

Even though some informal entrepreneurs engage in formal part-time jobs to earn additional income to support families and/or expand their businesses, the data also reveal that more than one-half (53.3%) of these business operators are seemingly less or not the burden of being the sole or primary breadwinners of their families. However, about 47.7% (14) of participants are primary income earners. To this, the researchers examine whether there is a nexus between the growth of businesses owned by female income earners (entrepreneurs) and their male counterparts. Hence, the question is, "Do female income earners' businesses grow faster than males?" In most parts of our world, especially in Africa, and precisely in Ghana, there is a proverbial saying in Akan: "*obaatan na'nim nea ne mma bƐ di. It* means *it is mostly the mother who knows best what/how her children would feed on/eat.*"

Hence, the number of dependents was also sought. The number of children in each household of respondents is considered to justify the question raised above and the relatedness of dependents on the expansion/growth of the entrepreneur's business venture. The concerns of the researchers are that if there are several dependents in a household with only one primary income earner, then is it likely to affect the growth of their various businesses significantly, if there are no additional streams of income such as part-time jobs, or contribution of income from other adult family members. Hence, the question: "Do informal business operations encounter less or delayed business growth due to the number of dependants of these business owners?" The investigation reveals from data that 13.3% (4) respondents have no extra 'mouths to feed' or provide for. Nonetheless, about half (50%) of the respondents have at least a child as a dependent. More than 16.7% of these participants have two children; 10% (3) of respondents have three children; 6.7% (2) respondents have four dependents, while only 3.3% (1) respondent has six dependents. Furthermore, there is only one income earner for the family.

From the above, it is clear that there is a direct relation between business growth and the number of children (dependents) entrepreneurs may have. Instead of reinvesting the little profit made into the business to ensure further growth, the opposite happens, as a larger portion of this money is used to maintain the home.

Lastly, more than three-thirds of the respondents have operated businesses for more than five years. This suggests the possibility of operating a sustainable informal business in Ghana for a long period. It might be linked to a weak regulatory system, causing the thriving of the informal economy in Ghana. The preceding discussions are summarized in Table 4.1.

Assessing the Marketing Strategies as a Growth Tool of Ventures in the Informal Economy

Any business' marketing strategy encompasses several plans used as tools to grow the business over time and preferably grow customers for life. Since the strategy is usually a long-term, forward-looking approach to planning to achieve a sustainable competitive advantage, developing the marketing strategy is essential. With this, it would be almost impossible

Table 4.1 Demographics of entrepreneurs

Characteristic	Percentage (%)
Gender	
Male	56.7
Female	43.3
Total	100.0
Age	
15–24	13.3
25–35	56.7
40–64	26.7
65+	3.3
Total	100.0
Employment status	
Own account worker	63.3
Employer	36.7
Total	100
Part-time formal job	
Yes	16.7
No	83.3
Total	100
Number of children	
1	50.0
2	16.7
3	10.0
4	6.7
6	3.3
None	13.3
Total	100
Main income earner	
Yes	47.7
No	53.3
Total	100
Age of business	
<1–5	23.3
6–10	36.7
11–15	20.0
16–20	13.3
20>	6.7
Total	100

Source: Field Data (2019)

to sustain clients or customers. Hence, the plan of action designed by the entrepreneur to promote and sell products and/or services is assessed to answer the question: *"What is/are your marketing strategy/strategies?"* It is assessed that some of these informal entrepreneurs still employ a

4 Enterprise Growth in the Informal Economy in Sub-Saharan...

Table 4.2 Marketing strategies commonly used by informal entrepreneurs

Themes	Percentage (%)
None	46.7
Marketing communications	43.3
Referrals/word-of-mouth	36.7
Discount/sales promotion	36.7
Customer service/delivery	30.0
Location, outlets, and ambience	26.7
Quality brand	26.7
Loyal customer promotion	23.3

Source: Field Data (2019)
Responses are more than 100% as respondents have more than one strategy

variety of tactics to attract customers to patronize their businesses. Notable among these approaches were captured in themes such as Referrals, Quality brand, Loyal Customer promotion, Discount/Sales promotion, Marketing communication, and Customer Service/Delivery (see Table 4.2):

Many informal entrepreneurs, representing 46.7% of the 30 total respondents, do not have marketing strategies in any form or shape, yet about three-fifths have at least one practice of reaching out to and keeping their customers. However, the other majority of 43.3% of respondents who use some form(s) of marketing strategy preferably deploy several marketing communications strategies. It is detected that informal entrepreneurs use online and offline marketing communications tools to engage in marketing communications. In line with this, IE 15 opines, *"I try to communicate about my products to customers and potential customers through an advert on the radio. Aside from this, I also market on Facebook and get several people patronizing my business from there."* Concerning offline marketing communications activities, actions such as announcements using megaphones, signage, billboards, television and radio advertisement, product displays, and personal selling, among others, are common among entrepreneurs in the informal economy. Regarding these offline marketing communications strategies, IE 23 maintains that *"I have a billboard directing people to my shop. So, others who did not know much about my business get information from the billboard."*

Similarly, IE 14 mentions, *"We have billboards at vantage points that give potential customers an idea about what we do."* However, to highlight the use of advertisement, IE7 says, *"I engage in verbal communication and advertisement through fliers."* To further show the usefulness of personal selling to informal entrepreneurs. *"I use a megaphone to communicate to customers and potential customers"* (IE18); *"I use the megaphone and wear branded shirts for my business"* (IE21); *"Telemarketing and banner display"* (IE3). Interestingly, a very traditional means of marketing communication is identified when a respondent said, *"I do much shouting to call customers"* (IE25)

On the flip side, online marketing communication strategies were carried out through social media and online marketing platforms. These have also become valuable tools for some informal entrepreneurs who are technologically savvy and thus take advantage of the Internet by posting product images, especially on Facebook, Instagram, and Twitter. In support of the preceding discussion, some respondents highlight the following:

> *"I do a lot of Cloud bulletins and displays."* (IE19)
> *"Social media is my thing because I am targeting the youth."* (IE1)
> *"I am on social media and engage in internet marketing a lot."* (IE5)
> *"We also engage in social media Ads and shelf display."* (IE14)

"*Tonaton*" and "OLX" are among the few popular online marketplaces in Ghana. On these platforms, buyers and sellers can trade in new and/or used products alike. *"Tonaton"* means "buy and sell" (in the Ghanaian Akan dialect) and has become a valuable tool for marketing enterprises in the marketplace via the Internet, regardless of their level of Informality. It reveals that informal entrepreneurs have their presence on online platforms, including OLX and Facebook, to reach a more comprehensive marketplace. Hence, irrespective of the level of (in)formality, several entrepreneurs could still communicate to audiences about their business ventures through social media/the Internet. Online and social media marketing has recently deepened the informal economy since it is difficult to physically locate them within the communities. New entrants into the informal economy do so by participating in the online business, partly or wholly unregistered by the state.

Regarding referral or word-of-mouth, a little above 36.7% of participants have benefited from referrals or recommendations; hence, the participants confirm that some customers are advocates for the enterprises. It becomes the marketing strategy for these entrepreneurs in the informal economy. As such, IE1 and IE15 demonstrate this by saying respectively: "I get *referrals from loyal customers, and this has been helpful.*" (IE1); "*I have reliable customers who make referrals*" (IE21). The data illustrates that entrepreneurs depend on customers to pass positive information (Word-of-mouth) about their products to friends, families, colleagues, and others in the marketplace. The evidence of customers to others helps drive customer traffic to these entrepreneurs. Hence, their informal businesses have acquired new customers through recommendations made by friends and existing customers. Therefore, it is crucial that business operators manage their customers well and not tarnish their business reputation, as negative word-of-mouth could be detrimental to growing any business venture. The referrals are also a factor for informal enterprise growth, especially online ones. The reason is that some security issues with doing business online, such as scammers, put some customers off. As a result, if their friends and family refer them to a particular online retailer, they feel more confident and assured about doing business with this enterprise.

Another 36.7% of businesspeople have resorted to sales promotion and discounts offering to capture buyers' hearts and influence their patronage. Therefore, some participants remark:

> "*There are discounts for customers on certain quantities.*" (IE26)
> "*Sometimes, I discount for large orders*" (IE30).

Further, data divulge that entrepreneurs in the informal economy use pricing strategies in addition to other marketing communication strategies; for example, participants' intonations infer that as the entrepreneur sells a product, he/she offers discounts to customers and then seizes that opportunity to introduce or promote other merchandise to same customers by encouraging them to sample or try the products for free. The vendor tries to use several approaches to influence the customer to sometimes act on impulse. Notwithstanding, because most customers seem to be price-sensitive, such marketable engagement with customers has usually increased the opportunity for further sales, which has sometimes led to repeat purchases and thus maintained the customer.

Consequently, some of these customers occasionally direct other prospects to the shop by referring to billboards and/or signposts of the business. Thus, to several of these entrepreneurs, price reductions, discounts, and higher commissions for other retailers increase market share and generate high returns. These actions influence marketing strategy, thereby engaging in competitive pricing strategies to maintain their customers. Customer service and delivery cover 30% of the entrepreneurs' informal marketing activities. According to these entrepreneurs, it is necessary to equip other workers with the requisite skills to serve customers better. These service/interpersonal skills are critically functional either during the point of sale by being polite and exhibiting extraordinary knowledge about the product being sold or the business activity that the entrepreneur is engaged in. To this, IE7 asserts that *"I make friends with my customers"* (IE14). IE30 presents a similar view by saying, *"We give good customer service."* Again, offering variants of the product line and further explaining the core benefits of products is of the essence, as IE3 mentions, *"Selling a variety of products."* The entrepreneurs also practice after-sales customer service when the business retails equipment, repairs, and/or installs electronics and machinery. At the same time, others have also lightened the transportation burdens of customers by delivering purchased or ordered items at customers' doorstep. These are reflected in the comments of some respondents: *"We offer some services in terms of fixing products for clients"* (IE5); *"I adequately talk to customers and deliver items at affordable cost"* (R11). Entrepreneurs sometimes distribute their call cards and further follow up on customers to keep in touch with customers, thereby building and bonding relationships with customers. Therefore, IE14 maintains that *"We also distribute complimentary cards to customers. Through we get other contacts to form them"* (IE5). In summary, being responsive to customer needs in a polite and friendly manner can keep the informal entrepreneur's safety net as he/she nurtures the growth business.

Further, 26.7% of participants reveal how they use location, outlets, and/or ambience of business to keep their pace in the business environment. According to Berman and Evans, "a location may let a retailer succeed even if its strategy is mediocre" because it significantly impacts the entrepreneur's strategy, especially when considering the target market and competition, among several factors. For instance, most of these entrepreneurs usually locate their businesses in a busy area such as the Kwame Nkrumah Circle (located in the heart/centre of the capital city) because it has the potential to direct customer traffic to their shops and/or eateries. Implicitly, locating a business in busy areas that are easily accessible with a dense population size and relative purchasing power for patronage may be a desirous strategy for most entrepreneurs due to market demand. Thus, the importance of location to a retailer must be emphasised. In support of this, some respondents opined:

> *"It is a good ambience for customers, considering my location (Circle)."* (IE7)
> *"I have a nice eating environment, and that is what attracts the customers"* (IE21)
> *"I have stores in different areas in the capital city."* (IE11)

Another 26.7% of the respondents believe that the quality of their product offerings (brands) and/or the name the business has built over time has solidified their operations. As a result, some respondents opine:

> "[A] *good name and quality food has also been our strategy.*" (IE21)
> "*Old Glory! We have made a name already.*" (IE11)

Nonetheless, 23.3% of the respondents allude that loyal customer promotions are a strategy being exploited by some informal entrepreneurs. Apart from this marketing strategy deployed, a portion of these respondents also sustains their businesses by offering credit sales to loyal customers when need be and rewarding loyal customers during festive periods or memorable events. These are usually in the form of 'freebies'—statements from respondents are shown:

> "*I give gifts to customers who make referrals to me.*" (IE17)
> "We *reward loyal customers we have over the years.*" (IE25)

Therefore, informal entrepreneurs, directly and indirectly, communicate with existing ones to keep the business afloat and win customers. Potential customers about their products through the distribution of fliers and other promotional materials and other media platforms such as social media, radio, and TV advertisement, as well as depending on loyal customers who have become advocates for their enterprises. It is, however, also evident from the responses that informal entrepreneurs have continually maintained traditional marketing strategies by using brands (products/services), pricing, place (location), and promotional activities to engage their customers and sustain their businesses in the marketplace. Invariably, these marketing strategies are bound to help the business grow, all things beings equal. Hence, the entrepreneurs' growth strategies are subsequently assessed.

Assessing the Growth Strategies of Informal Entrepreneurs

Several businesses across different economic sectors have growth as a business objective. As such, different entrepreneurs employ different strategies to achieve the growth objective. The growth strategies employed should be competitive; thus, competitive strategies are necessary for the growth of any business (Machado, 2016). The views of the respondents regarding the growth strategies used by entrepreneurs in the informal economy covered: expansion/acquisition; diversification; financial support; ploughing back of profit, as well as having the correct number of employees (Table 4.3).

Table 4.3 Growth strategies commonly used by informal entrepreneurs

Themes	Percentage (%)
Expansion/acquisition	53.3
Diversification	36.7
Financial support	30.0
Plough back profits	20.0
Employ/number of workers	16.7
None	10.0

Source: Filed Data (2019)
Responses are more than 100% because some respondents have more than one strategy

To begin with, a more significant percentage of respondents (53.3%) say that expanding and/or acquiring assets drives business growth. Respondents believe that one growth strategy is to expand the business by expanding the customer base or assets. In this direction and within the informal economy in Ghana, assets expansion is more about acquiring more businesses in the exact location or other locations. The acquisition of a larger number of customers and assets is expected to be reflected in the firm's profits, in this situation, higher profits. Some responses of the participants' responses to expansion as a strategy are presented:

"I will expand operation and premises with time." (IE24)
"[W]in one new major customer a week and improve on quality. These will help expand my business, and that is how it will grow." (IE 10)
"Outlets in key areas like Labone and Cantonments are instrumental to my business growth." (IE7)

A key conclusion on the growth through multiple outlets is that the stores used by informal operators are usually small and in no time get congested when the business starts to grow. The only remedy to decongest is to find another store nearby or move to a new location to ensure efficiency and effectiveness.

Also, 36.7% of the respondents hold that diversifying into other areas (unrelated) other than the original (related) business activity is a sure way of growing. Diversification allows the business to spread risks associated with business operations. Since the term diversification is usually associated with a change in the characteristics of the firm's product line and or market, these entrepreneurs crave and engage in product-market strategy alternatives. Given this, some respondents maintain:

"[I]ntroduce new business related to this business." (IE16)
"[E]xpand into other building materials such as iron rods and others." (IE10)

The issue with diversification in the informal economy is that the entrepreneurs need to assess the further growth potential of their current business before moving into other areas (sometimes unfamiliar) of business. Again, there needs to be more assessment of the new business's growth potential. However, it relies on the success of a few enterprises in the new industry to make their diversification decision.

Again, 30% of the respondents opine that having financial support helps a business to grow and thus always to grow; there is a need to solicit funds by acquiring loans from financial institutions. These informal entrepreneurs believe that without a solid financial capacity, the growth of the business is in limbo. Here are some responses from participants:

> *"I applied for a loan, which I would use to grow my business by increasing my stock in the future."* (IE24)
> *"I would apply for a loan to expand my business."* (IE27)
> *"[I]t all boils down to finance. Once I have money, I will be able to grow my business in desirable ways, like expanding to other territories."* (4)

In terms of accessing extra money for growth, the evidence from the interview suggests that most informal entrepreneurs do not need extra money for further growth because they can grow without a new cash injection. However, these entrepreneurs believe that business growth always requires more cash injection. It is what we regard as the "growth myth." The informal entrepreneurs captured in this study have grown their businesses by sometimes purchasing on credit and receiving financial support from suppliers through discounts on payables as they purchase in bulk. Hence, they can make more purchases due to reduced costs. However, most of this category usually source loans from banks and other non-financial institutions, but at high-interest rates. It is risky to lend money to them since most of these entrepreneurs have yet to register officially. The high-interest rate promotes non-payment of loans as these vulnerable entrepreneurs struggle to make ends meet.

Moreover, 20% of the respondents reveal that their approach to business growth is reinvesting business proceeds for growth purposes. These respondents, therefore, do not view the profits made from the business as meant for personal consumption. For a planned period, the proceeds of the business are reinvested to grow the business to a desired state. As IE11 opines, *"I intend to invest my profits into the business from now to like six months so that I can increase production"* (IE13). It is, however, observed that the practice of ploughing back of profit is common with respondents who have other jobs aside from the business and those who were not sole providers at home.

Additionally, 16.7% of participants rely on the business' workforce to enhance business growth. They believe that getting more employees leads to greater productivity, which translates into business growth. It is also seen as a growth myth in that from classical management; productivity is not using more resources to achieve more output, but rather the opposite. However, these crops of entrepreneurs who often disregard classical management thinking believe that the more resources you have, the higher the growth you can attain. It is deduced from respondents' responses like: *"I get more distributors monthly"* (IE10). Several entrepreneurs depend on family members for human resources. Some respondents note that this is used as a strategy for growth. They argue that because these employees are family members, their actions will be in the interest of the business and hence promote growth. Hence, IE13 says, *"I employ relatives that see the business as their own"* (IE6). To these employers, getting another workforce to help cater for the job indicates their growth in the business. Viewing this from a different angle, more resources are seen as a cause and consequence of growth. We are growing. That is why we need more hands or more hands because we want to grow, IE14 remarked again.

Nonetheless, 10% of entrepreneurs have no growth strategy even though they have operated their business for some time. However, it is observed that even though these informal entrepreneurs do not directly point to a particular strategy, they are indirectly involved in a strategy that has helped sustain their activity in the marketplace. For these entrepreneurs, business growth has a spiritual underpinning; thus, God gives business growth to entrepreneurs. Some even cite Bible quotations to buttress their claim. For example, Proverbs 10:22 "The blessing of the LORD enriches, and He adds no sorrow to it." With such a notion, minimal effort is made towards developing a growth plan or strategy. It is more worrying that some of these entrepreneurs are successful with this notion.

Discussion of Findings

The study's findings suggest that conducting organized and planned marketing activities or developing growth plans/strategies is unique to Ghana's informal economy. The study's conclusion is that only some informal entrepreneurs treat growth/marketing as a planned activity. Therefore, participation in formal marketing activities in the informal economy is not a standard or common practice. The data also shows that almost half of the respondents have not planned and intended marketing practices. Not surprisingly, there is a paucity in the academic discourse of studies examining the marketing skills or activities of informal entrepreneurs or firms. The most commonly practised marketing activity is marketing communications. The few informal entrepreneurs that are marketing-oriented understand the essence of marketing communications in the business field even though they operate informally. A range of marketing communications activities involving informal entrepreneurs include the use of signage, product displays, radio adverts, and billboards, regardless of their size and limitations. The study unearths that informal entrepreneurs also leverage social media marketing to market their enterprises. Other marketing strategies have been identified, such as business referrals, discount sales, customer service delivery, location and ambience, and the sale of quality goods. The discovery of customer service delivery and convenient location as marketing tools echoes the findings of Khan (2017), who examined informal entrepreneurs in the food vending business in Kenya. However, whereas Khan (2017) finds the idea of convenient location as a critical marketing tool from the customer's perspective, this study finds it from the perspective of the enterprises. This difference in findings could be linked to contextual differences. Whilst Khan (2017) examined just the food retail sector, this study included and covered various sub-sectors in the informal economy.

Although some of the informal entrepreneurs have yet to learn marketing activities, they have identified growth strategies. The relatable growth strategies identified are expansion, diversification, financial support, ploughing back of profits, and hiring the right employees. The reliance on financial support and qualified employees as a growth strategy echoes the findings of Baporikar et al. (2016), who emphasize that access to finance, appropriate marketing strategies, excellent customer service, and skilled human resources or labour are the bedrock of growth of enterprises. Our study revealed that business expansion is a crucial growth strategy in the informal economy. The study participants strongly associate the expansion of enterprises with their growth. Unlike existing literature (Ghosh, 2016; Koryak et al., 2015) considering innovation as a critical growth factor, it is largely absent from this study as none of the participants mentioned it in the growth of firms. Our findings suggest that business expansion, diversification, and ploughing back of profits are key strategies for firm growth in the informal economy.

The study argues that part of Gilbert's law that states that enterprise growth is proportionate to enterprise size, applies to this study. We opine so, considering that several informal enterprises remain small for an extended period despite having explicit growth strategies. Evidence from this study shows that although 76.6% of the respondents have been in business for over five (5) years, only 36.7% have employees. They are yet to experience enough growth to employ others. Other things being equal, expanding the business to a certain level required hiring more workers. The absence of these employees shows that the growth of the informal enterprises concerned reflects or is proportionate to their size. However, we argue that firm growth is not based on random factors, as Gibrat's law asserts. Our position is that enterprise growth factors are not random, but based on a deliberate decision made by the entrepreneur and not a coincidence. Business growth is by choice (voluntary) and chance (accidental); as such, the entrepreneur must identify those key factors that achieve maximum growth rates and focus on them, as suggested by the Critical Success Factors Theory.

The findings of this study have various policy implications, and therefore some policy directions are required. The findings demonstrate that public policy towards enterprise growth needs to focus on the growth objectives of individual entrepreneurs and not on a particular sector or industry. One-size-fits-all policies will only lead to meaningful enterprise development in the informal economy. This requires empirical research to uncover the growth challenges facing informal entrepreneurs. The outcome of such research forms the basis for any formulation of growth policies by stakeholders. The results of this research will help eliminate a situation where uniform policies are developed for different needs.

Second, the development of accelerators to scale entrepreneurs' growth. There should be more avenues for entrepreneurs to educate themselves, particularly in managing and sustaining business growth. More so, helping entrepreneurs to create uncontested market spaces, especially during diversification as was seen as a key growth strategy in this study. The creation of uncontested market space gives entrepreneurs the first-mover advantage and a competitive edge over their peers.

Additionally, more money is critical to sustaining business growth. In this context, it is important to ensure easy access to credit facilities and other financial incentives (subsidies, interest-free credit, etc.). The current financial situation makes it more difficult for entrepreneurs to access the credit they need to continue growing. Public policy must create avenues through which entrepreneurs can easily access financial resources at a reasonable interest rate, lower than the prevailing market rate, in order to purposefully drive the growth of companies.

Limitations and Future Research Directions

This research has some limitations. First, the scope is limited as only Accra (the capital of Ghana) is included. Future studies could expand the scope of the present study. Also, this study applied purely qualitative research methods to uncover issues related to the research problem given the lack of studies in this field. We encourage future research to consider the use of quantitative methods to measure the extent to which the factors and strategies identified impact enterprise growth.

Conclusion

The study aimed to examine the marketing and growth strategies of informal entrepreneurs in Ghana. We based the study in Accra (the capital of Ghana), as we consider it the centre of the informal economy with informal entrepreneurs from diverse backgrounds. Using a sample size of

30 respondents, data were drawn from three contrasting neighbourhood types, ranging from the disadvantaged to the affluent: Nima (very disadvantaged), Madina (middle of the continuum), and East Legon (affluent). Based on this, the study captured enterprises with target markets of people with different economic skills. The study hinged on the critical success factors to examine the key activities of informal entrepreneurs that lead to growth or successful outcomes. Data were collected through in-depth interviews, transcribed and manually via thematic analysis. Getting involved in planned marketing activities is not typical of the informal economy in Ghana. Entrepreneurs must be educated to undertake marketing activities, including marketing communications, referrals, discount sales, customer service delivery, location, and ambience, and selling quality merchandizes. However, even without planned marketing activities for several informal enterprises, informal entrepreneurs consciously develop growth strategies for their firms. In other words, they are aware of the critical success factors for their firms. The growth strategies pursued include expansion, diversification, financial support, ploughing back of profits, and hiring the right employees. It can be concluded that informal entrepreneurs in the study context consistent with the critical success factors theory. However, most of them do not consider marketing a critical success factor. The few who believe in marketing rely heavily on marketing communications as opposed to discounts, referrals, customer service delivery, location, ambience, and selling quality products.

References

Adom, K. (2014). Beyond the marginalization thesis: An examination of the motivations of informal entrepreneurs in sub-Saharan Africa: Insights from Ghana. *The International Journal of Entrepreneurship and Innovation, 15(2), 113–125.*

Adom, K. (2017). Formalisation of entrepreneurship in the informal economy in sub-Saharan Africa and the role of formal institutions: An analysis of Ghana's experience. In *In the informal economy in global perspective* (pp. 277–291). Palgrave Macmillan.

Adom, K., & Williams, C. C. (2012). Evaluating the motives of informal entrepreneurs in Koforidua, Ghana. *Journal of Developmental Entrepreneurship, 17*(01), 1250005.

Adom, K., & Williams, C. C. (2014). Evaluating the explanations for the informal economy in third world cities: Some evidence from Koforidua in the eastern region of Ghana. *International Entrepreneurship and Management Journal, 10*(2), 427–445.

Altındağ, O., Bakış, O., & Rozo, S. V. (2020). Blessing or burden? Impacts of refugees on businesses and the informal economy. *Journal of Development Economics, 146*, 102490.

Angen, M. J. (2000). Evaluating interpretive inquiry: Reviewing the validity debate and opening the dialogue. *Qualitative Health Research, 10*(3), 378–395.

Antonopoulos, G. A., & Mitra, J. (2009). The hidden enterprise of bootlegging cigarettes out of Greece: Two schemes of illegal entrepreneurship. *Journal of Small Business & Entrepreneurship, 22*(1), 1–8.

Aryeetey, E. (2015). The informal economy, economic growth, and poverty in sub-Saharan Africa. In *Economic growth and poverty reduction in sub-Saharan Africa: Current and emerging issues* (p. 159). Oxford University Press.

Baporikar, N., Nambira, G., & Gomxos, G. (2016). Exploring factors hindering SMEs' growth: Evidence from Nambia. *Journal of Science and Technology Policy Management, 7*(2), 190–211.

Benjamin, N., & Mbaye, A. A. (2012). *The informal sector in Francophone Africa: Firm size, productivity, and institutions*. The World Bank.

Benjamin, N., & Mbaye, A. A. (2014). *Informality, growth, and development in Africa* (No. 2014/052). WIDER working study.

Boynton, A. C., & Zmud, R. W. (1984). An assessment of critical success factors. *Sloan Management Review, 25*(4), 17–27.

Bravo-Biosca, A., Criscuolo, C., & Menon, C. (2016). What drives the dynamics of business growth? *Economic Policy, 31*(88), 703–742.

Cherubini, S., Iasevoli, G., & Michelini, L. (2015). Product-service systems in the electric car industry: Critical success factors in marketing. *Journal of Cleaner Production, 97*, 40–49.

Creswell, J. W., & Creswell, J. D. (2017). *Research design: Qualitative, quantitative, and mixed methods approaches*. Sage Publications.

Damayanti, M., Scott, N., & Ruhanen, L. (2017). Competitive behaviours in an informal tourism economy. *Annals of Tourism Research, 65*, 25–35.

Elgin, C. (2020). *The informal economy: Measures, causes, and consequences*. Routledge.

Gelb, A., Mengistae, T., Ramachandran, V., & Shah, M. K. (2009). "To formalize or not to formalize?", Comparisons of microenterprise data from Southern and East Africa. *Comparisons of Microenterprise Data from Southern and East Africa*, July 20.
Ghosh, S. (2016). Does mobile telephony spur growth? Evidence from Indian states. *Telecommunications Policy, 40*(10-11), 1020–1031.
Godfrey, P. C. (2015). Introduction: Why the informal economy matters to management. In *Management, society, and the informal economy* (pp. 11–28). Routledge.
GSS. (2012). *Population and housing census: Provisional summary report for final results*. Accra: Ghana Statistical Service.
Hart, K. (1973). Informal income opportunities and urban employment in Ghana. *Journal of Modern African Studies,11*(1), 61–89.
Hart, K. (1985). The informal economy. *Cambridge Anthropology*, 54–58.
Hormeku, T. (1998). The transformation and development of the informal economy and the role of trade unions. Retrieved April 10, 2008.
ILO. (2002). *Decent work and the informal economy*. Geneva: International Labour Organization.
ILO. (2015). *Academy on formalisation of the informal economy*. International Labour Organisation. Geneva: ITC.
Khan, E. A. (2017). An investigation of marketing capabilities of informal microenterprises: A study of street food vending in Thailand. *International Journal of Sociology and Social Policy, 37*(3/4), 186–202.
Kim, J., & Rhee, J. (2012). An empirical study on the impact of critical success factors on the balanced scorecard performance in Korean green supply chain management enterprises. *International Journal of Production Research, 50*(9), 2465–2483.
Kistruck, G. M., Webb, J. W., Sutter, C. J., & Bailey, A. V. (2015). The double-edged sword of legitimacy in base-of-the-pyramid markets. *Journal of Business Venturing, 30*(3), 436–451.
Kitchen, R., & Tate, N. (2001). *Conducting research in human geography: Theory, practice and methodology*. Prentice Hall.
Koh, S. L., Gunasekaran, A., & Goodman, T. (2011). Drivers, barriers and critical success factors for ERPII implementation in supply chains: A critical analysis. *The Journal of Strategic Information Systems, 20*(4), 385–402.
Koryak, O., Mole, K. F., Lockett, A., Hayton, J. C., Ucbasaran, D., & Hodgkinson, G. P. (2015). Entrepreneurial leadership, capabilities and firm growth. *International Small Business Journal, 33*(1), 89–105.

Kumar, D. (2016). *Enterprise growth strategy: Vision, planning and execution*. Routledge.

Leidecker, J. K., & Bruno, A. V. (1984). Identifying and using critical success factors. *Long Range Planning, 17*(1), 23–32.

Li, Y., Zhao, X., Shi, D., & Li, X. (2014). Governance of sustainable supply chains in the fast fashion industry. *European Management Journal, 32*(5), 823–836.

Lubell, H. (1991). *The informal economy in the 1980s and 1990s*. https://www.cabdirect.org/cabdirect/abstract/19916711642 (on what date was it accessed please).

Luthra, S., Garg, D., & Haleem, A. (2015). An analysis of interactions among critical success factors to implement green supply chain management towards sustainability: An Indian perspective. *Resources Policy, 46*, 37–50.

Machado, H. P. V. (2016). Growth of small businesses: A literature review and perspectives of studies. *Gestão & Produção, 23*(2), 419–432.

Madichie, N. O., Nkamnebe, A. D., & Ekanem, I. U. (2020). Marketing in the informal economy: An entrepreneurial perspective and research agenda. *Entrepreneurship Marketing*, 412–428.

Marshall, M. N. (1996). Sampling for qualitative research. *Family Practice, 13*(6), 522–526.

Meagher, K. (2010). *Identity economics: Social networks & the informal economy in Nigeria*. Boydell & Brewer Ltd.

Miles, M. B., Huberman, A. M., Huberman, M. A., & Huberman, M. (1994). *Qualitative data analysis: An expanded sourcebook*. Sage.

Morris, M. H., Pitt, L. F., & Berthon, P. (1996). Entrepreneurial activity in the Third World informal economy: The view from Khayelitsha. *International Journal of Entrepreneurial Behavior & Research, 2*(1), 59–76.

Morris, H. M., Mayasiki, N. N., Watters, C. E., & Coombes, M. S. (2006). The dilemma of growth: understanding venture size choices of women entrepreneurs. *Journal of Business Management, 44*(2), 221–224.

Mróz, B. (2012). Entrepreneurship in the shadow: Faces and variations of Poland's informal economy. *International Journal of Economic Policy in Emerging Economies, 5*(3), 197–211.

Nnamseh, M., & Akpan, S. S. (2015). Revitalising small business growth strategies: Exploring the risk-benefit of strategic management approaches. *International Business Research, 8*(7), 87.

Nobert, O., David, N., & Robert, O. O. (2020). The challenges affecting tax collection in Nigerian informal economy: Case study of Anambra State. *Journal of Accounting and Taxation, 12*(2), 61–74.

Nyamekye, M., Koboré, N., Bonégo, E. R., Kiéma, E., Ndour, B., Jallo, S., & Tarawally, M. S. (2009). Organizing informal sector workers in West Africa: Focus on women workers, trade union strategies: Case studies from Ghana, Sierra Leone, Senegal and Burkina Faso. In *Accra, Ghana Trades Union Congress*.

Osei-Boateng, C., & Ampratwum, E. (2011). *The informal sector in Ghana*. Friedrich-Ebert-Stiftung, Ghana Office.

Penrose, E., & Penrose, E. T. (2009). *The theory of the growth of the firm*. Oxford University Press.

Pinto, J. K., & Slevin, D. P. (1987). Critical factors in successful project implementation. *IEEE Transactions on Engineering Management, 1*, 22–27.

Richey, R. G., Pettit, S., & Beresford, A. (2009). Critical success factors in the context of humanitarian aid supply chains. *International Journal of Physical Distribution & Logistics Management*.

Rizea, R. D. (2015). Growth Strategies of Multinational Companies. *Petroleum-Gas University of Ploiesti Bulletin, Technical Series, 67*(1).

Rockart, J. F. (1979). Chief executives define their own data needs. *Harvard Business Review, 57*(2), 81–93.

Routroy, S., & Pradhan, S. K. (2013). Evaluating the critical success factors of supplier development: A case study. *Benchmarking: An International Journal, 20*(3), 322–341.

Shibia, A. G., & Barako, D. G. (2017). Determinants of micro and small enterprises growth in Kenya. *Journal of Small Business and Enterprise Development, 24*(1), 105–118.

Simbaña-Taipe, L. E., Franco Chasi, P. A., Pacheco Pillajo, P. A., Rodríguez-Gulías, M. J., & Rodeiro-Pazos, D. (2019). The validity of Gibrat's Law: Evidence from Ecuadorian service SMEs. *Latin American Business Review, 20*(2), 135–156.

Stanculescu, M. (2017). *The social impact of informal economies in Eastern Europe*. Routledge.

Stuart, E., Samman, E., & Hunt, A. (2018). *Informal is the new normal. Improving the lives of workers at risk of being left behind*. Overseas Development Institute.

Suehiro, A. (2017). New growth strategies of Thailand's big firms in the ASEAN economic community era. In *Southeast Asia beyond Crises and Traps* (pp. 35–69). Palgrave Macmillan.

Sutter, C., Webb, J., Kistruck, G., Ketchen, D. J., Jr., & Ireland, R. D. (2017). Transitioning entrepreneurs from informal to formal markets. *Journal of Business Venturing, 32*(4), 420–442.

Swamy, R., & Singh, A. (2018). Creating a supportive entrepreneurial ecosystem for street vendors: The case of the National Association of Street Vendors of India (NASVI). In *Entrepreneurial, innovative and sustainable ecosystems* (pp. 151–172). Springer.

Symon, G., & Cassell, C. (2012). Assessing Qualitative Research 12. In *Qualitative organizational research: Core methods and current challenges* (p. 204).

Webb, J. W., Bruton, G. D., Tihanyi, L., & Ireland, R. D. (2013). Research on entrepreneurship in the informal economy: Framing a research agenda. *Journal of Business Venturing, 28*(5), 598–614.

Welter, F., & Smallbone, D. (2011). Institutional perspectives on entrepreneurial behavior in challenging environments. *Journal of Small Business Management, 49*(1), 107–125.

Welter, F., Smallbone, D., & Pobol, A. (2015). Entrepreneurial activity in the informal economy: A missing piece of the entrepreneurship jigsaw puzzle. *Entrepreneurship & Regional Development, 27*(5-6), 292–306.

Williams, C. C. (2007). The nature of entrepreneurship in the informal economy: Evidence from England. *Journal of Developmental Entrepreneurship, 12*(02), 239–254.

Williams, C. C. (2009). Beyond legitimate entrepreneurship: The prevalence of off-the-books entrepreneurs in Ukraine. *Journal of Small Business and Entrepreneurship, 22*(1), 55–68.

Williams, C. C. (2015). Cross-national variations in the scale of informal employment: An exploratory analysis of 41 less developed economies. *International Journal of Manpower, 36*(2), 118–135.

Williams, C. C., & Lansky, M. A. (2013). Informal employment in developed and developing economies: Perspectives and policy responses. *International Labour Review, 152*(3–4), 355–380.

Williams, C. C., & Nadin, S. (2011). Evaluating entrepreneurs in the shadow economy: Economic or social entrepreneurship. International Journal for Management and Enterprise Development, 11(1), 20–33.

Yin, R. K. (2014). *Case study research, Design and methods.* Sage.

5

Social Entrepreneurship in Focus: Evidence from Ghana

Atsu Nkukpornu, Kwame Adom, and Etse Nkukpornu

Introduction

In the face of mounting social problems in Africa, governments and multilateral agencies increasingly need help to provide timely and effective interventions. The astronomical rate of social ills has motivated firms to conduct business with embedded social drive. Social entrepreneurship acts as a catalyst for social change. The chapter introduces the evolution of social entrepreneurship, highlighting that though not new in practice,

---

A. Nkukpornu (✉)
Department Entrepreneurship and Agribusiness, Cape Coast Technical University, Cape Coast, Ghana

K. Adom
School of Business, Burman University, Lacombe, AB, Canada
e-mail: kwameaadom@burmanu.ca

E. Nkukpornu
Department of Accounting and Finance, Christian Service University College, Kumasi, Ghana
e-mail: enkukpornu@csuc.edu.gh

it is undoubtedly enjoying heightened attention. In this chapter, the authors shed light on the initiatives of some social entrepreneurs/enterprises towards mitigating some social problems in Africa, with a particular focus on Ghana.

Evolution of Social Entrepreneurship

The concept of social entrepreneurship was coined by William (Bill) Drayton, the founder and CEO of the international association Ashoka: Innovators for the Public (Sen, 2007). This association has existed since 1980 to identify, select, and empower social entrepreneurs (Sen, 2007). Social entrepreneurship has a long history but has exploded in popularity recently, impacting multiple sectors of society and culture (Tan et al., 2020; Weerakoon, 2021). This is because problems like environmental pollution, poverty, climate change, unemployment, health challenges, and others have grown at an alarming rate in recent years (Almeida, 2021; Tan et al., 2020; Roan, 2021; Bacq & Lumpkin, 2021). Social entrepreneurship is a novel construct based on Mahatma Gandhi's ideology, that is, "be the change you want to see in the world."

The Nobel Peace Prize awarded in 2006 to Dr Muhammad Yunus, founder of the Grameen Bank in Bangladesh, was likely the event that elevated the increased interest in social entrepreneurship on academic research and teaching agendas and promoted the concept onto the radar screen of many governments and practitioners. Based on reciprocal lending without needing collateral (Mair & Marti, 2006), the Grameen Bank has successfully lent to the lowest of the poor (specifically, women in rural Bangladesh).

Among other things, the argument over how to approach and define the concept of social entrepreneurship has been sparked because the idea is conceptualised differently in different countries (Monroe-White et al., 2015). The multitude of definitions of social entrepreneurship is a testament to the growing interest in the subject (Bedi & Yadav, 2019; Dees, 1998; Huybrechts & Nicholls, 2012). Social entrepreneurship is often described as an initiative a social entrepreneur/social enterprise takes to invest time and resources to benefit society (Bedi & Yadav, 2019). In other words, "social entrepreneurship" refers to individuals and organisations that engage in entrepreneurial activities with social objectives. A social entrepreneur "combines the passion of a social purpose with a business-like image of discipline, inventiveness, and tenacity" (Dees, 1998). A social enterprise is a business that focuses on a particular social issue as its primary goal (Alvord et al., 2004). Social entrepreneurship is the sector in which entrepreneurs modify their activity to create social benefit as a final objective. In doing so, they often behave with little or no aim to benefit themselves. Social entrepreneurship is integral to making the world a better place because they fill the social voids left by government and private ownership (Santos, 2012).

One of the most challenging issues confronting most social entrepreneurs is acquiring resources (Desa & Basu, 2013; Kickul et al., 2010). Social entrepreneurs in developing countries face scarce resources and weak institutional financing activities (Zahra et al., 2008). Even in developed countries, the tensions between social mission and financial returns can create resource mobilisation challenges (Austin et al., 2006). The plight of social enterprises is their inability to access capital from the traditional market (Lumpkin et al., 2013) and their inability to recruit qualified human resources due to the inherent salary competitiveness (Austin et al., 2006; Dorado, 2006). Notwithstanding these, social entrepreneurs survive and grow despite resource limitations (Desa & Basu, 2013).

This is because they relied on resources such as; personal abilities and knowledge, networks, volunteers, and stakeholder engagements (Dwivedi & Weerawardena, 2018). This mode of resource mobilisation is anchored in the effectuation theory (Sarasvathy, 2001). Therefore, social entrepreneurs deviate from conventional causative approaches and adapt to what works in a context to achieve social objectives. This is evidenced in Yunus' approach to alleviating poverty among impoverished communities in Bangladesh (Yunus, 2005). By implication, social entrepreneurship is the collaboration of different practices that effectively solves (and can solve) social problems. It is about presenting new solutions for old problems; in essence, it challenges the traditional methods by which things are done (Visser, 2011). These achievements underscore the efficacy of social entrepreneurship as a mechanism for addressing social voids.

What Is Social Entrepreneurship

The concept of social entrepreneurship means different things to different people (Jokela & Elo, 2015; Martin & Osberg, 2015; Williams & Kadamawe, 2012; Bacq & Janssen, 2011; Dacin et al., 2011). Williams and Kadamawe (2012) opine that the definition of social entrepreneurship would be incomplete if there is the absence of accountability, empathy, responsibility, solidarity, and transparency. Meanwhile, Martin and Osberg (2015) and Bacq and Janssen (2011), and Dacin et al. (2011) suggest that the recognition of context in defining social entrepreneurship is paramount. The implications deduced from these scholars' point to the fact that, the growing interest in the subject area coupled with the heterogeneous nature of the social environments has contributed significantly to the myriad meanings to social entrepreneurship.

This chapter adopted Jokela and Elo's (2015) definition to social entrepreneurship. Jokela and Elo (2015) define social entrepreneurship as *"focusing on ventures that are founded to fulfil a social mission, based on the observed opportunity and innovation, to create sustainable social value for the target audience."*

The first element identified in this definition is the social mission. Scholars have acknowledged as the fundamental purpose that overrides its economic gain (Austin et al., 2006). The social mission aspect is the core of distinguishing social entrepreneurs and social enterprises from business entrepreneurs (Tracey & Phillips, 2007). The second element is opportunity identification. Peredo and McLean (2006) contend that priority should be given to the social mission in the opportunity identification rather than profitable activities. The third element is the creation of sustainable social value for the target audience. Sustaining the social value creation is one of the key points that make social entrepreneurship unique.

Fundamentally, social entrepreneurship is how social entrepreneurs develop social enterprises (Defourny & Nyssens, 2010). Social entrepreneurs are individual heroes, visionaries, and change agents who solve social issues while overcoming resource constraints (Najafizada & Cohen,

2017). Social entrepreneurs look for both a return on investment and a return to society (Betts et al., 2018). Social enterprises are businesses that trade for a social purpose (Doherty et al., 2014). A social enterprise's vision and mission differ from a commercial enterprise (Austin et al., 2006). Table 5.1 shows the difference in social entrepreneurship between non-governmental organisations (NGOs) and commercial entrepreneurs based on some indicators.

Notwithstanding the differences, it is essential to point out some similarities between social entrepreneurship and not-for-profit organisations. This is shown in Table 5.2.

Table 5.1 Differences between social entrepreneurship, not-for-profit organisations, and commercial enterprises

Indicators	Not-for-profit organisation	Social enterprises	Commercial enterprises
Motives, methods, and goals	Appeal to goodwill Mission-driven social value	Mixed motives Mission- and market-driven social and economic value	Appeal to self-interest, market-driven, economic value
Beneficiaries	Pay nothing	Subsidised rates, or mix of full payers and those who pay nothing	Market-rate prices
Capital	Donations and grants	Below-market capital, or mix of donations and market-rate capital	Market-rate capital
Workforces	Volunteers	Below-market wages, or mix of volunteers and fully paid staff	Market-rate compensation
Suppliers	Make in-kind donations	Special discounts, or mix of in-kind and full-price donation	Market-rate prices

Source: Dees (1998) cited in Nicholls (2008, p. 280)

Table 5.2 Similarities between social entrepreneurship and not-for-profit organisation

Indicators	Social entrepreneurship	Not-for-profit organisation
Mission	Address social problems and vulnerability	Vulnerability
Impact	Address social problems and vulnerability	Vulnerability

Source: Dees (1998) cited in Nicholls (2008, p. 280)

Social Entrepreneurship in Africa

Africa is characterised by widespread poverty, limited access to financial resources, a lack of commercial and community infrastructure, colonialism-centred economic activity exploiting natural (and human) resources, and a post-colonial legacy of oppressive governmental bureaucracy and corruption, hunger, poor health care, and education. In an ironic twist, a number of these same conditions create ideal ground for social entrepreneurship. Social businesses (and the non-profit sector in general) arise when both markets and government fail (Santos, 2012). Market failures plague emerging nations characterised by a mismatch between demand and supply, inefficient manufacturing, a lack of confidence, and inadequate infrastructure. The government is therefore anticipated to regulate markets and provide public goods. Government failure occurs when the state intervenes ineffectively or lacks the means or political will to meet unmet social requirements. In this environment, social companies that are not entirely reliant on market pricing and predictable earnings and have a strong emphasis on satisfying social needs might flourish.

Notwithstanding the opportunities the African continent presents for social entrepreneurship, the prospect of being a wealth-creator is appealing to many Africans today. How about being a social entrepreneur?

In the meantime, social entrepreneurs are spreading across Africa, starting enterprises that aim to improve society rather than maximise profit. Sub-Saharan Africa has the world's highest number of social entrepreneurs per capita, according to the Global Enterprise Monitor (Bosma et al., 2016), outside Australia and the USA. Among adults aged 18–34 in

Northern and sub-Saharan Africa, more are involved in early-stage social entrepreneurship than commercial entrepreneurship (Mirvis & Googins, 2018). However, there are still barriers to entry for social entrepreneurs trying to launch or expand their firms in these sectors (Mirvis & Googins, 2018). Compared to their global contemporaries, African social entrepreneurs have lower levels of education and invest less of their own money in their ventures, as found by a study conducted by GEMS (Mirvis & Googins, 2018). They have restricted access to resources such as credible role models who could serve as mentors, venture capital and bank finance, and professional management tools and skills (Mirvis & Googins, 2018).

The emergence of social entrepreneurship in Africa is thus linked to the traditional Ubuntu philosophy. It emphasises interdependence and reciprocity over individualism and self-interest (Chilufya & Kerlin, 2017). These animating cultural values are central to the mindset of "society-minded" entrepreneurs in parts of Africa and core tenets of an emerging philosophy of Africapitalism (Amaeshi & Idemudia, 2015).

The concept of social entrepreneurship in Africa is at the developmental stage. The Southern African Development Community (SADC) and East Africa have produced most of the literature on the concept in sub-Saharan Africa (Rivera-Santos et al., 2015). It is acknowledged in the developing world that most of the social services provided by local and national governments will not be able to fulfil their intended purpose. Consequently, we need to think entrepreneurially about solving social problems, and, at the same time, social entrepreneurship must be regarded as a process of creating value. Examples of value addition in a social context in South Africa are the PlayPump (in which the energy of children at play is harnessed to draw water from underground to supply clean water to storage tanks for community use in poor areas) and Q-Drum inventions (a cylindrical unit that eases the hauling of water overland in poor communities) (Visser, 2011).

Littlewood and Holt (2015) studied the African social entrepreneur ecosystem. They discovered that South Africa's enabling legislation on black economic empowerment and its hybrid-friendly regulatory environment facilitated the growth of the country's social business sector. On the capacity-building side, social entrepreneurs can find resources like training materials, mentors, and peer networks through organisations like the Social Enterprise Academy Africa (SEAA), the African Society Entrepreneurs Network (ASEN), South Africa.

Social Entrepreneurship Landscape in Ghana

Ghana's government began structural adjustment initiatives in the 1980s to open up the economy by limiting state engagement and increasing private sector involvement with macroeconomic stability and growth objectives. Despite the achievements of the government's development programmes, severe poverty and social issues continued (World Bank, 2014). Ghana has had some success in democracy and commerce growth in sub-Saharan Africa. The Gross Domestic Product (GDP) has fluctuated (PWC, 2014). Ghana has been underrepresented in West African research on social entrepreneurship. The "status and landscape of social entrepreneurship in Ghana" was studied by Agyeman-Tobogo et al. (2016) and Darko and Koranteng (2015). A study by Adom et al. (2018) examined the impact of environmental factors on Ghanaian social entrepreneurship.

Being in sub-Saharan Africa, Ghana is a fertile social entrepreneurship field. An ecosystem commissioned by the British Council in Ghana to provide an overview of social entrepreneurship activities revealed that the phenomenon was embryonic, now receiving little practitioner and scholarly attention (Adom et al., 2018; Darko & Koranteng, 2015).

In Ghana, the operations of social entrepreneurs exist at regional, national, and international levels. Agyeman-Tobogo et al. (2016) discovered that 46% of social entrepreneurs work at the regional level, 39% operate nationally, and 14% operate worldwide. Regarding regional dispersion, the report revealed that 75% and 60% of social entrepreneurs who operate regionally were found in the Western and Northern Regions, respectively. Greater Accra Region has the highest (22%) of those working internationally, followed by the Ashanti Region, accounting for 17% operating in the international arena (Agyeman-Tobogo et al., 2016). This analysis exemplifies the typologies of Ghana's social entrepreneurs based on their operation boundaries.

Regulatory backing on the operations of social entrepreneurs in Ghana has received little attention from policymakers and the government. The public body is Reach for Change, also known as Social Entrepreneurs (SE) Ghana. The role of SE Ghana is to host data and monitor the activities of social entrepreneurs and enterprises in Ghana. SE Ghana seeks a balance between social, economic, and environmental values and avoids a concentration on maximising shareholder wealth.

The lack of legal support for social entrepreneurs in Ghana has inhibited their registration as social enterprises from scratch. The option to them is to register a commercial business entity and a separate not-for-profit organisation to take care of the social objective. Ghanaian social entrepreneurs are burdened with financial obligations since their commercial ventures are not exempt from tax obligations. Ghanaian social entrepreneurs' activities are developing skills, creating jobs and livelihood, women empowerment in agriculture, technology, health and sanitation, education, environment, childcare, and inclusion (blind and deaf).

These dynamic activities are a testament to social entrepreneurial activities in Ghana as being multifaceted. There is anecdotal evidence of the initiatives of social entrepreneurs in Ghana. These are explained.

Social Entrepreneurship Initiative on Health and Sanitation

Human well-being and human capital are intertwined, and good health is a vital component. It is critical for reducing poverty because of the positive impact better health has on household income and economic growth (Bloom & Canning, 2003). When people are sick, their financial resources are depleted, making it harder to improve one's financial situation. It also lessens the amount of effort and time that those who are already poor for time may commit to locating better deals on basic essentials. By training and engaging a cadre of local community health workers, social entrepreneurs feel they are investing directly in the communities they serve. These community health workers are responsible for providing health services to patients and their families.

In Ghana, many social enterprises provide health care and sanitation products and services that often provide additional benefits of improved health for women and their communities. Some names of social enterprises in this category include Pride Sanitary Pads, Maza, and Clean team (Agyeman-Tobogo et al., 2016; Darko & Koranteng, 2015).

For instance, *Pride Sanitary Pads* observed that, in Ghana, many girls miss school or even drop out altogether due to their monthly period. This social enterprise sought to provide a sustainable solution to this menace, particularly in rural communities where young girls use unclean rags and newspapers to manage their flow, leading to infections and other health complications. The theory of change used by Pride Sanitary Pads is to locally produce sanitary products made from banana fibre, local cotton, and paper pulp, which are biodegradable. They also provide education about menstrual hygiene and are working to dispel the harmful stigmas surrounding female menstruation.

Maza is another social enterprise that operates under the health and sanitation category. Their operation is based on providing transports to pregnant women to hospital to give birth. This social enterprise seeks to reduce the death rate of pregnant women and infant mortality rate in rural communities, particularly in the northern region of Ghana, which is the most affected with the highest rate of premature deaths among the pregnant and infants. To sustain this project, Maza provides a network of motorised tricycles, and the drivers obtain the tricycles at a subsidised rate and "work-and-pay" to own them over two years.

Clean Team, a social enterprise, observed that, in addition to health and sanitation problems, women and girls are susceptible to facing the risk of sexual violence when using public toilets. To solve this social problem, Clean Team provide home toilets for low-income families. Their customers pay an initial deposit of a small amount, and Clean Team provides the toilet and collects the waste weekly in sealed containers for safe disposal. Their operation is in the Ashanti region, particularly Kumasi, and they are hopeful to scale to other regions.

Social Entrepreneurship Initiative on Education, Skills Development, Creating Jobs, and Livelihood

Education is an enabler for the socioeconomic upliftment of countries around the world. As a result, social entrepreneurs believe that educating the impoverished opens new career prospects (Bloom, 2009). Social entrepreneurs who adhere to this concept are concerned with assisting those needing employment training and career advancement. Pandey et al. (2006) discovered that education is critical to the economic well-being of women with kids. Social entrepreneurs believe that quality education would result in the well-being of societies.

For example, *Devio Arts* is a social enterprise that aims to promote the creative educational rights and inclusion of young people, especially those from marginalised backgrounds. It is reforming education in Ghana by scaling its impact learning curriculum, which includes a unique combination of arts, design thinking, personal development, games, and sign language lessons. Devio Arts supports the creative education of both boys and girls, and by introducing sign language, they have a compelling impact on the education of deaf children. To scale the impact, Devio Arts was supported through the Reach for Change Incubator program to develop Devio Arts into a sustainable, scalable social enterprise. In 2016, Devio Arts impacted the lives of 2000 and trained 135 teachers (Agyeman-Tobogo et al., 2016; Darko & Koranteng, 2015).

Similarly, *ANOPA*, an international sports project based in Cape Coast, Ghana, uses sports, such as swimming, football, and basketball, as an instrument for individual development, promotion of gender equity, peacebuilding, inclusion, and other essential soft and social skills for kids in the Central Region of Ghana. ANOPA project's theory of change is anchored on the philosophy that—sport is not just an end in itself but also an effective tool to help improve the lives of children, families, and communities. ANOPA's module spans various areas such as coaching, all-inclusive, educational support, awareness of disability support programmes (deaf and blind), and vocational and technical skills. To scale the impact, ANOPA uses the proceeds from its restaurant to support and sustain the project (ANOPA Project.com).

Initiatives of Technology Social Ventures in Ghana

Technology social venture (TSV) represents a unique genre of social ventures which attempts to satisfy a social need through technological innovation in a financially sustainable manner (Ismail et al., 2012). The merger of social and technology entrepreneurship uses a knowledge-bridging mechanism for technological innovation to serve social needs (Ismail et al., 2012). Like social entrepreneurship, TSVs address the double keystones of social value creation (Austin et al., 2006) and financial return (Peredo & McLean, 2006). However, they do so by using advanced technology. TSV's differ from social ventures in some unique ways. Traditional social ventures are driven by human power, rely on volunteers, and employ social workers as human resources. The growth of the social venture requires more human resources, which demands more funding for the hiring and training of additional human resources to ensure growth (Ismail et al., 2012).

On the contrary, although TSV's often require more initial funding than traditional social ventures, they can be replicated across regions or projects at less expense and a faster rate (Desa & Kotha, 2006). The replication quality helps the TSVs maximise the social impact, achieve the principle of scale, and reach sustainability. TSVs in Ghana include but are not limited to mPedigree and Soronko Solution (Agyeman-Tobogo et al., 2016; Darko & Koranteng, 2015; mPedigree.com).

Trade in fake medicines became a primary social concern globally. *mPedigree* is building innovative and technological tools to solve such social problems. mPedigree is the global leader in using mobile and web technologies to secure products against faking, counterfeiting, and diversion. mPedigree has as partners more than two dozen telecom operators, Fortune 500 technology companies, and regulatory agencies in several countries. mPedigree renders service to the world's leading pharmaceutical and consumable companies with the shared goal of protecting consumers, enriching their lives, and transforming their communities through a cleaner, better supply chain.

Despite initial optimism that information technology (IT) would offer a new gender-neutral form of work, another social problem identified is that women's interest in IT is underrepresented in both developed and developing economies (Kenny & Donnelly, 2020). Such a stark gender imbalance makes it one of the country's most male-skewed, white-collar occupations and one that faces a growing shortfall of much-needed IT professionals (Kenny & Donnelly, 2020). The situation in developing countries like Ghana is dire.

To address this social problem, *Soronko Solutions*, a for-profit ICT company, uses its profit to fund ICT skills development work through its foundation. One of its projects, dubbed "Tech Need Girls," has trained over 4500 girls to code using 200 volunteer mentors; all are computer scientists or engineers. Soronko Solution prioritises working with girls from slums, helping many go to university instead of being forced into early marriages (Agyeman-Tobogo et al., 2016; Darko & Koranteng, 2015).

Findings

This study provides a snapshot of the initiatives of social entrepreneurs in Africa, focusing on Ghana. We observed that social entrepreneurs in Ghana are relentlessly pursuing their social mission agenda in areas such as girl's empowerment in ICT, youth development in education, skills development, job creation, health and sanitation. These initiatives are contributing to better the socioeconomic life of the identified target groups in deprived communities. For instance, the educational impacts of some social enterprises contribute to meeting long-term educational goals. Health impacts from social entrepreneurial initiatives could result in improved human health and clean environment.

The authors further observed that the identified social entrepreneurs operate as individuals with little collaborations. In terms of scholarly works to validate the initiatives of the social entrepreneurs, the authors realised that little attention has been given to the discourse. These present an opportunity for studies to be conducted in this context.

Conclusion and Recommendation

The following recommendations are made having identified the initiatives of some Ghanaian social entrepreneurs:

- The authors recommend institutional collaboration because most social enterprises in developing countries like Ghana are created and operated by individuals with restrained resource access. It makes it difficult to scale the social impact. The Ghanaian government needs to develop a supportive framework embodying a public-private partnership. Organisations collaborating to address societal issues on a local level can result in improving local conditions.
- Social entrepreneurial activities are highly influenced by contextual settings. We recommend that social entrepreneurial initiatives should be developed on the principle of "what works" in the context.
- The authors identified that most initiatives of social entrepreneurs lack empirical validation. Therefore, empirical studies are needed to substantiate the initiatives of social entrepreneurs in Ghana.
- Setting up business incubation centres could also help breed local social entrepreneurs capable of solving social problems since social entrepreneurship is in its nascent stage in Ghana.

References

Adom, K., Abdul-Rahaman, A., & Duah-Agyemang, F. (2018). Social entrepreneurship: An emerging market perspective, some fresh evidence from Ghana. *International Journal of Social Entrepreneurship and Innovation, 5*(2), 77–94.

Agyeman-Tobogo, K., Tobogo, L. G., Darko, E., & Sharp, S. (2016). *The state of social enterprises in Ghana*. Retrieved October 10, 2022, from www.britishcouncil.org/society/socialenterprise

Almeida, F. (2021). Innovative response initiatives in the European Union to mitigate the effects of COVID-19. *Journal of Enabling Technologies, 15*(1), 40–52.

Alvord, S. H., Brown, L. D., & Letts, C. W. (2004). Social entrepreneurship and societal transformation: An exploratory study. *The Journal of Applied Behavioural Science, 40*(3), 260–282.

Amaeshi, K., & Idemudia, U. (2015). Africapitalism: A management idea for business in Africa. *Africa Journal of Management, 1*(2), 210–223.

Austin, J., Stevenson, H., & Wei-Skillern, J. (2006). Social and commercial entrepreneurship: Same, different, or both? *Entrepreneurship Theory and Practice, 30*(1), 1–22.

Bacq, S., & Janssen, F. (2011). The multiple faces of social entrepreneurship: A review of definitional issues based on geographical and thematic criteria. *Entrepreneurship & Regional Development, 23*(5–6), 373–403.

Bacq, S., & Lumpkin, G. T. (2021). Social entrepreneurship and COVID-19. *Journal of Management Studies, 58*(1), 285.

Bedi, H. S., & Yadav, N. (2019). Social entrepreneurship: A conceptual clarity. Bedi, HS & Yadav, N., Social Entrepreneurship: A Conceptual Clarity. *Our Heritage, 67*(10), 1006–1016.

Betts, S. C., Laud, R., & Kretinin, A. (2018). Social entrepreneurship: A contemporary approach to solving social problems. *Global Journal of Entrepreneurship, 2*(1), 31–40.

Bloom, D., & Canning, D. (2003). The health and poverty of nations: From theory to practice. *Journal of Human Development, 4*(1), 47–71.

Bloom, P. N. (2009). Overcoming consumption constraints through social entrepreneurship. *Journal of Public Policy & Marketing, 28*(1), 128–134.

Bosma, N., Schøtt, T., Terjesen, S. A., & Kew, P. (2016). Global entrepreneurship monitor 2015 to 2016: special topic report on social entrepreneurship. Available at SSRN 2786949.

Chilufya, R., & Kerlin, J. A. (2017). Zambia: Innate resource legacies and social enterprise development: The impact of human agency and socio-spatial context in a rural setting. In *Shaping social enterprise* (pp. 217–252). Emerald Publishing Limited.

Dacin, M. T., Dacin, P. A., & Tracey, P. (2011). Social entrepreneurship: A critique and future directions. *Organization Science, 22*(5), 1203–1213.

Darko, E., & Koranteng, K. (2015). *Social enterprise landscape in Ghana*. Retrieved October 10, 2022, from www.britishcouncil.org.gh

Dees, J. G. (1998). The meaning of social entrepreneurship.

Defourny, J., & Nyssens, M. (2010). Conceptions of social enterprise and social entrepreneurship in Europe and the United States: Convergences and divergences. *Journal of Social Entrepreneurship, 1*(1), 32–53.

Desa, G., & Basu, S. (2013). Optimization or bricolage? Overcoming resource constraints in global social entrepreneurship. *Strategic Entrepreneurship Journal, 7*(1), 26–49.

Desa, G., & Kotha, S. (2006). Ownership, mission and environment: An exploratory analysis into the evolution of a technology social venture. In *Social entrepreneurship* (pp. 155–179). Palgrave Macmillan.

Doherty, B., Haugh, H., & Lyon, F. (2014). Social enterprises as hybrid organizations: A review and research agenda. *International Journal of Management Reviews, 16*(4), 417–436.

Dorado, S. (2006). Social entrepreneurial ventures: Different values so different process of creation, no? *Journal of Developmental Entrepreneurship, 11*(04), 319–343.

Dwivedi, A., & Weerawardena, J. (2018). Conceptualizing and operationalizing the social entrepreneurship construct. *Journal of Business Research, 86*, 32–40.

Huybrechts, B., & Nicholls, A. (2012). Social entrepreneurship: Definitions, drivers and challenges. In *Social entrepreneurship and social business* (pp. 31–48). Gabler Verlag.

Ismail, K., Sohel, M. H., & Ayuniza, U. N. (2012). Technology social venture: A new genréof social entrepreneurship? *Procedia-Social and Behavioural Sciences, 40*, 429–434.

Jokela, P., & Elo, M. (2015). Developing innovative business models in social ventures. *Journal of Entrepreneurship, Management and Innovation, 11*(1), 103–118.

Kenny, E. J., & Donnelly, R. (2020). Navigating the gender structure in information technology: How does this affect the experiences and behaviours of women? *Human Relations, 73*(3), 326–350.

Kickul, J., Griffiths, M. D., & Gundry, L. (2010). Innovating for social impact: Is bricolage the catalyst for change? In *Handbook of research on social entrepreneurship*. Edward Elgar Publishing.

Littlewood, D., & Holt, D. (2015). Social and environmental enterprises in Africa: Context, convergence and characteristics. In *The business of social and environmental innovation* (pp. 27–47). Springer.

Lumpkin, G. T., Moss, T. W., Gras, D. M., Kato, S., & Amezcua, A. S. (2013). Entrepreneurial processes in social contexts: How are they different, if at all? *Small Business Economics, 40*(3), 761–783.

Mair, J., & Marti, I. (2006). Social entrepreneurship research: A source of explanation, prediction, and delight. *Journal of World Business, 41*(1), 36–44.

Martin, R. L., & Osberg, S. (2015). *Getting beyond better: How social entrepreneurship works*. Harvard Business Review Press.

Mirvis, P., & Googins, B. (2018). Catalysing social entrepreneurship in Africa: Roles for western universities, NGOs and corporations. *Africa Journal of Management, 4*(1), 57–83.

Monroe-White, T., Kerlin, J. A., & Zook, S. (2015). A quantitative critique of Kerlin's macro-institutional social enterprise framework. *Social Enterprise Journal*.

Najafizada, S. A. M., & Cohen, M. J. (2017). Social entrepreneurship tackling poverty in Bamyan Province, Afghanistan. *World Development Perspectives, 5*, 24–26.

Nicholls, A. (Ed.). (2008). *Social entrepreneurship: New models of sustainable social change*. OUP Oxford.

Pandey, S., Zhan, M., & Kim, Y. (2006). Bachelor's degree for women with children: A promising pathway to poverty reduction. *Equal Opportunities International, 25*(7), 488–505.

Peredo, A. M., & McLean, M. (2006). Social entrepreneurship: A critical review of the concept. *Journal of World Business, 41*(1), 56–65.

PWC. (2014). Growth Accelerated Doing Business and Investing in Ghana. March 2014.

Roan, C. (2021). *Lessons from social entrepreneurs fighting COVID-19*. Retrieved from https://www.hbr.org/sponsored. Accessed on May, 2021. Harvard Business Review.

Rivera-Santos, M., Holt, D., Littlewood, D., & Kolk, A. (2015). Social entrepreneurship in sub-Saharan Africa. *Academy of Management Perspectives, 29*(1), 72–91.

Santos, F. M. (2012). A positive theory of social entrepreneurship. *Journal of business ethics, 111*(3), 335–351.

Sarasvathy, S. D. (2001). Causation and effectuation: Toward a theoretical shift from economic inevitability to entrepreneurial contingency. *Academy of Management Review, 26*(2), 243–263.

Sen, P. (2007). Ashoka's big idea: Transforming the world through social entrepreneurship. *Futures, 39*(5), 534–553.

Tan, L. P., Le, A. N. H., & Xuan, L. P. (2020). A systematic literature review on social entrepreneurial intention. *Journal of Social Entrepreneurship, 11*(3), 241–256.

These two examples of the improvement in the quality of life of poor communities are listed by the non-profit media organization. Retrieved October 13,

2022, from Worldchanging.com: http://www.worldchanging.com/archives/000462.html

Tracey, P., & Phillips, N. (2007). The distinctive challenge of educating social entrepreneurs: A postscript and rejoinder to the special issue on entrepreneurship education. *Academy of Management Learning & Education, 6*(2), 264–271.

Visser, K. (2011). Social entrepreneurship in South Africa: Context, relevance and extent. *Industry and Higher Education, 25*(4), 233–247.

Weerakoon, C. (2021). A decade of research published in the Journal of Social Entrepreneurship: A review and a research Agenda. *Journal of Social Entrepreneurship*, 1–23.

Williams, D. A., & Kadamawe, A. K. (2012). The dark side of social entrepreneurship. *International Journal of Entrepreneurship, 16*, 63.

World Bank. (2014). GINI index. Washington, DC: Author. Retrieved from http://data.worldbank.org/indicator/SI.POV.GINI/. Accessed on January 14, 2018.

Yunus, M. (2005). Eliminating poverty through market-based social entrepreneurship. *Global Urban Development Magazine, 1*(1), 1–10.

Zahra, S. A., Rawhouser, H. N., Bhawe, N., Neubaum, D. O., & Hayton, J. C. (2008). Globalization of social entrepreneurship opportunities. *Strategic Entrepreneurship Journal, 2*(2), 117–131.

6

Exploring International Joint Ventures

Henry Boateng, Stanley Cofie, Robert E. Hinson, and John Paul Kosiba

Introduction

Entrepreneurial businesses are local and international. In international entrepreneurship, joint ventures represent some of the most fertile modes for developing entrepreneurial businesses in Africa and the global south. Research has shown that international Joint Venture (JV) has been on the rise in the last decade and has become one of the preferred alternatives for

---

H. Boateng (✉)
Institutional Research, D'Youville University, Buffalo, US
e-mail: boatengh@dyc.edu

S. Cofie
Ghana Institute of Management and Public Administration, Accra, Ghana
e-mail: scofie@gimpa.edu.gh

R. E. Hinson
Ghana Communication Technology University, Accra, Ghana

University of the Free State Business School, Bloemfontein, South Africa
e-mail: rehinson@gctu.edu.gh

J. P. Kosiba
Department of Marketing, University of Professional Studies, Accra, Ghana

business growth apart from mergers and acquisitions (Piaskowska, Nadolska & Barkema, 2019; Rinaudo & Uhlaner, 2014). Some researchers have studied international joint ventures from the Resource-Based View (RBV). For instance, Choi and Beamish (2013) liken joint ventures to the resource-based pool of the partnering firms involved. They argue that the ability of firms to effectively complement each other's resource strengths lies in the sustained synergy in using these resources to their greatest of promises. One of the purposes of joint ventures is to have access to other firms' resources for gaining otherwise unavailable competitive advantages (Shah, 2015). The resource-based view proposes that complementarity amongst resources for partners of international joint ventures is vital for joint venture performance (Ainuddin et al., 2007; Chand & Katou, 2012). From these views, it is logical to argue that the social capital theory is insightful in understanding joint venture. However, limited studies exist on how social capital explains joint venture (Piaskowska et al., 2019). According to the social capital theory, people and organizations obtain intangible and tangible resources from social interactions and connections (Adler & Kwon, 2002; Coleman, 1988; Bourdieu, 1986). Social capital has been explored at the individual level, group or organizational level, and community level (Nahapiet & Ghoshal, 1998). The social capital theory has been approached differently by scholars. For example, while Bourdieu (1986) approaches social capital from an investment perspective, Coleman (1988) and Putnam (1995) approach social capital from relational and civic engagement perspectives respectively. However, they all acknowledge that social capital is a potential and actual intangible resource embedded in social relations that facilitate an individual and a collective action (Putnam, 1995; Coleman, 1988; Bourdieu, 1986).

In this study, we draw on the social capital theory to explain why home firms initiate joint venture with international firms. We also seek to understand the challenges home firms face that are in a joint venture with an international firm. Lastly, our study seeks to explore the resources that home firms access from their foreign partners in a joint venture relationship.

The rest of the chapter is divided as follows: theoretical background, literature review, methodology, data analysis, and presentation of findings, discussion, and implications.

Theoretical Background: Social Capital Theory

The focal tenet of the social capital theory is that individuals and organizations obtain both intangible and tangible resources via social interactions and relations (Adler & Kwon, 2002; Putnam, 1995; Coleman, 1988; Bourdieu, 1986). Social capital has been defined differently by scholars. Coleman, for example, asserts that "social capital is defined by its function. It is not a single entity, but a variety of different entities having two characteristics in common: They all consist of some aspect of a social structure, and they facilitate certain actions of individuals who are within the structure" (Coleman, 1990, p. 302). It has also been defined via social structures, cognitive, and social relation (Nahapiet & Ghoshal, 1998). Thus, it can be argued that social relations constitute a social capital that firms and individuals can utilize to achieve a specific goal. According to Coleman (1990) there are elements of social relations and social structures that constitute a social capital. These help the individual or organization situated in the structure or social relation to access resources.

Individuals or organizations in a social relationship have obligations and expectations to each other which create a social capital. For the parties in the social relations to enjoy this form of social capital, each must perform his or her obligations and fulfil the other's expectations. Coleman (1990) is of the view that social capital results from activities performed by members in a social structure; however, there are social capital that results from members' investment with the intentions of "receiving a return on their investment" (Coleman, 1990, p. 313). This means, accessing social capital requires investment in social relations. The amount of investment which might take the form of time, commitment, or even money that one makes in a social relation can earn the person a social capital. In this view we believe that the social capital theory can explain joint venture especially in international joint venture. Yan and Luo (2016) define international joint ventures as joint ventures that include firms from different countries cooperating across national and cultural restrictions. To Shah et al. (2014), international joint venture is a way through which indigenous firms, which were facing difficulties in entering foreign markets, easily penetrate such markets. The formation of an international joint venture has hence become a significant market entry strategy that most multinational firms adopt (Huang et al., 2015).

In this study, we conceptualize social capital from two perspectives: structural capital and relational capital. Relational capital is defined as all forms of relationships—"market relationships, power relationships and cooperation—established between firms, institutions and people, which stem from a strong sense of belonging and a highly developed capacity of cooperation typical of culturally similar people and institutions" (Capello & Faggian, 2005 cited in Welbourne & Pardo-del-Val, 2009, p. 486). Structural capital are results situated in networks and organizational structures. Such resources may include routines, capabilities, methods, and procedures within an organization (Khavandkar et al., 2016).

Coleman (1990) sees the potentials of information existing within social relations as a form of social capital. This enables people within the social structure to perform action. However, he believes that acquiring information is costly and therefore, people rely on their social relations for information (Coleman, 1990, 1988). Coleman is of the view that social capital results from activities performed by members in a social structure; however, there are social capital that result from members' investment with the intentions of "receiving a return on their investment" (Coleman, 1990, p. 313). This means, social capital requires investment in social relations. In this case investing in social relations and social structures can enable firms to access resources including knowledge.

Literature Review

Defining Joint Ventures

The concept of joint venture, in recent decades, has received attention in academic discourse and practice. This can be attributed to the upsurge in the dynamic nature of international business opportunities (Išoraltė, 2014; Sahebi et al., 2015). Lin (2017) observes that there is no universally accepted definition for joint venture. Different scholars present different views on the concept. However, definitions for joint venture can be traced as far back as 1976 when Pfeffer and Nowak conceptualized it as a legally and economically discrete organizational entity that is set up by two or more parent organizations which collate resources such as finance and human resources to pursue identified objectives. Hence, the concept cannot be considered as new. Xuan et al. (2011) view a joint venture as an agreement between two or more legally independent companies which merge resources and capabilities to undertake a shared business. To Georgieva et al. (2012), a joint venture is when a group of individual firms engage in a contract to share certain resources in operating another separate and new venture which will be jointly owned and governed by all participating individual firms. They add that the participating firms do not establish new infrastructure for the joint venture but maintain their places of operation. Hence, the concept is more of a top management decision and product collaborations rather than the creation of a separate firm. Again, Ahmed and Ahmed (2013) simply put it that a joint venture is a strategic decision. Lin (2017) indicates that joint ventures occur from the combination of resources by two or more parent companies. From the foregoing discourse, the link among varied definitions is the agreement that joint ventures occur between two or more firms, maintaining that a single firm cannot undertake a joint venture. There is also a consensus regarding the pooling of resources by the firms concerned. Therefore, two crucial activities are key to joint ventures; the agreement between two or more firms, and the pooling of resources. Also, per the view of Moxuan (2011), a joint venture becomes an international joint venture when at least one of the participating firms is a foreign company. This notion is iterated by Bryson et al. (2015), who positions that in the quest to explore new and emerging markets, overseas firms often enter into joint venture arrangements with firms in other international jurisdictions, making the term international joint venture increasingly popular.

Why Firms Enter into Joint Venture Relationships

Firms, as entities that are concerned about profitability and going concern, aim at making strategic decisions. Hence, firms do not just contract joint venture agreements for nothing but have motives for such actions. Over the years, scholars have shown interest in understanding the motivations for the establishment of joint ventures as noted by Wright et al. (2005). Egger and Egger (2006) explain that joint venture agreements are catalysts to productivity. As such, Morgan et al. (2012) suggest that firms are attracted to joint ventures considering the continual achievement of world economy and progress in the globalization agenda. Likewise, Kotler and Armstrong (2014) propose that organizations should explore several international markets and tap into the global market through joint ventures.

Extant literature identifies several reasons for joint venture agreements. Dunning (1995) identifies four major motives for firms, especially foreign ones, engaging in joint ventures. These are as follows: resource seeking, strategic assets seeking, market seeking, and efficiency seeking. According to Kotler and Armstrong (2014), most firms operate joint ventures to gain advantages such as strategic positions, resources, and local content advantages. Further, Kwarteng et al. (2018) consider knowledge acquisition from partnering firms a key reason why firms attempt joint ventures. These researchers further point out that knowledge of the host country's competitive conditions, culture, language, political systems, and business systems are mostly convincing factors that firms consider which make them opt for joint ventures other than other forms of entry into foreign countries. Additionally, Capaldo (2014) posits that companies involve in joint venture to share information, transfer knowledge, and co-produce knowledge. This is echoed by Child and Yan (2001), who believe that international joint ventures are a great source of knowledge transfer, particularly for firms in developing countries. On the contrary, Tortoriello and Krackhardt (2010) find no knowledge transfer advantages in joint venture agreements.

Biggs (2013) however states that the desire to increase sales is a motive for firms participating in joint ventures. He explains that joint ventures allow firms with distinct customer base to reach more customers and hence a wider market share. Biggs (2013) further connects the search for innovativeness and skills to reasons why a firm would consider a joint venture; through joint ventures, firms are able to explore combined skills and managerial innovativeness.

Makino et al. (2007) give account that firms enter joint ventures to take advantage of foreign markets to exploit growth potential as well as gain access to cheaper labour. Market saturation is also found to be a motive for joint venture (Gross et al., 2017). To these scholars, firms from smaller markets such as Singapore tend to quickly experience market saturation and therefore seek foreign exposure through joint ventures. Tang (2013) and Malhotra and Gaur (2014) establish that a firm may enter a joint venture to share economic risks and costs with its partners. Correspondingly, Gross et al. (2017) find the availability and cost of capital as a strong motivation for joint venture by hotel chains in the United States of America, Europe, and Asia.

Resources Home Firms Access from Foreign Firms in Joint Venture Relationship

International joint ventures have generally been found to have a positive impact on indigenous firms and their subsequent performance (Beamish & Lupton, 2009). The formation of joint ventures is based on the idea that economic value will be created for participating firms (Sahebi et al., 2015). In an international joint venture, the allocation and usage of resources is often a combined effort of both local and foreign firms. Zhang and Wen (2016) believe that through joint ventures, firms can combine imperfectly mobile and perfectly imitable but value-creating corresponding resources of partners. It is usually expected that partner firms work to achieve business goals that would have otherwise not been effectively accomplished had the joint agreement not existed (Gaur et al., 2018; Zhan & Chen, 2013). This presupposes that local and foreign firms both benefit from joint venture agreements.

The benefits available to local firms in joint venture agreements are enormous. To begin with, Beamish and Lupton (2009) and Lin (2017) mention that just as foreign firms, local firms gain knowledge on emerging markets through joint ventures and can subsequently exploit opportunities in these markets based on the knowledge gained. This is iterated by Lu et al. (2011), who admit that local firms gain knowledge from foreign firms in joint partnerships especially if the foreign firms are multinational ones. International joint ventures also serve as a vital means of knowledge transfer. Resultantly, local entities are linked with global partners and are able to create networks through associational learning, as Khan et al. (2015) espouse. Local firms are also able to gain brands and product knowledge from foreign firms in joint venture agreements (Nuruzzaman, Gaur & Sambharya, 2022). The knowledge that home firms gather from joint venture agreements aids them to sustain or advance their international competitiveness (Dunning & Lundan, 2008; Wiersema & Bowen, 2008). However, Liu, Ghauri, and Sinkovics (2010) argue that the failure of a firm to gain valuable knowledge from partner(s) may lead to dissatisfaction with the partnership, which increases the possibility of termination of the agreement. On another strand, Makino et al. posit that organizations in the local terrain mostly access marketing, technology and management resources, and expertise from joint ventures.

Methodology

This study used a case study research design. We used the case study design because our study addresses "why" and "what" questions and this is consistent with Yin (2014). According to Yin, case study must be used when research seeks to address why and what research questions. Following the choice of research design, we selected three firms in Ghana that are currently in international joint venture. These firms operate in the real estate and advertising industries. Since it was difficult to access the CEOs/managers of these firms, we decided to rely on people who are connected with these CEOs/managers. This is in line with Creswell (2007), who advised that researchers should rely on gatekeepers to access participants who are difficult to reach. In all, we were able to reach nine people who are either CEOs or hold managerial positions in the companies. For the purposes of confidentiality, we have decided not to name the firms and the individual participants. We have used pseudonyms (e.g., interviewee A, B, C) to identify the participants of the study. After getting in touch with the participants, we made appointments with them to conduct a face-to-face interview with them. The interviews took place in the participants' respective offices. We chose this option to conform to the operations of the firms and also to create an environment which can help the respondents relate many of the questions to their operations in the firm. On an average, each interview lasted for 40 minutes. With the participants' permission, we recorded all the interviews and transcribed them later for analysis. We used a thematic analysis technique to analyse the data. In using this technique, we read all the transcripts to familiarize ourselves with the response. After that, we read each transcript again to identify the emerging themes and partners. This resulted in major and minor themes. To ensure the trustworthiness (reliability and validity) of this study we used various methods. Yin (2014) proposes that to ensure rigour in qualitative studies, researchers should use established research design. Thus, following Yin (2014), we used a case study research design which is an established qualitative research design. Additionally, following Guba (1981) and Shenton (2004), we have used excerpts from the interviews to support all our findings. These excerpts augment the themes derived from the analysis and help us to incorporate the exact words of the participants into the study. We have also used member checking and peer debriefing where each author of this paper verified the themes and the data we have used to support them.

Presentation and Discussions of Findings

In this section of the paper, we present the findings of the study. We have presented the findings in accordance with the objectives of the study. The results of this study show that the need for financial resources and credibility triggers local firms to enter into joint ventures with foreign firms. The findings of this study also indicate that home firms that enter into joint venture experience challenges in the form of cultural differences, and inadequate information technology infrastructure. We also found that joint venture grants home firms access to resources in the form of knowledge and customers.

Why Home Firms Initiate Joint Venture

There were two major themes derived from the analysis: financial support and credibility. These have been elaborated in the next paragraphs.

Financial Support

We noticed that the major reason for the firms to enter into joint venture was to have access to funds. The firms have many projects to undertake but have limited financial resources. As a way of solving this challenge, they enter into joint venture with a foreign firm that can provide financial support to them. The following excerpts from the interviews support our findings:

> …*We had this international venture in 2015, when one Senegalese company called Atlantic Coast Regional Fund came to partner us in one of our developments named Rumbus, located at Kanda. Basically, they were supposed to provide funds in the nature of debt for us to be able to put up the development. Then we will service the debt from the sale or rental proceeds from the development*—**Interviewee A**

From this quote it can be observed that the firm entered the joint venture in order to obtain funds from the foreign partner to enable them to undertake projects. That is, the need for financial resources necessitates home firms to enter into joint venture with a foreign firm that has the needed financial resources. Relationship building in this case is a conscious effort based on the need for financial resources.

We find another support from one of the managers we interviewed.

> *The company was initially a subsidiary of and investment banking firm which was a multinational known as Renaissance Capital. Then later became a*

fully-fledged real estate company. So, basically the relationship was established when the company was an investment banking firm. **Interviewee C**

Similarly, a manager of another firm confirmed this view:

Appolonia is a project of a mother company called Rendeavour and that is what Rendeavour does, it invests in land banks.—**Interviewee F**

The home firms see the foreign partner as investors in this case. From the results, it is clear that the home firms build network with foreign firms and obtain resources from the same.

Credibility of Home Firm

The results also show that the firms enter into joint venture with foreign firms to leverage on the foreign firms' reputation. When a home firm is in a joint venture with a reputable foreign firm, potential customers perceive the home firms to be credible. This suggests that entering a joint venture will require that the home firm does a comprehensive background check of the foreign firm in order to ensure that the foreign partner they choose in this instance is credible. This is what one of our interviewees said:

I can only guess why it started, but it has been in existence for 4 to 5 years now. I guess we entered the joint venture because it puts us on a better stead. In that, when we were trying to get MTN accounts abroad, the MTN group required that, we are part of a certain agency to be able to handle the business. So that was a motivation for us to affiliate with DDB. I think the affiliation puts us in a better stead to get things you wouldn't normally get if you didn't have the strength of that affiliation.—**Interviewee C**

Another interviewee had this to say:

.....what I know about these joint ventures is that it strengthens your hold on the business and gives you a bit more credibility, sought of endorsement. When an international agency wants to collaborate with you, then you must have some clouts that they can be confident about.—**Interviewee G**

Similarly, a CEO of one of the firms we studied said that:

> *For me, it is because of the benefits that it brings. In Ghana, there are a lot of foreign firms which are more used to advertising space like, DDB, and Saatchi and Saatchi. When the foreign firms come to Ghana, they look to see where they would be comfortable, and their brand well handled. Taking INNOVA alone, the foreign firms might not be comfortable to work with, but when they know that it's not just INNOVA but INNOVA DDB, because of the standard and quality of DDB, their brand strength and awareness draws them in.*—**Interviewee C**

From these two excerpts, the credibility of the home firm is equally important as the foreign firm when it comes to joint venture. By entering into a joint venture with a credible foreign firm, the home firm is able to instil confidence in potential clients. Another interviewee shared a similar opinion:

> *Also, business security by virtue of the venture we are privileged to get some business proposals that wouldn't have come to us if we were just on the local market. But being out there, the group will share some businesses and tell them: we have partners in Ghana, so if you go there, they will take care of you. And with the confidence that they have in the global agency, they expect same from us. That notwithstanding, it gives us a big responsibility to make up to what the global partners have done.*—**Interviewee D**

This excerpt confirms that by associating themselves with a credible foreign firm, the home firm is able to attract some clients who are normally recommended by the foreign firm.

Resources Derived from Joint Venture

We noticed that joint venture enables the home firm to access resources in the form of knowledge and clients.

Access to Knowledge

The analysis shows that the home firms that are in joint venture relationship mainly access knowledge, although they enter into joint venture in order to access financial resources. All the interviewees acknowledged that the joint venture enables them to access knowledge from the foreign firms. The home firms adopt the best practices of the foreign firms and utilize them in their operations. They also access global market knowledge. The following views offered by some of our interviewees support this point:

I guess in terms of knowledge sharing and best practices, because they have been doing this much longer than we have, they have got a lot in terms of the best industry practices that some can be implemented here. Also, we get case studies that we can refer to when we are working on similar projects. **Interviewee A**

Another interviewee had this to say:

In knowledge transfer, DDB has a very big network, and ensure that its members are well versed with whatever happens globally from every market. Every year, there are several training programmes; they send invitations around so that if we are in the position to go for it, then yes. We have been going for training programmes for various levels of staff. There are some for junior levels, creatives, account managers, and management staff as well. Last year, we went for one training for management staff, and it was a big eye opener. Because you realize that some of the trends that you feel are peculiar to your market is not actually just in your market but global. There have been times that we complain about clients cutting budget left, right, centre, and we thought it was in our market only, but we went there and realised that every one that came there was also saying same. There are other peculiar things that happen in other markets that you can learn from and get to probably solve before it hits your market. **Interviewee C**

These excerpts show that different types of knowledge are accessed by the home firms from their foreign partners. Some of the knowledge about the foreign market are sometimes similar to those in the home market. In this case the knowledge accessed from the foreign firms may affirm the existing knowledge possessed by the home firms.

How Knowledge Is Transferred and Accessed

Our results show that the home accessed the knowledge by building a relationship with the employees of the foreign firms. The foreign firms also make a conscious effort to transfer knowledge to the home firms using case studies and workshops:

> *It's both ways, depending on who needs what at what time. But it's also got to do with the interpersonal relationship built between our company and the other partner's members. We also work through emails and phone calls, so it's dual. They also ask for help from us sometimes.*—**Interviewee B**

For this interviewee, personal relationship with employees of their partners in the joint venture enables them to access knowledge. This confirms Coleman's (1990) position that social relations constitute social capital which help people in the social relations to access knowledge (Coleman, 1990). From the results it can also be observed that apart from the formal relationship built at the institutional level, the members of the firms built informal relationships. In this case, through joint venture, knowledge is transferred and accessed through formal and informal channels.

The formal channels include training and workshop:

> The call in is mandatory and normally initiated by the other partner. The training sessions are also organized by them. But on occasions we tell them that we need particular capacity building, and they will specially organize or get somebody who can give us the necessary training. Sometimes we travel to South Africa to do training.

Accessing knowledge via this formal channel is the responsibility of both partners. Although the foreign firms normally take the initiative to transfer knowledge to their partners in the home country, the home firms sometimes request for the training.

Access to Clients

We noticed that it is not only knowledge that home firms access from their foreign partners. Entering into a joint venture with foreign firms grants the home firms access to clients. This is consistent with Makino et al. (2007), who found that by entering into a joint venture home firms are able to access new market as well as expertise. The following excerpts from the interviews affirm the position:

> *I can't say who benefits most but I guess there are benefits for both sides. For example, if France has a client, and the client wants to come to Ghana, it is quite easy for them to do that through us. They can tap into the knowledge that we have. Sometimes they might be pitching for a project, and they can tap into our local knowledge. Most of the time it's free, and with that we can win their pitches. Or if a client wants to expand and he approaches them, it is an advantage for them to refer him to agency partner in other countries. Therefore, the client can expand with the team that they already know. So it's mutual.—* **Interviewee B**

From this extract, the home firm also enables the foreign firm to access the local market. They offer the foreign firms knowledge about the home market.

> *We are currently working on Lucozade which is managed by DDB elsewhere. DDB referred Lucozade to us in Ghana, so we get to work with them. So, in my view, the local partner [DDB] benefits more by capitalizing on the brand strength to get more business to work with.* **Interviewee C**

These excerpts suggest that joint venture relationship between a home firm and a foreign firm enables both foreign and home firms to access knowledge and new market.

Conclusions and Recommendations on the Way Forward

The purpose of this study was to explore why home firms decide to enter joint venture with foreign firms and the resources they obtain from their foreign partners. Our study also explored some of the challenges home firms encounter in joint venture relationship. The findings of the study show that the home firms normally take initiative to enter international joint venture to access financial resources and also build their credibility. Thus, the need for tangible and intangible resources drives home to firms to enter into joint venture with international firms. Therefore, the motive of these firms is to access strategic intangible resources and financial resources. An earlier study by Dunning (1995) states the motive of some firms that enter into a joint venture had been to access strategic assets. Thus, our study supports this finding. We see credibility as a strategic asset which the home firms can utilize to achieve their business goals. For example, the firms can rely on the reliability of the foreign firms to attract new clients as opined by one of the interviewees. By this finding, it can be said that firms build social relations and social structures in order to utilize the social capital therein to access financial and strategic assets.

Although the home firms enter into a joint venture with the above motives, they rather get access to knowledge and clients while they are into the joint venture relationship. Kwarteng et al. (2018) found that access to knowledge is one of the motives for firms to enter into joint ventures; however, in our study we found that access to knowledge is not a motive for the firms to enter into a joint venture but the firms' access to knowledge about foreign market becomes accessible to the home firm after they have entered into the joint venture. This becomes possible because of the social relations the employees of the home firms build with the employees of the foreign. Again, by the joint venture agreement the home firm is integrated into the foreign firms' structures which facilitate the transfer of knowledge to the home firms. We also noticed that the home firms also transfer knowledge to the foreign firms once they enter into a joint venture. This means that when firms enter into international joint venture knowledge is shared at the institutional and individual levels rather than transferred at the institutional level. Knowledge accessed from the foreign firms are stored through knowledge sharing among employees of the home firms. Knowledge sharing is one of the ways of retaining knowledge obtained from foreign firms.

Studies such as Gross et al. (2017) indicate that access to new market is a motive for home firms to enter into international joint venture; however, our study shows that access to new market comes as a result of the joint venture, thereby supporting Makino et al. (2007)'s finding.

Our findings have implications for theory and practice. From a theoretical perspective, the findings of our study show that social capital is formed at the organizational and individual levels. The social capital situated at the organizational level trickles down to the individual level enabling the individuals within the organization access to resources. At the organizational level social capital is formed within structures of the organization, while at the individual level social capital is formed within social relations. From this perspective, organization's social capital, it's the ties it has with other organization which relates to structural capital contributes to resources access and the individual members relational capital which contributes knowledge sharing. The findings also imply that social capital can be built and requires investment and commitment to relationships. The results also suggest that motive for investing in social capital may change once relationships are formed. At this stage organizations may focus on other benefits than their motives for investing in social capital.

Practically our findings suggest that building social capital at the organizational level will require that organizations manage the social capital formed at the individual level. This will enable the firm to obtain the maximum benefit from their social capital investment at the organizational level. The findings also mean that organizations in contractual agreement should not only fulfil their legal obligations but they must also build and maintain social relations. This will help them obtain some benefits that might be part of the contractual agreement.

References

Adler, P. S., & Kwon, S. W. (2002). Social capital: Prospects for a new concept. *Academy of Management Review, 27*(1), 17–40.

Ahmed, R. S. H., & Ahmed, S. S. H. (2013). The future of joint ventures: Literature review. *International Journal of Business and Management Studies, 5*(2), 230–240.

Ainuddin, R. A., Beamish, P. W., Hulland, J. S., & Rouse, M. J. (2007). Resource attributes and firm performance in international joint ventures. *Journal of World Business, 42*(1), 47–60.

Beamish, P. W., & Lupton, N. C. (2009). Managing joint ventures. *Academy of Management Perspectives, 23*(2), 75–94.

Biggs, R. P. (2013). *10 Reasons to go international*. http://choosewashingtonstate.com/wp-content/uploads/2013/06/10_Reasons_to_go_International.pdf

Bourdieu, P. (1986). The Forms of Capital. In J. Richardson (Ed.), *Handbook of theory and research for the sociology of education* (pp. 241–258). New York: Greenwood.

Bryson, J. M., Crosby, B. C., & Bloomberg, L. (2015). *Public value and public administration*. Georgetown University Press.

Capaldo, A. (2014). Network governance: A cross-level study of social mechanisms, knowledge benefits, and strategic outcomes in joint-design alliances. *Industrial Marketing Management, 43*(4), 685–703.

Chand, M., & Katou, A. A. (2012). Strategic determinants for the selection of partner alliances in the Indian tour operator industry: A cross-national study. *Journal of World Business, 47*(2), 167–177.

Child, J., & Yan, Y. (2001). National and transnational effects in international business: Indications from Sino-foreign joint ventures. *MIR: Management International Review, 41*, 53–75.

Choi, C. B., & Beamish, P. W. (2013). Resource complementarity and international joint venture performance in Korea. *Asia Pacific Journal of Management, 30*(2), 561–576.

Coleman, J. S. (1988). Social capital in the creation of human capital. *American Journal of Sociology, 94*, S95–S120.

Coleman, J. S. (1990). *The Foundations of Social Theory*. Cambridge, Mass: Harvard University Press.

Creswell, J. W. (2007). *Research design: Qualitative, quantitative and mixed methods approaches* (4th ed.). Thousand Oaks, CA: Sage

Dunning, J. H. (1995). Reappraising the eclectic paradigm in an age of alliance capitalism. *Journal of International Business Studies, 26*, 461–491.

Dunning, J. H., & Lundan, S. M. (2008). *Multinational enterprises and the global economy*. Edward Elgar Publishing.

Egger, H., & Egger, P. (2006). International outsourcing and the productivity of low-skilled labour in the EU. *Economic Inquiry, 44*(1), 98–108.

Gaur, A. S., Ma, X., & Ding, Z. (2018). Home country supportiveness/unfavorableness and outward foreign direct investment from China. *Journal of International Business Studies, 49*(3), 324–345.

Georgieva, D., Jandik, T., & Lee, W. Y. (2012). The impact of laws, regulations, and culture on cross-border joint ventures. *Journal of International Financial Markets, Institutions and Money, 22*(4), 774–795.

Gross, M. J., Huang, S., & Ding, Y. (2017). Chinese hotel firm internationalisation: Jin Jiang's joint venture acquisition. *International Journal of Contemporary Hospitality Management, 29*(11), 2730–2750.

Guba, E. G. (1981). Criteria for assessing the trustworthiness of naturalistic inquiries. *Educational Communication and Technology Journal, 29*(2), 75–91.

Huang, M. C., Hsiung, H. H., & Lu, T. C. (2015). Re-examining the relationship between control mechanisms and international joint venture performance: The mediating roles of perceived value gap and information asymmetry. *Asia Pacific Management Review, 20*(1), 32–43.

Išoraitė, M. (2014). Importance of strategic alliances in company's activity. *Intellectual Economics, 1*(5), 39–46.

Khan, Z., Lew, Y. K., & Sinkovics, R. R. (2015). International joint ventures as boundary spanners: Technological knowledge transfer in an emerging economy. *Global Strategy Journal, 5*(1), 48–68.

Khavandkar, E., Theodorakopoulos, N., Hart, M., & Preston, J. (2016). Leading the diffusion of intellectual capital management practices in science parks. In *Human resource management, innovation and performance* (pp. 213–231). Palgrave Macmillan.

Kotler, P., & Armstrong, G. (2014). *Principles of marketing* (Fifteenth Global ed.). Pearson.

Kwarteng, A., Dadzie, S. A., Famiyeh, S., & Aklamanu, A. M. K. (2018). Institutional dimensions and conflict resolution strategy in international joint ventures: An empirical examination. *Thunderbird International Business Review, 60*(4), 591–604.

Lin, J. Y. (2017). Knowledge creation through joint venture investments: The contingent role of organizational slack. *Journal of Engineering and Technology Management, 46*, 1–25.

Liu, C. L. E., Ghauri, P. N., & Sinkovics, R. R. (2010). Understanding the impact of relational capital and organizational learning on alliance outcomes. *Journal of World Business, 45*(3), 237–249.

Lu, J., Liu, X., & Wang, H. (2011). Motives for outward FDI of Chinese private firms firm resources, industry dynamics, and government policies. *Management and Organization Review, 7*(2), 223–248.

Makino, S., Chan, C. M., Isobe, T., & Beamish, P. W. (2007). Intended and unintended termination of international joint ventures. *Strategic Management Journal, 28*(11), 1113–1132.

Malhotra, S., & Gaur, A. S. (2014). Spatial geography and control in foreign acquisitions. *Journal of International Business Studies, 45*, 191–210.

Morgan, N. A., Katsikeas, C. S., & Vorhies, D. W. (2012). Export marketing strategy implementation, export marketing capabilities, and export venture performance. *Journal of the Academy of Marketing Science, 40*(2), 271–289.

Moxuan, A. O. (2011). Factors Affecting Malaysia-China Construction Joint Venture (MCCJV) Projects. *Journal of Academic Research in Economics, 3*, 317–329.

Nahapiet, J., & Ghoshal, S. (1998). Social capital, intellectual capital, and the organizational advantage. *Academy of Management Review, 23*(2), 242–266.

Nuruzzaman, N., Gaur, A., & Sambharya, R. B. (2022). WTO accession and firm exports in developing economies. *Journal of International Business Policy, 5*(4), 444–466.

Piaskowska, D., Nadolska, A., & Barkema, H. G. (2019). Embracing complexity: Learning from minority, 50-50, and majority joint venture experience. *Long Range Planning, 52*(1), 134–153.

Putnam, R. D. (1995). Tuning in, tuning out: The strange disappearance of social capital in America. *PS: Political Science & Politics, 28*(4), 664–683.

Rinaudo, K. E., & Uhlaner, R. (2014). Joint ventures on the rise. *McKinsey Quarterly*, 1–3.

Sahebi, H., Nickel, S., & Ashayeri, J. (2015). Joint venture formation and partner selection in upstream crude oil section: Goal programming application. *International Journal of Production Research, 53*(10), 3047–3061.

Shah, K. U. (2015). Choice and control of international joint venture partners to improve corporate environmental performance. *Journal of Cleaner Production, 89*, 32–40.

Shah, K. U., Philippidis, G., Dulal, H. B., & Brodnig, G. (2014). Developing biofuels industry in small economies: Policy experiences and lessons from the Caribbean basin initiative. *Mitigation and Adaptation Strategies for Global Change, 19*(2), 229–253.

Shenton, A. K. (2004). Strategies for ensuring trustworthiness in qualitative research projects. *Education for Information, 22*(2), 63–75.

Tang, J. A. (2013). Joint venture formation and internationalization: A Japanese MNEs' perspective. *Journal of Asia-Pacific Business, 14*(2), 107–129.

Tortoriello, M., & Krackhardt, D. (2010). Activating cross-boundary knowledge: The role of Simmelian ties in the generation of innovations. *Academy of Management Journal, 53*(1), 167–181.

Welbourne, T. M., & Pardo-del-Val, M. (2009). Relational capital: strategic advantage for small and medium-size enterprises (SMEs) through negotiation and collaboration. *Group Decision and Negotiation, 18*, 483–497.

Wiersema, M. F., & Bowen, H. P. (2008). Corporate diversification: The impact of foreign competition, industry globalization, and product diversification. *Strategic Management Journal, 29*(2), 115–132.

Wright, M., Filatotchev, I., Hoskisson, R. E., & Peng, M. W. (2005). Strategy research in emerging economies: Challenging the conventional wisdom. *Journal of Management Studies, 42*(1), 1–33.

Xuan, M., Omran, A., & Pakir, A. H. K. (2011). Factors affecting Malaysia-China construction joint venture (MCCJV) projects. *Journal of Academic Research in Economics, 3*(3).

Yan, A., & Luo, Y. (2016). *International joint ventures: Theory and practice: Theory and practice*. Routledge.

Yin, R. K. (2014). *Case study research: Design and methods*. Los Angeles, CA: Sage.

Zhan, W., & Chen, R. R. (2013). Dynamic capability and IJV performance: The effect of exploitation and exploration capabilities. *Asia Pacific Journal of Management, 30*(2), 601–632.

Zhang, X., & Wen, J. (2016). The impacts of economic importance difference of a joint venture (JV) held by partners and partners' size difference on the extraction of rivalrous and non-rivalrous private benefits in a JV. *International Review of Financial Analysis, 48*, 46–54.

Part IV

Technology and Entrepreneurial Development

7

The Impact of 4IR Technologies on Venture Creation and Technology Commercialisation: Insights and Exemplars from an Emerging Economy Context

Patience Rambe and Ratakane Maime

Introduction

The advent of the Fourth Industrial Revolution (4IR) technologies, which spans technologies that integrate the physical, biological, and digital domains in novel ways and interconnects populations (Tripathi & Gupta, 2021), has been embraced with great anticipation in South Africa. The initial excitement with these technologies has been fuelled by their inherent and instrumental promise to accelerate the realisation of global development goals such as the provision of sustainable water security (Stankovic et al., 2020), the unlocking of global value chains (Amsden, 2001; Nyagadza et al., 2022), unleashing of lean manufacturing, proliferation of smart factories (Morrar et al., 2017; Benassi et al., 2022),

---

P. Rambe (✉)
University of the Free State, Free State, South Africa
e-mail: prambe@cut.ac.za

transformation of job opportunities, and their re-engineering of human skills needs (Citi Insight, 2020). Punctuated by a strong technology focus and emphasising the nexus between multiple technologies and their impact on the configuration of production and changes in business processes (Benassi et al., 2022), these technologies have also granted the South African government an aura of fervent and justified hope to create more humane job opportunities and roll back the frontiers of unemployment in the country. For instance, the Presidential Commission on the 4IR postulates that 4IR technologies, enabled by the National Development Plan 2030, present possibilities and pathways for the material realisation of poverty reduction, the reduction of unemployment, and the eradication of extreme inequality (Presidential Commission on the Fourth Industrial Revolution, 2020).

The euphoria surrounding institutional, infrastructural, and financial 4IR preparedness has manifested in the strong state intervention approach to 4IR, leading to the materialisation of multiple national and regional initiatives in the Free State Province. Following the establishment of the Presidential Commission on 4IR and later the production of its report on architectures and developments on 4IR, other regional and local responses proliferated in the province. These interventions include inter alia, the convening of the multi-stakeholder 4IR Summit in the province in 2019 (Ngowi et al., 2019) and the pledging of R6 million by the Free State Provincial government to establish a science park for high-technology start-ups. Other initiatives include the revitalisation of special economic zones for industrial and high-technology firms (Department of Trade and Industry, 2021) and the implementation of quadruple helix (university-business-industry-community) partnerships through the Entrepreneurship Development in Higher Education (EDHE) in South Africa (Pivot Global Education, 2020). Despite the work of these institutions, 4IR preparedness documentation and some financial deployments, some compelling and demonstrable high-tech venture creation outcomes are yet to emerge in the province and in the country. Some South African Universities have also joined the 4IR bandwagon by creating Higher Education Research Development in the Central Region (HERDIC), a consortia of universities

---

R. Maime
Central University of Technology, Free State, Bloemfontein, South Africa

and technical and vocational education training (TVET) colleges in the Central region of South Africa (especially Central University of Technology, Free State, University of the Free State, Sol Plaatje University and TVET colleges in the central region) aimed at commercialising the outputs of research and development through venture development, venture capitalisation, and technology innovations. Though these initiatives constitute positive gestures at embracing 4IR technologies as vehicles for technology commercialisation, these actions remain sporadic, incohesive, and lack sufficient resource orchestration to stir compelling, groundbreaking technology innovations and the founding of high-technology start-ups.

The aforesaid instrumentation of 4IR technologies as silver bullets for high-tech start-up development and the commercialisation of technology innovation are not devoid of teething problems. Technology commercialisation, which denotes a process of translating promising discoveries and inventions into streams of economic returns that involve product conceptualisation, development, production, and product launch activities (Gans & Stern, 2003; Mattila et al., 2019), is fraught with inherent and potential challenges. From an infrastructural perspective, South Africa is reeling under erratic power supply due to rolling blackouts, which interrupt consistent and stable internet connectivity for digital and technology-based businesses. From an entrepreneurial perspective, South Africa experiences high rate of start-up failure (Martin, 2018), and entrepreneurs acutely lack critical digital expertise (Adendorff & Putzier, 2018). From a functional perspective, appropriating digital technologies to support high-technology venture development is hampered by inherent uncertainty and ambiguity that accompanies radical novelty and anticipations of rapid growth and impact (Rotolo et al., 2015). Moreover, devising a feasible digital strategy, understanding potential customers, creating credibility, expecting support from the surrounding network and ecosystem, overcoming adoption barriers to generates sales (Aarikka-Stenroos & Lehtimäki, 2014; Salehi et al., 2022) are not an easy feat in emerging economies where it would be argued that digital competencies remain unsophisticated, and the financial markets are largely underdeveloped.

In view of the ambivalent venture creation and technology commercialisation outcomes of 4IR technologies, this chapter seeks to conduct a reality check of the compendium of digital technologies that can be harnessed to foster high-technology venture development and promote the commercialisation of technology outcomes. Following Maynard's (2015) argument that 4IR not only draws on digital technologies but exploits variances in technologies' computational power and integrates devices with human-like intelligence, and brings greater interconnectivity among material objects, we build on this argument to demonstrate which 4IR technologies are amenable for adoption, exploitation, and commercialisation by small high-tech firms in resource poor contexts. We draw on entrepreneurial ecosystems theory to argue that entrepreneurs themselves must be architects and drivers of the institutionalisation of the entrepreneurial ecosystems (Stam, 2015), with governments serving as "feeders" in the entrepreneurial ecosystem that provide finance, professional services, and adjust laws (Feld, 2012). Drawing on this hands-free approach, we challenge the monolithic, government-driven approach to 4IR and propose a bottom-up approach in which serial technology entrepreneurs and their local entrepreneurial ecosystems serve as cogs and nodes for the exploitation of 4IR technologies to support effective venture creation and the commercialisation of technology innovations.

The chapter makes two main contributions: first, the study combines the instrumentality of technological affordances and contextual nuances to develop an understanding of technologies that might coalesce in shaping venture development and technology commercialisation. This is critical because the realisation of technology entrepreneurship through the founding of high-tech firms requires "recognising, creating and exploiting opportunities, and assembling resources around a technological solution" in specific organisational contexts (Ratinho et al., 2015). Second, the chapter develops a bottom of the pyramid approach, drawing on participants of entrepreneurial ecosystems, to develop a more nuanced appreciation of a technology-mediated strategy to technology venture development and commercialisation (e.g., through high-technology ventures, patents, industrial designs, prototypes, and intellectual property outcomes) that could be more contextually grounded and participant driven. This is critical because the founding of technology ventures requires not only entrepreneurs' knowledge and expertise but also a recognition of institutional resources and incentives availed in the entrepreneurial ecosystem and the influence of contextual factors (McAdams &

Pals, 2006; Mitchell et al., 2002) as well as technology venture development frameworks situated at different levels where multiple relationships unfold between internal and external players (McAdam et al., 2016).

The Conceptual Overview

Entrepreneurial Ecosystems

The realisation of venture creation and technology commercialisation is one of the functions of entrepreneurial ecosystems. The term "ecosystem" describes the complex interaction of economic communities based on engagements of individuals, roles, infrastructure, organisations (business and government), and events (Bloom & Dees, 2008; Moore, 1993). At the heart of entrepreneurial ecosystems are individual entrepreneurs who interact with their entrepreneurial environment and such engagements provide some deep insights into the founding of new ventures (Valdez, 1988). As such, entrepreneurial ecosystem outcomes such as venture creation and technology commercialisation are not just consequences of technology appropriation and adoption for value capture and creation alone but also outcomes of the interaction between ecosystem stakeholders such as venture capitalists, incubators, government representatives, entrepreneurs, employees, and communities, in areas where these high-tech firms are located.

Entrepreneurial ecosystems theory describes components of entrepreneurial ecosystems as comprising opportunities (e.g., entrepreneurial opportunities), skilled people (e.g., technology entrepreneurs), and resources (e.g., finance, expertise, and physical resources) (Ahmad & Hoffman, 2008; Cowell et al., 2018). Other literature conceives of entrepreneurial ecosystems as comprising five C's: capital (financial resource), capability (the entrepreneurs and owners' skillset), connections (resource and relationship networks), culture (the local communities' perception and support of entrepreneurship), and climate (regulatory institutions, economic development, and policy environment) (Macke et al., 2014). For the purposes of this study, the resources that merge to facilitate technology commercialisation are 4IR context, 4IR technologies, knowledge and expertise of high-technology entrepreneurs, physical resources (e.g., capital, machinery, buildings, offices, and laboratories), social and business networks that facilitate high-tech business development, and a supportive regulatory environment. The presence or absence of these ingredients and the extent to which they merge differentiate ecosystems from one another and explain the robustness of entrepreneurial ecosystems (Colin, 2015).

South Africa

There are some compelling reasons to believe that 4IR technologies have the potential to transform the South African economy and society. First, the ICT sector now constitutes approximately 10% of South Africa's GDP. Regarding the labour force, it is estimated that there are approximately 600,000 workers that operate in the ICT sector across South Africa, with 41% in media, IT, communications, and electronics; 13% in academia; 8% in banking; 4% in local government; and 1% in national and provincial government (Citi Insight, 2020). Compared with other sub-Saharan countries, South Africa presents a promising climate for the maturity of 4IR due to the high rate of electrification, internet access, and better infrastructure (Nyagadza, 2019). On the other hand, if it was not for the slow policy and legislative developments, expensive data, poor quality infrastructure among other challenges, the level of digitalisation would have been much more pervasive than it has been for other sub-Saharan countries (Nyagadza et al., 2022).

4IR Technologies

The term 4IR describes a set of convergent technologies and applications that merge physical, digital, and biological domains (Gilchrist, 2016). The concept 4IR was popularised at the World Economic Forum Annual meeting in 2016 by the founder and chairman, Klaus Schwab. He conceived it as comprising a fusion of technologies (e.g., ubiquitous and mobile Internet, powerful sensors, artificial intelligence, and machine learning) blurring the lines between the physical, digital, and biological spheres (Schwab, 2016). The 4IR supersedes previous revolutions that were driven by the mechanisation of tasks (the first being the first industrial revolution), the second being the industrial revolution characterised by electrification, and the third characterised by digitalisation which facilitated automation (Drath & Horch, 2014; Marnewick & Marnewick, 2020; Schmidt et al., 2015). The heartbeat of 4IR is the seamless fusion and integration of technologies, devices, applications, and networks blurring the role of space and physical location in transacting products and services.

At the coalface of 4IR are a range of new, emerging, and disruptive technologies, such as artificial intelligence (AI), big data, the Internet of Things (IoT), blockchain, drones, and virtual and augmented reality (VR/AR) (Stankovic et al., 2020), autonomous driving cars, and machine learning, to name a few. The main argument is that these technologies can revolutionise methods of organisation, production, and distribution based on digital transformation and automatisation that erase the limits between physical objects, turning them into a comprehensive complex system of interconnected and interdependent elements (Sukhodolov, 2019). Such an argument is relevant to technology entrepreneurship that focuses on the recognition, creation, and exploitation of opportunities and the assembling of resources (technology, human, capital, and physical resources around technological solutions) (Ratinho et al., 2015).

High-Tech Venture Creation

Venture creation describes the process that unfolds between the intention to start a business and making the first sale (Liao et al., 2005). These temporal, non-linear activities that lead to venture founding are conceived differently by different authors. For Galbraith (1982), the venture creation process involves several stages ranging from the proof of principle stage, prototype stage, model shop stage, and start-up stage. For Brockner (2004), the process involves idea generation, idea screening, procuring the necessary resources, proving the business model, business rollout, maturity, renewal, and growth decline. Despite the different characterisations of venture development in literature, start-up development is a well-orchestrated and resource-driven process that culminates in the founding of a new venture. Moreover, it is an event-driven and outcome-based development, in which opportunity identification culminates in the first sale of a product or service (Muniz-Avila et al., 2019).

High-Technology Venture Development

High-tech start-ups contribute to the development of organisations and products that are unique to the market and draw on sophisticated technology and high technical knowledge. At the coalface of technology venture development are a range of inputs and actors that facilitate research and development, engineering, equipment tests, certifications, and the launch of innovative technology-based products in technology-intensive markets (Vargas & Plonski, 2019). Venture development in technology-intensive industries such as biotechnology, robotics, biomedical engineering, and microelectronics involve the embedding of high levels of specialised technical knowledge in products and services (Vargas & Plonski, 2019). Yet the development process of high-tech firms does not only involve exploration of technology opportunities, dissection of complex market needs, development of competitive product strategies (Rozenfeld et al., 2006) but also the development of high value-added technology products or services and their wide-scale rollout or commercialisation at the industrial scale.

Technology Commercialisation

Commercialisation is the transformation of a business idea into a revenue-generating product or service and the attainment of competitive advantage within a specific market (Jamil et al., 2015). It captures the process of transitioning technologies from the research lab to the marketplace at an industrial scale (University of California, n.d.) through various processes such as patenting, licencing, and start-up activity (Link & Siegel,

2007). Datta et al. (2014) noted that commercialisation of technology has two main phases. The first involves a small demand for a product by technology "enthusiasts" also known as "initial adopters" even though there are no significant returns realised from selling a product. The second phase involves a significant penetration of technology innovation products in a large market beyond the initial adopters (Datta et al., 2014).

In the context of South Africa, the Directorate of Innovation, Technology Transfer and Commercialisation at the University of South Africa (2020) lists some of the disruptive technologies that have been amenable to commercialisation in energy, ICT, and manufacturing at the institution. These are tubular fixed-bed reactors, low-cost household wind turbine, solar energy harvesting system, plastic-to-energy anaerobic gasification, high-performance lithium ion batteries, membrane distillation for desalination, acid mine drainage using maghemite nanoparticles, predictive index software, photonic data processing and sensors on chip, chitosan-based resistive switching memory device, grocery delivery app, automatic healthcare assistance device, flotation device, and waste beer recovery (Directorate of Innovation, Technology Transfer and Commercialisation at the University of South Africa, 2020). Although this Directorate's report lists the range of these technologies that have commercialisation potential, it does not capture the complexity of commercialisation in developing economies due to lack of financial resources, complexities in the formalisation of R&D and the lack of effective networks that undermine the benefits that small, micro, and medium enterprises (SMMEs) derive from pursuing open innovations (Bigliardi & Galati, 2016) such as technology commercialisation.

The Inter-American Development Bank Report (2020) also articulates different technologies that can be commercialised such as the use of AI in smart water management and the use of machine learning for assessment of conditions of portable water mains, enabling significant optimisation in utility maintenance. The study also provides a range of technology start-up firms that have been created that deploy AI and machine learning to improve water management services such as eWaterPay (specialising in smart water connections), Intelliflux (specialising in artificial intelligence-guided adaptive cleaning for membrane and filtration processes), and WatchTower Robotics (a firm that designs, manufactures, and operates small-scale robots to identify and pinpoint pipe leaks early and accurately) (Stankovic et al., 2020).

4IR Technologies, Technology Commercialisation, and Venture Creation

We provide some exemplars of the appropriation, institutionalisation, and domestication of 4IR technologies with a view to develop a model that serves as a techno-infrastructural dashboard for informing the future pipeline for technology business development and the commercialisation of technology innovation outcomes. These technologies are the Internet of Things, big data, artificial intelligence, augmented reality, and blockchain technology.

Internet of Things

The Internet of Things (IoT) is defined as "a network of advanced sensors and actuators in different locations embedded with software, network connectivity and computer capability, that can collect and exchange data over the internet and enable automated solutions to multiple problem sets" (PWC, 2017). The network of objects (e.g., devices, vehicles, machines, containers), embedded with sensors and software have the ability to collect and communicate data over the internet (Edwards & Hopkins, 2018), allowing "things" to be identified, located, sensed, and controlled via the global platform (Borgia, 2014). At the basic level, a *smart home system* employs IoT to improve efficiency in the use of the internet, connects home appliances and applications with built-in sensors while making the home more habitable and desirable to stay in. For instance, smart thermostats that regulate home temperature, thereby diminishing electricity costs significantly, smart refrigerators that monitor the availability of products every time when the door is opened and order new ones, offer recipes, smart locking systems, and other devices that limit the risk of fire, electricity accidents, and damage by adjusting power supply (Angelova et al., 2017) are all instantiations of the application of IoT. Similar technologies, such as the smart bin (as is the one installed at the Central University of Technology, Free State), a sensor installed bin for monitoring waste management and waste management routes resonate with Guna et al.'s (2022) view on the importance of promoting environmentally sustainable behaviours. Smart health-sensing systems deploy small intelligent equipment and devices to check and monitor the different health issues and fitness levels or the amounts of calories burned in the fitness centre, and so on (Kumar et al., 2019). Other sensor-controlled smart devices and applications have been used for regulating temperature of freezers for storing medicines and vaccines; monitoring of patients in hospitals and in their homes; calibrating biometric data and sending them to doctors without the need for consultations; and sensors that trigger signals to remind patients to take their medication according to the prescriptions (Angelova et al., 2017).

From a venture creation perspective, firms can use IoT for generating innovative ideas, prototype development, product development, and design through real-time data inputs and customisation of marketing strategies (McGinnis, 2020). For instance, the Stable Kernel website (2021) provides some simple ways of developing an IoT ecosystem from an idea to commercialisation involving the conduct of rigorous market research to test product viability in the market and the creation of an IoT kit for developing a low-cost, low-risk entry into IoT with sensors. The next stage is to develop a proof of concept for testing connectivity, transfering data, and gathering user feedback without significant financial risk and moving production to a quality cloud infrastructure for scaling the system with data and developing a customer base using Google Cloud, Microsoft Azure, or Amazon Web Services (Stable Kernel website, 2021).

Regarding technology commercialisation, the use of IoT is deemed critical to improving supply chains for products, improving customer shopping experiences, and improving inventory controls. Using IoT can close the gap between the physical and the digital world by synchronising the information flow with the physical flow (Ping et al., 2011), thereby enhancing demand-driven retail supply chains using digital connectivity and coordination in supply chains when supplying goods, products, and services (Fleisch & Tellkamp, 2005). Moreover, IoT reduces dissatisfaction with the purchasing experience by assisting customers to interact with products, often in a virtual or augmented reality environment before purchase (Middleton, 2018). The use of IoT has enabled start-ups to not only provide a seamless shopping experience at reduced cost but also facilitate improved stock/inventory control and supply chain management by tracking and gathering real-time data on popular products in different settings and creating up- or cross-selling opportunities (Middleton, 2018).

Big Data Analytics

Big data analytics (BDA) is defined as an organisation's analytical capability to collect, process, analyse, and interpret large datasets to extract insights relevant for effective decision-making and operational performance (Akter et al., 2016; Moktadir et al., 2019). The prevalence of diverse emerging technologies such as smart devices, social network platforms, the improvements in cloud computing and Internet of Things is credited with enabling and enhancing the BDA phenomenon (Babu et al., 2021; Dumbill, 2013). The BDA phenomenon is conceived to drive business intelligence and cognitive computing, business innovation, and performance (Akter et al., 2020; Davenport & Kudyba, 2016). For customers, BDA presents them with a better understanding of new products and provides new simplified modes of large scale interaction between them and firms (Zhan et al., 2018).

The use of big data analytics is, however, not without its limitations and challenges. For instance, the use of data analytics generates a penetrating gaze into consumers' and service users' lives as big data relies predominantly on data streams from social and online media, as well as personal devices designed to share data (Ball & Webster, 2020). Research suggests that consumers have limited opportunities to opt out of data sharing and experience challenges in ascertaining the use to which their data is put once it is shared (Ball et al., 2016). Apparently, when BDA is deployed, consumers and service users exert less control over their personal information flows and their mundane consumption activities become subject to scrutiny (Ball & Webster, 2020) often with(out) their authorisation.

Although the use of big data is credited with providing new business insights, improving core operating processes, enabling faster and better decision-making surreptitiously, taking advantage of changing industry value chains (Brock et al., 2013), the commercialisation of big data is not a clear and straightforward exercise. While big tech companies such as Alphabet, Amazon, Apple, Facebook, and Microsoft have deployed appropriate technologies and predictive algorithms to extract powerful insights into their customers' shopping habits and predict their product preferences (Choi & Taylor, 2018), the development of big data analytics strategies remain unclear because of the lack of training of senior and middle management in data science and machine learning, poor data quality or poor application of big data models (Novikov, 2020).

While commercialisation of big data denotes how big data itself is monetised as an asset rather than analysed and the resulting insights combined with existing or new products and services (Chen et al., 2012), commercialisation appears to be an afterthought, or at best, conceived as a generalised notion of value that is created by improved internal analysis and decision-making (Thomas & Leiponen, 2016). Yet the use of data as an asset has a fundamental effect on streamlining business operations and creating a holistic purchasing experience for customers. For example, Microsoft streamlined its sales operations by decreasing employee time devoted to each potential sale by 10 to 15 minutes by centralising data on each sales opportunity. The data was then enhanced using predictive analytics software, thereby allowing sales employees to gauge the chance that a shopping opportunity would lead to a sale while also providing the company with critical information needed to make a successful sale (Choi & Taylor, 2018).

Acknowledging the importance of data as a key resource in big data analytics, Novikov (2020) employed a six-stage model for commercialising big data that involves business understanding (to define business goals and requirements), data understanding (to locate data quality problems and identifying interesting data subsets), data preparation (for data mining and processing of raw data), modelling (to define modelling techniques and parameters), evaluation (evaluation of model quality against business objectives), and deploying (e.g., report development or automating data analysis processes) (Novikov, 2020). Although the model is not completely foolproof as it fails to take cognisance of the environment in which the business operates, it provides a useful point of departure for matching big data with business imperatives and goals. In short, the commercialisation of big data creates more accurate and detailed performance data on all aspects of a company from product inventory management to succession planning (Manyika et al., 2011).

Artificial Intelligence

Artificial intelligence (AI) may be defined as "Computer science learning algorithms that are capable of performing tasks that normally require human intelligence and beyond such as visual perception, speech recognition and decision-making" (PWC, 2017). AI describes computers that can "think" like humans by recognising complex patterns in unstructured data, process information, draw conclusions, and make some recommendations (McGinnis, 2020). Technologies such as image recognition, video recognition, semantic understanding, speech synthesis, machine translation, and sentiment analysis are categories of AI which manifest themselves as the simulation, extension, and expansion of human intelligence (Li & Yao, 2021).

The advent of the AI wave is facilitating new developments such as the scaling up of AI through scenarios where technology innovation and business model innovation are happening concurrently, resulting in the disruption of verticals, development of unsupervised learning—an approach in AI in which algorithms learn from data without human-provided labels or guidance, and Transformer model of Open AI that produces functioning code, compose thoughtful business memos, write articles using massive layers of data (Global Partnership on Artificial Intelligence, 2020). Despite these opportunities, the use of AI also presents multiple challenges. For instance, the use of smartphones, connected devices, sensors, machines, and satellites can generate data overload as a vast digital footprint pervades consumers' lives (Stankovic et al., 2020). Moreover, while empirical data can benefit consumers though spotting hidden patterns, unexpected relationships, market trends, or references, consumers tend to bear the brunt of engaging in data markets that they may not even be aware they are participating in (Stankovic et al., 2020).

From a venture creation perspective, AI-supported automation can contribute to relieving employees from repetitive tasks and supporting knowledge-intensive activities that promote productivity and innovation (Vocke et al., 2019). The venture creation functions where AI could be critical include automated data collection and analysis (e.g., during market research), development of hypotheses (e.g., business propositions), as well as creation of business models and their verification (Vocke et al., 2019). However, enterprises that deploy advanced AI systems will need a cadre of employees who can explain the inner workings of complex algorithms to non-technical professionals (Wilson et al., 2017).

Despite the various complexities outlined earlier, AI presents multiple opportunities for technology commercialisation. For example, AI computer-aided engineering can facilitate automated product designs (Krahe et al., 2019). AI can also be commercialised through full stack start-ups. Mannes (2019) contends that that the most overlooked strategy of commercialising AI is for companies to do it themselves through building full stack start-ups. A full stack start-up is a company that "builds a complete, end-to-end product or service that bypasses existing companies" (Dixon, 2014) and companies such as Uber and Tesla were built on full stack methodology prior to the zenith of the deep-learning revolution (Mannes, 2019). Companies such as Cognition IP, a BSV portfolio company, and Atrium have benefited from automation of some of their services and data labelling (Mannes, 2019). Despite these expected benefits, the use of AI data for commercialisation is not without its own hurdles. For example, the collection of large volumes of data on a consistent basis, which is at the heart of AI data commercialisation (Pandya, 2021), is beyond the capability limits of start-ups with resource constraints. Moreover, the collection of large corpuses of data means that for systems with computer vision (CV) capabilities used for human activity recognition (HAR), long durations of video footage for analysis, and the need for supervised learning to fully understand the operations of AI systems, including manual analysis and labelling of data by experts to produce the desired results will be required (Pandya, 2021).

Blockchain Technology

Blockchain is defined as "a distributed electronic ledger that uses cryptographic software algorithms to record and confirm immutable transactions and/or assets with reliability and anonymity without a central authority and automates contracts that relate to those assets and transactions" (PWC, 2017). Based on a peer-to-peer distributed and decentralised computational architecture, which puts emphasis on value and trust rather than the controlled exchange of information (Ahmad et al., 2019; Ali et al., 2019), blockchain provides a secure and transparent way of recording and sharing data, with no need to rely on third-party intermediaries (McGinnis, 2020). As such, blockchain technologies displaced traditional trading mechanisms, by diminishing reliance on traditional intermediaries and replacing them with new forms of electronic intermediaries (Cort, 1999).

In a context where data security, data protection, and information security are increasingly becoming important in the face of cyberattacks and unauthorised use of information, blockchain technology has been proposed as a convenient, secure, and safe way of promoting information security. Antwi et al. (2021) contend that in contemporary times where cyberattacks on the health care industry are threatening patients' privacy and security and causing financial and reputation damages to healthcare firms, blockchain technology provides robust and reliable ways to ensure data security, confidentiality, and availability to authorised users exclusively. Apart from providing data privacy, blockchain technology such as bitcoin increases trust among parties through (1) improving transparency in the interactants and reducing conflict between them; (2) supporting data integrity by verifying transactions between peers using cryptography; and (3) enhancing immutability of agreed transactions (Seebacher & Schüritz, 2017). The adoption of cryptographic hashes and distributed consensus mechanisms does not only provide cryptocurrency users with greater control of their personal data to ensure greater data integrity and consistency but also renders greater protection and compliance with General Data Protection Regulation (GDPR) Act 2018 (Antwi et al., 2021; Council of the European Union, 2018).

At the level of venture creation, healthcare firms have employed blockchain technology to enhance the interoperability of electronic health records and patient self-governance over their data (Tama et al., 2017). From a business model development perspective, blockchain technologies can offer decentralised ecosystems of interactions where service seekers seek services and providers can provide services through this secure unitary system. The business models based on digital platforms, such as Airbnb and Uber, have employed an ecosystem similar to blockchain technology where centralised digital systems connect service providers and seekers (Lage et al., 2022). In the provision of business-to-consumer (B2C) commerce, blockchain technologies are deemed to circumvent click fraud and enable creative loyalty programmes (Rejeb et al., 2020). To the extent that customer loyalty programmes constitute ways of promoting consumer retention, systematically collecting and storing their customer data (Cvitanović, 2018), blockchain technology has potential to provide a database management software on customer data (e.g., purchasing patterns, transactional history, preferences), the tailoring of effective loyalty programmes and enabling sophisticated and personalised tracking of customers (Buss, 2002).

From a technology commercialisation perspective, blockchain technology allows for the enforcing of smart contracts. For Kshetri (2017), smart contracts are digitally signed, computable, self-executing agreements among participants triggered by external events, and these contracts automatically verify and enforce the terms of the agreement. Unlike other forms of technology commercialisation such as technology leasing and technology licencing that are enforced through contracts that require documentation and physical contract signing, smart contracts save time and effort and money (contract signing fees) as they are self-enforcing and self-verifying.

Augmented and Virtual Reality

Virtual reality (VR) involves a computer-based technology simulating a new environment (Sherman & Craig, 2018) via a display that isolates a user from the real world by offering new opportunities such as a specially created world that may simulate reality or could be completely different from it (Kulkov et al., 2021). In turn, augmented reality (AR) is an interactive system consisting of a display, smartphone, or tablet that combines digital and real objects (Bimber & Raskar, 2005). While augmented reality *"augments"* the real-life situations with a digital one, a virtual reality offers only a completely virtual experience.

The ventures that have exploited the benefits of VR/AR the most are located in education, specialist training, diagnostics, teleconferencing, and patient rehabilitation (Iserson, 2018; Kim et al., 2017). Fade (2019) provide several ways in which augmented reality can be employed in venture operations. First, in the retail industry, augmented reality can improve the digital shopping experience by transforming the ways that customers interact with digital products by blurring of the lines between digital and physical shopping. For instance, the use of AR in digital clothing stores can allow shoppers to digitally view clothing items in a 3D format. Second, in the design and creative industries, AR is being deployed to superimpose 3D models into physical spaces, allowing product designers to iterate on designs and model them in a 3D space, thereby improving the quality of products produced. AR allows the design process to be targeted to a specific market while allowing product designers to visualise the image of a finished product or experience it in real life. Third, in the healthcare sector, some companies such as CAE Healthcare are integrating Microsoft's HoloLens into their training programmes, allowing physicians to practice complex medical procedures in a 3D environment (Fade, 2019). Despite this, compared with other industries, medicine remains one of the most conservative industries regarding uptake of innovations and new technology (Barlow, 2016; Shaikh & O'Connor, 2020) owing to the fact that human lives are at the heart of the medical field operations and training in new technologies would be costly and time-consuming.

The aviation industry is one domain where VR has been widely used and commercialised at the level of training. To reduce the risks of accidents and injuries, VR simulators have been employed for training pilots as well as in high-risk fields such as oil and gas and heavy industries such as the chemical industries (Nichols, 2019). In elaboration, Nichols (2019) provides a range of industries where VR/AR are being applied at a commercial scale. In the real estate industry, VR is creating opportunities for customers to visualise themselves in upmarket properties. For instance, Matterport Company is using virtual tour of high-end properties and Sotheby's is using its AR home staging application to put users in virtual furniture of their choice in properties of their interest. Automobile companies like BMW and Volvo are using Head-Up Displays (HUDs) as deployments of AR for estimating speed and gas consumed by cars, allowing drivers to concentrate on driving without distractions (Nichols, 2019).

Proposed Conceptual Model

Drawing on the review of literature, the following observations were made which formed the basis for developing a techno-infrastructural dashboard that could inform the development of a pipeline for high-technology venture development and commercialisation of innovations. First, 4IR is driving a deluge of emerging and digital technologies, applications, and devices which are transforming different industries and sectors. Second, these swathes of technologies and applications are being embraced, integrated, adopted for the development of high-technology ventures, modifying their operations and transforming their corporate practices. Third, while high-technology venture development is just one way of realising technology outcomes, commercialising innovations takes many forms such as patents, industrial designs, leasing companies, licencing, joint ventures, and partnerships. These issues are summarised in the simple model (see Fig. 7.1).

While the model presents 4IR as the main driver of 4IR technologies and illustrates 4IR technologies' contribution to entrepreneurial outcomes such as venture creation and technology commercialisation, it is important to acknowledge that venture creation can also be conceived as a dimension of technology commercialisation as much as it can be a commercial end on its own. Also, the interaction of the four variables unfolds in an environment comprising institutions, individuals, and processes in organisational settings. These include incubators, universities, venture investors, government institutions, and local communities.

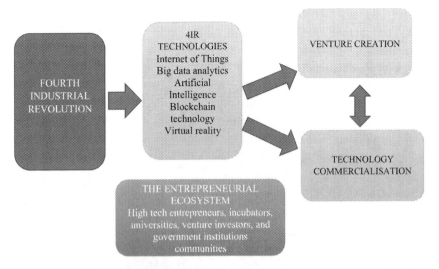

Fig. 7.1 The flow diagram illustrating the interaction between 4IR, 4IR technologies, and their entrepreneurial outcomes within an entrepreneurial ecosystem

Study Implications

The study into the role of 4IR technologies in promoting high-tech venture creation and technology commercialisation presents several implications for practice. First, the study presented only five examples of 4IR technologies that have greater potential to impact high-technology venture creation and technology commercialisation. Since these technologies are inexhaustive, future studies can explore a range of 4IR technologies (e.g., autonomous driving cars, robotics, drones, actuators, machine learning) to provide a more comprehensive understanding of the impact of various 4IR technologies on high-tech venture creation and technology commercialisation.

Second, since 4IR was conceived as a driver of the enunciation, adoption, and application of 4IR technologies in an efficiency-driven economy of South Africa, future studies must examine what role the environmental context (e.g., factor-driven, efficiency-driven, and innovation-driven economies) plays in the enactment, adoption, and appropriation of technologies for high-tech venture creation and technology commercialisation.

Third, although our study concentrated on two aspects of technology entrepreneurial outcomes, namely high-technology venture creation and technology commercialisation, we dwelt much on the impact of 4IR technologies on the technology commercialisation process rather than variants of technology commercialisation. Future studies may concentrate on these variants of technology commercialisation such as spinoffs, joint ventures, technology leasing, technology licencing, and strategic and collaborative alliances to establish the influence of 4IR technologies on these technology commercialisation variants.

Fourth, the study took a generic posture on the role of entrepreneurial ecosystems in shaping technology commercialisation and high-technology venture creation. Future studies may examine the individual effects of each entrepreneurial ecosystem dimension on 4IR technologies, technology commercialisation, and high-technology venture development. Such studies could, for instance, examine how different forms of entrepreneurial traits (e.g., entrepreneurial cognition, entrepreneurial efficacy) direct different aspects of the venture development process or how the provision of different tangible resources (e.g., venture capital or crowdfunding) impacts different processes of technology commercialisation. Other studies could also examine how government interventions such as different incentives and support mechanisms facilitate the implementation of 4IR technologies and different technology entrepreneurial outcomes such as high-technology venture creation and technology commercialisation.

Conclusion

This literature review-based investigation drew on entrepreneurial ecosystem theory and exemplars of 4IR technology implementation to explore the intersection between 4IR technologies and specific outcomes such as technology commercialisation and high-technology venture creation. The study drew on five instances of 4IR technologies, namely, Internet of Things, big data analytics, artificial intelligence, blockchain technology, and virtual reality or augmented reality, to provide some insights into the range of 4IR technologies that could provide a techno-infrastructural dashboard for the pipeline for start-ups targeting technology commercialisation and venture creation as their entrepreneurial outcomes in emerging economies.

References

Aarikka-Stenroos, L., & Lehtimäki, T. (2014). Commercialising a radical innovation: Probing the way to the market. *Industrial Marketing Management, 43*, 1372–1384.

Adendorff, C., & Putzier, M. (2018). 4IR, the role of universities – Trends for the future. South African Technology Network International Conference, 11–13 September 2018, Durban.

Ahmad, F., Ahmad, Z., Kerrache, C.A., Kurugollu, F., Adnane, A., & Barka, E. (2019). Blockchain in internet-of-things: Architecture, applications and research directions. In *International Conference on Computer and Information Sciences* (ICCIS), 2019, Saudi Arabia, 3–4 April 2019.

Ahmad, N., & Hoffman, A. (2008). *A framework for addressing and measuring entrepreneurship*. Working Paper, Organisation for Economic Cooperation and Development.

Akter, S., Michael, K., Uddin, M. R., McCarthy, G., & Rahman, M. (2020). Transforming business using digital innovations: The application of AI, blockchain, cloud and data analytics. *Annals of Operations Research.* https://doi.org/10.1007/s10479-020-03620-w

Akter, S., Wamba, S. F., Gunasekaran, A., Dubey, R., & Childe, S. J. (2016). How to improve firm performance using big data analytics capability and business strategy alignment? *International Journal of Production Economics, 182*, 113–131.

Ali, M. S., Vecchio, M., Pincheira, M., Dolui, K., Antonelli, F., & Rehmani, M. H. (2019). Applications of blockchains in the internet of things: A comprehensive survey. *IEEE Communications Surveys Tutorials, 21*(2), 1676–1717.

Amsden, A. H. (2001). *The rise of the rest: Challenges to the West from late-industrializing economies.* Oxford University Press.

Angelova, N., Kiryakova, G., & Yordanova, L. (2017). The great impact of internet of things on business. *Trakia Journal of Sciences, 15*(Suppl. 1), 406–412.

Antwi, M., Adnane, A., Ahmad, F., Hussain, R., Rehman, M. H., et al. (2021). The case of HyperLedger Fabric as a blockchain solution for healthcare applications. *Blockchain: Research and Applications, 2*(2021). https://doi.org/10.1016/j.bcra.2021.100012

Babu, M. M., Rahman, M., Alam, A., & Dey, B. L. (2021). Exploring big data-driven innovation in the manufacturing sector: Evidence from UK firms. *Annals of Operations Research*. https://doi.org/10.1007/s10479-021-04077-1

Ball, K., DiDomenico, M., & Nunan, D. (2016). Big data surveillance and the body subject. *Body & Society, 22*(2), 58–81.

Ball, K., & Webster, W. (2020). Big Data and surveillance: Hype, commercial logics and new intimate spheres. *Big Data & Society*, January–June, 1–5.

Barlow, J. (2016). *Managing innovation in healthcare*. World Scientific Publishing Company.

Benassi, M., Grinza, E., Rentocchini, F., & Rondi, L. (2022). Patenting in 4IR technologies and firm performance. *Industrial and Corporate Change, 31*, 112–136.

Bigliardi, B., & Galati, F. (2016). Which factors hinder the adoption of open innovation in SMEs? *Technology Analysis and Strategic Management, 28*, 869–885.

Bimber, O., & Raskar, R. (2005). *Spatial augmented reality: Merging real and virtual worlds*. AK Peters/CRC Press.

Bloom, B. Y., & Dees, J. G. (2008). Cultivate your ecosystem. *Stanford Social Innovation Review*, 47–53.

Borgia, E. (2014). The Internet of Things vision: Key features, applications and open issues. *Computer Communications, 54*, 1–31.

Brock, J., Dreischmeier, R., Platt, J., & Souza, R. (2013). Opportunity unlocked: Big data's five routes to value-IT Advantage. Boston Consulting Group, 2–6. https://web-assets.bcg.com/img-src/BCG_Opportunity_Unlocked_Oct_2013_tcm9-93856.pdf

Brockner, J. E. (2004). Regulatory focus theory and the entrepreneurial process. *Journal of Business Venturing, 19*(2), 203–220.

Buss, D. (2002). *As loyalty programs expand, customer fatigue forces creativity and caution*. Resource Centre Article, MCI.COM.

Chen, H., Chiang, R. H., & Storey, V. C. (2012). Business intelligence and analytics: From big data to big impact. *MIS Quarterly, 36*, 1165–1188.

Choi, Z. J., & Taylor, C. G. (2018). Optimal data commercialisation: Transforming raw data into revenue-generating insights. Special report: Technology in business: Strategy. Financier Worldwide.

Citi Insight. (2020). Research on the Fourth Industrial Revolution. Implications for local government in the context of skills development. Final Report. Local Government, Sector Education and Training Authority.

Colin, N. (2015). What makes an entrepreneurial ecosystem? Retrieved March 10, 2017, from https://salon.thefamily.co/what-makes-an-entrepreneurial-ecosystem-815f4e049804#.gij6oqmum

Cort, S. G. (1999). Industry corner: Industrial distribution: How goods will go to market in the electronic marketplace. *Business Economics, 34*, 53–55.

Council of European Union. (2018). Reform of EU Data Protection Rules, European Commission, 2018.

Cowell, M., Lyon-Hill, S., & Tate, S. (2018). It takes all kinds: Understanding diverse entrepreneurial ecosystems. *Journal of Enterprising Communities: People and Places in the Global Economy, 12*(2), 178–198.

Cvitanović, P. L. (2018). New technologies in marketing as competitive advantage. In *2018 ENTRENOVA conference proceedings*. Split: Econstor, pp. 294–302.

Datta, A., Mukherjee, D., & Jessup, L. (2014). Understanding commercialisation of technological innovation: Taking stock and moving forward. *R&D Management, 45*(3). https://doi.org/10.1111/radm.12068

Davenport, T. H., & Kudyba, S. (2016). Designing and developing analytics-based data products. *MIT Sloan Management Review, 58*(1), 83–88.

Department of Trade and Industry. (2021). South Africa's special economic zones. https://www.thedtic.gov.za/wp-content/uploads/SEZ-brochure_2021.pdf

Directorate of Innovation, Technology Transfer and Commercialisation at the University of South Africa. (2020). Technologies: Opportunities for Commercialisation. University of South Africa.

Dixon, C. (2014). a16z podcast: For Buzzfeed sharing is the matric that matters. Retrieved March 22, 2022, from https://soundcloud.com/a16z/a16z-podcast-sharing-is-the-metric-that-matters-building-buzzfeed-for-a-socialmobile-world

Drath, R., & Horch, A. (2014). Industrie 4.0: Hit or Hype? *IEEE Industrial Electronics Magazine, 8*(2), 56–58.

Dumbill, E. (2013). Making sense of big data. *Big Data, 1*(1), 1–2.

Edwards, C., & Hopkins, J. (2018). The Australian supply chain tech survey. Retrieved March 22, 2022, from https://sclaa.com.au/2018-australian-supply-chain-tech-survey-results

Fade, L. (2019). Augmented reality in business: How AR may change the way we work. Retrieved March 19, 2022, from https://www.forbes.com/sites/theyec/2019/02/06/augmented-reality-in-business-how-ar-may-change-the-way-we-work/?sh=48aaae8a51e5

Feld, B. (2012). *Startup communities: Building an entrepreneurial ecosystem in your city.* Wiley.

Fleisch, E., & Tellkamp, C. (2005). Inventory inaccuracy and supply chain performance: A simulation study of a retail supply chain. *International Journal of Production Economics, 95*(3), 373–385.

Galbraith, J. (1982). The stages of growth. *Journal of Business Strategy, 3*(4), 70–79.

Gans, J. S., & Stern, S. (2003). The product market and the market for "ideas": Commercialization strategies for technology entrepreneurs. *Research Policy, 32*, 333–350.

Gilchrist, A. (2016). Introducing industry 4.0. In A. Gilchrist (Ed.), *Industry 4.0* (pp. 195–215). Springer.

Global Partnership on Artificial Intelligence (GPAI). (2020). Innovation & Commercialisation. Working Group Report November 2020 – GPAI, Montréal Summit, Canada.

Guna, J., Horvat, K. P., & Podjed, D. (2022). People-centred development of a smart waste bin. *Sensors, 22*, 1288. https://doi.org/10.3390/s22031288

Iserson, K. V. (2018). Ethics of Virtual Reality in medical education and licensure. *Cambridge Quarterly of Healthcare Ethics, 27*(2), 326–332.

Jamil, F., Ismail, K., & Mahmood, N. (2015). A review of commercialization tools: University incubators and technology parks. *International Journal of Economics and Financial Issues, 5*(Special Issue), 223–228.

Kim, Y., Kim, H., & Kim, Y. O. (2017). Virtual reality and augmented reality in plastic surgery: A review. *Archives of Plastic Surgery, 44*(3), 179–187.

Krahe, C., Iberl, M., Jacob, A., & Lanza, G. (2019). AI based computer aided engineering for automated product design – A first approach with a multi-view -based classification. 7th CIRP Global Web conference. *Procedia CIRP, 86*, 104–109.

Kshetri, N. (2017). Blockchain's roles in strengthening cybersecurity and protecting privacy. *Telecommunications Policy, 41*(10), 1027–1038.

Kulkov, I., Berggren, B., & Hellstr¨om, M., Wikstr¨om, K. (2021). Navigating uncharted waters: Designing business models for virtual and augmented reality companies in the medical industry. *Journal of Engineering and Technology Management, 59*(2021). https://doi.org/10.1016/j.jengtecman.2021.101614

Kumar, S., Tiwari, P., & Zymbler, M. (2019). Internet of Things is a revolutionary approach for future technology enhancement: A review. *Journal of Big Data, 6*, 111. https://doi.org/10.1186/s40537-019-0268-2

Lage, O., Saiz-Santos, M., & Zarzuelo, J. M. (2022). Real Business Applications and Investments in Blockchain Technology. *Electronics, 2022*(11), 438. https://doi.org/10.3390/electronics11030438

Li, J., & Yao, M. (2021). New framework of digital entrepreneurship model based on artificial intelligence and cloud computing. *Hindawi Mobile Information Systems*, 2021, Article ID 3080160, 11 pages. https://doi.org/10.1155/2021/3080160

Liao, J., Welsch, H., & Tan, W. L. (2005). Venture gestation paths of nascent entrepreneurs: Exploring the temporal patterns. *Journal of High Technology Management Research, 16*(1), 1–22.

Link, A. N., & Siegel, D. S. (2007). *Innovation, entrepreneurship and technological change*. Oxford University Press.

Macke, D., Markley, D., & Fulwider, J. (2014). *Energizing entrepreneurial communities: A pathway to prosperity*. Centre for Rural Entrepreneurship.

Mannes, J. (2019). The most overlooked path to commercialize AI is for companies to do it themselves. TechCrunch. Retrieved March 19, 2022, from https://techcrunch.com/2019/04/15/the-most-overlooked-path-to-commercialize-ai-is-for-companies-to-do-it-themselves/#:~:text=it%20themselves%20%7C%20TechCrunch-,The%20most%20overlooked%20path%20to%20commercialize%20AI,companies%20to%20do%20it%20themselves&text=Editor's%20note%3A%20John%20Mannes%20is,address%20big%20problems%20across%20industries

Manyika, J., Chui, M., Brown, B., Bughin, J., Dobbs, R., et al. (2011). *Big data: The next frontier for innovation, competition and productivity*. McKinsey Global Institute, McKinsey & Company.

Marnewick, C., & Marnewick, A. L. (2020). Technology readiness: A precursor for Industry 4.0. *Journal of Contemporary Management, 17*(1), 1–21.

Martin, J. P. (2018). *Skills for the 21st century: Findings and policy lessons from the OECD survey of adult skills*. OECD Education Working Paper No. 166. OECD Publishing.

Mattila, M., Yrjölä, M., & Lehtimäki, H. (2019). Drivers of and barriers to networked commercialization: A business model perspective. *International Journal of Entrepreneurship and Innovation Management, 23*, 479–495.

Maynard, A. D. (2015). Navigating the fourth industrial revolution. *Nature Nanotechnology, 10*(12), 1005–1006.

McAdam, M., Miller, K., & McAdam, R. (2016). Situated regional university incubation: A multi-level stakeholder perspective. *Technovation, 50–51*, 69–78.

McAdams, D. P., & Pals, J. L. (2006). A new Big Five: Fundamental principles for an integrative science of personality. *American Psychologist, 61*, 204–217.

McGinnis, D. (2020). What is the fourth industrial revolution? Salesforce. Retrieved March 8, 2022, from https://www.salesforce.com/blog/what-is-the-fourth-industrial-revolution-4ir/

Middleton, C. (2018). *Five ways the Internet of Things is transforming businesses today*. IoTBuild. Retrieved March 18, 2022, from https://internetofbusiness.com/5-ways-the-internet-of-things-is-transforming-businesses-today/

Mitchell, R. K., Busenitz, L., Lant, T., McDougall, P. P., Morse, E. A., & Smith, B. (2002). Entrepreneurial cognition theory: Rethinking the people side of entrepreneurship research. *Entrepreneurship: Theory and Practice, 27*(2), 93–104.

Moktadir, M. A., Ali, S. M., Paul, S. K., & Shukla, N. (2019). Barriers to big data analytics in manufacturing supply chains: A case study from Bangladesh. *Computers & Industrial Engineering, 128*, 1063–1075.

Moore, J. F. (1993). Predators and prey: A new ecology of competition. *Harvard Business Review, 71*(3), 75–86.

Morrar, R., Arman, H., & Mousa, S. (2017). The fourth industrial revolution (industry 4.0): A social innovation perspective. *Technology Innovation Management Review, 7*(11), 12–20.

Muniz-Avila, E., Silveryra-Leon, G., & Segarra-Perez, L. (2019). Startup Path: The development of the entrepreneur and his/her journey in creating a start-up. In M. Corrales-Estrada (Ed.), *Innovation and entrepreneurship: A New mindset for emerging markets* (pp. 31–63). Emerald Publishing.

Ngowi, A. B., Awuzie, B., & Mapiyeye, S. (2019). Report on the Free State Provincial Fourth Industrial Revolution (4IR) Summit 28–29th November 2019, Central University Of Technology, Free State.

Nichols, G. (2019). The business guide to AR and VR: Everything you need to know. ZD Net. Retrieved March 20, 2022, from https://www.zdnet.com/article/the-business-guide-to-ar-and-vr-everything-you-need-to-know/

Novikov, S. V. (2020). Data science and big data technologies' role in the digital economy. *Technology, Education, Management, Informatics Journal, 9*(2), 756–762.

Nyagadza, B. (2019). Responding to change and customer value improvement: Pragmatic advice to banks. *The Marketing Review (TMR), 19*(3), 235–252.

Nyagadza, B., Pashapa, R., Mazuruse, C. G., & Hove, P. K. (2022). Digital technologies, Fourth Industrial Revolution (4IR) & Global Value Chains (GVCs) nexus with emerging economies' future industrial innovation dynamics. *Cogent Economics and Finance, 10*(1), 2014654. https://doi.org/1 0.1080/23322039.2021.2014654

Pandya, S. (2021). Understanding the challenges of commercializing AI from a provider's perspective. Forbes Technology Council. Retrieved March 21, 2022, from https://www.forbes.com/sites/forbestechcouncil/2021/04/02/understanding-the-challenges-of-commercializing-ai-from-a-providers-perspective/?sh=4e976b532a99

Ping, L., Liu, Q., Zhou, Z., & Wang, H. (2011). Agile supply chain management over the internet of things. *Paper presented at the International Conference on Management and Service Science* (MASS), August 12, 2011.

Pivot Global Education. (2020). National university entrepreneurship ecosystem baseline report, Universities South Africa, Pretoria, South Africa.

Presidential Commission on The Fourth Industrial Revolution. (2020). Presidential Commission on the 4IR Report Summary Report and recommendations. Government Gazette, Vol 122, No. 43834, 23 OCTOBER 2020, Department of Communications and Digital Technologies

PriceWaterCoopers (PWC). 2017. Fourth Industrial Revolution for the Earth Harnessing the 4th Industrial Revolution for Sustainable Emerging Cities. World Economic Forum.

Ratinho, T., Harms, R., & Walsh, S. T. (2015). Structuring the technology entrepreneurship publication landscape: Making sense out of chaos. *Technological Forecasting and Social Change, 100*, 168–175.

Rejeb, A., Keogh, J. G., & Treiblmaier, H. (2020). How blockchain technology can benefit marketing: Six pending research areas. *Frontiers in Blockchain, 3*(3), 1–12. https://doi.org/10.3389/fbloc.2020.00003

Rotolo, D., Hicks, D., & Martin, B. (2015). What is an emerging technology? *Research Policy, 44*, 1827–1843.

Rozenfeld, H., Forcellini, F., Amaral, D., Toledo, J., Silva, S., et al. (2006). *Management of the product development process: A reference for improvement of processes.* Saraiva.

Salehi, F., Shapira, P., & Zolkiewski, J. (2022). Commercialization networks in emerging technologies: The case of UK nanotechnology small and midsize enterprises. *The Journal of Technology Transfer.* https://doi.org/10.1007/s10961-022-09923-3

Schmidt, R., Möhring, M., Härting, R.-C., Reichstein, C., Neumaier, P., & Jozinović, P. (2015). Industry 4.0 – Potentials for creating smart products: Empirical research results. In W. Abramowicz (Ed.), *Business information systems* (pp. 16–27). Springer International Publishing.

Schwab, K. (2016). The fourth industrial revolution: What it means, How to respond. World Economic Forum. Retrieved January 12, 2022, from https://www.weforum.org/agenda/2016/01/the-fourth-industrial-revolution-what-it-means-and-how-to-respond/

Seebacher, S., & Schüritz, R. (2017). Blockchain technology as an enabler of service systems: A structured literature review. In *Proceedings of the international conference on exploring services science*, Rome, Italy, 24–26 May 2017, pp. 12–23.

Shaikh, A., & O'Connor, G. C. (2020). Understanding the motivations of technology managers in radical innovation decisions in the mature R&D firm context: An agency theory perspective, *Journal of Engineering. Technology Management, 55*(2020), 10155.

Sherman, W. R., & Craig, A. B. (2018). *Understanding virtual reality: Interface, application, and design*. The Morgan Kaufmann Series in Computer Graphics. Elsevier.

Stable Kernel. (2021). Internet of things: Building an IoT ecosystem: From idea to commercialization. Retrieved March 19, 2022, from https://stablekernel.com/article/building-an-iot-ecosystem-from-idea-to-commercialization/

Stam, E. (2015). Entrepreneurial ecosystems and regional policy: A sympathetic critique. *European Planning Studies, 23*(9), 1759–1769.

Stankovic, M., Hasanbeigi, A., & Neftenov, N. (2020). Use of 4IR technologies in water and sanitation in Latin America and the Caribbean. Inter-American Development Bank Report. Water and Sanitation Division. Technical Note No IDB-TN-1910.

Sukhodolov, Y. A. (2019). The notion, essence, and peculiarities of Industry 4.0 as a sphere of industry. In Industry 4.0: Industrial revolution of the 21st century. https://www.researchgate.net/publication/326547788_The_Notion_Essence_and_Peculiarities_of_Industry_40_as_a_Sphere_of_Industry

Tama, B. A., Kweka, B. J., Park, Y., & Rhee, K. H. (2017). A critical review of blockchain and its current applications. In: *Proceedings of the 2017 International Conference on Electrical Engineering and Computer Science* (ICECOS), Sriwijaya, Indonesia, 22–23 August 2017; 2017, pp. 109–113.

Thomas, L. D., & Leiponen, A. (2016). Big data commercialization. *IEEE Engineering Management Review, 44*(2). https://doi.org/10.1109/EMR.2016.2568798

Tripathi, S., & Gupta, M. (2021). A holistic model for global industry 4.0 readiness assessment. *Benchmarking: An International Journal, 28*(10), 1463–5771.

University of California. (n.d.). Technology commercialization process. Retrieved March 2, 2022, from https://www.ucop.edu/knowledge-transfer-office/innovation/training-and-education/technology-commercialization-process.html

Valdez, J. (1988). The entrepreneurial ecosystem: Toward a theory of new business formation. Small Business Institute Director's Association (SBIDA), pp. 102–119.

Vargas, C. A., & Plonski, G. A. (2019). The contribution of technology parks to high-tech startups. In M. Oliveira, F. Cahen, & F. Borini (Eds.), *Startups and innovation ecosystems in emerging markets, a Brazilian perspective* (pp. 99–118). Palgrave Macmillan.

Vocke, C., Constantinescu, C., & Popescu, D. (2019). Application potentials of artificial intelligence for the design of innovation processes. *Procedia CIRP, 84*, 810–813.

Wilson H. J., Daugherty P. R., & Morini-Bianzino N. (2017). The jobs that artificial intelligence will create. *MIT Sloan Management Review*, p. 201. https://sloanreview.mit.edu/article/will-ai-create-as-many-jobs-as-it-eliminates/

Zhan, Y., Tan, K., Li, Y., & Tse, M. (2018). Unlocking the power of big data in new product development. *Annals of Operations Research, 270*(1-2). https://doi.org/10.1007/s10479-016-2379-x

8

The Impact of Digital Platforms on SMEs' Development and Performance

Judith Ochinanwata and Nonso Ochinanwata

Introduction

Digital technologies are drastically transforming how small and established firms develop new products and services (Soto Setzke et al., 2023). The significance of digitalization and the digital transformation of business cannot be overemphasized due to advancements in technology. Digital platform is referred to as an online community that facilitates interaction—the exchange of information, goods, and services between producers and consumers (Parker et al., 2017).

Evans and Gawer (2016, p. 4) assert that "enterprises that leverage the power of platform business models have grown dramatically in size and scale over the past decade. Platform ecosystems are gaining ground

J. Ochinanwata (✉) • N. Ochinanwata
African Development Institute of Research Methodology, Enugu, Nigeria
e-mail: judith@adirmng.com; nonsoochi@adirm.com.ng

through the digitalization of products, services and business processes and the processes are reshaping the global landscape." Evans (2016) identified that multisided platform enterprises connect distinct groups of customers who need to transact business with each other.

Jin and Hurd (2018) identified that previous literature has traditionally explored the implementation of digital technologies in large firms with little study on the implementation of digital platforms in entrepreneurial SMEs. Some scholars highlight that, insufficient digital skills are associated with a barrier to digital platform adoption in small businesses (Giotopoulos et al., 2017). Also, Parker et al. (2016) identified that entrepreneurial SMEs attempt to digitalize their offering through digital platforms but with little or no knowledge of how the different digital platforms work, nor do they have a strategy in place to succeed in their digital transformation. Thus, exploring how entrepreneurial SMEs can leverage digital platforms to achieve their goal and performance is a crucial aspect of current research (Parker et al., 2016).

Understanding how SMEs develop, create, and capture value through digital platforms will be crucial to developing countries' business transformation, competitiveness, and economic development. The problem is that much of the research on technology development and strategies has concentrated on developed nations, which are characterized by stable institutional environments (Amankwah-Amoah et al., 2021). Due to the relevance of emerging digital technologies in developing economies, research is required to examine the sector and how to improve the business environment. Moreover, the digital economy has a major impact on the growth of small-medium enterprises (SMEs) since firms utilize technologies to achieve a competitive advantage (Amankwah-Amoah et al., 2021). Digital platforms increase job opportunities and promote competition, innovation, and improved products and services. Despite its impact, there has been little research on the impact of the digital platform on SME development and performance in Nigeria. Therefore, studies like this are required to develop the knowledge of how small-scale businesses can use digital platforms to develop and increase performance of their business.

This study focuses on how digital platforms enable entrepreneurial SMEs' development. Specifically, the study explores how digital platforms will help entrepreneurs and individuals to develop online small businesses and how the platform fosters the performance of existing ones. The findings of the present research will enrich the literature on digital platform capabilities on entrepreneurial SMEs' development through digital platforms (Li et al., 2016). To achieve the objectives of this article, the following research questions (but not limited to these questions) were pursued:

- How do digital platforms facilitate SME development?
- What are the challenges associated with adopting digital platforms for business owners?
- What are the frameworks for adopting digital platforms to create and foster online small businesses?

Literature Review

Overview of Digital Platform

Several scholars have attempted to define the term "digital platform" with variations dependent on the sector or context it's being used. Some scholars conceptualized digital platforms based on a non-technical view that emphasizes platforms as a commercial network or market which empowers transactions such as Business-To-Business (B2B), Business-To-Customer (B2C), or even Customer-To-Customer (C2C). However, the definition adopted in this research is that which focuses on SMEs establishing and promoting their offerings in the digital space. Parker et al. (2017) see digital platforms as an online community that facilitates interaction—the exchange of information, goods, and services between producers and consumers.

According to Keisha (2020), there exists a categorization of digital platforms into four groups. This research highlights two of her categorizations relevant to this study—(a) digital platforms as intermediaries and (b) digital platforms as network effects, both of which can uphold an informed understanding of digital platforms and entrepreneurship. She explained digital platforms as an intermediary to mean enabling direct interaction between two or more groups within or outside markets in a manner that supports co-creation and co-development, consequently decreasing the cost of searching for information, clients, products, and services, and assisting a person with discovering what they require or connect with those they need to reach. Thus, connecting entrepreneurs with customers and customers with entrepreneurs likewise, made possible through platforms, hence, providing value to all sides (Hagiu & Wright, 2015). Keisha (2020) further explained the categorization of digital platforms as network effects as an occurrence where the value of consuming or purchasing a product or service for one user increases or decreases depending on the number of other users who consume or purchase that product or service.

Platforms are multifaceted networks that incorporate two or more distinct users and promote interactions/transactions between users depending on the infrastructure, usually taking the form of an online resource (Gawer, 2014). A digital platform has been described as "a building block that provides an important role to a technological framework and serves as a basis upon which complementary goods, technologies, or services can be developed" (Spagnoletti et al., 2015, p. 364). There are many examples of digital platform models, such as Amazon, Alibaba, Facebook, eBay, Uber, Didi Chuxing, and Airbnb. A key distinction between the platforms is that they serve as either transaction platforms or innovation platforms (Gawer, 2014; Parker et al., 2016). Also, platforms serve as infrastructures on which various parties or users depend to build their businesses. For instance, Facebook connects users, advertisers, developers, companies, and others, while Uber connects riders and drivers. In addition, users can create profile pages on Facebook, and software developers can create apps for Apple's App Store.

E-commerce Platforms

The term e-commerce has been defined and argued differently by scholars. Huy and Filiatrault (2006) see e-commerce as any economic or business activity that uses ICT applications to enable the buying and selling of products and services, facilitating business transactions between and among businesses, individuals, governments, and other organizations. Lai and Turban (2008) defined e-commerce as "the process of selling, buying, transferring, or exchanging products, services, and/or information through the Internet." However, some extant literature refers to e-commerce and e-business interchangeably. This study argues that the concept of e-business as defined by Chaffey and Ellis-Chadwick (2016) is that which integrates the use of Information Technology to increase the viability and competitiveness of an organization. Also, Laudon and Laudon (2017) define e-business as "the use of the internet and digital technology to execute all of the activities in the enterprise." Hence, following these definitions, the concept of e-business is not adopted here.

Many empirical studies have examined the impact of e-commerce on SMEs and the aggregate economy. Cohen et al. (2000) identified that e-commerce enabled businesses in developing countries to overcome the traditional boundaries associated with limited access to information, high market-entry costs, and isolation from potential markets. Molla and Licker (2005) argued that SMEs should take advantage of the opportunities in the utilization of e-commerce platforms to expand their market reach, gain from economies of scale, become more profitable, and contribute to economic development.

However, further research on the adoption of e-commerce in developing countries as identified by Wynn and Olayinka (2021) has shown the challenges inhibiting the adoption and use of e-commerce platforms. Some literature conducted on e-commerce in developing countries identifies factors responsible for adoption, barriers to adoption (Janita & Chong, 2013), challenges of adoption (Agwu & Murray, 2015) and the benefits of e-business and consumer attitude to e-business adoption (Emeti & Onyeaghala, 2015). Raghavan et al. (2018) explored e-commerce adoption and trends in Indian SMEs. Like existing studies in other developing countries, their research identified owner-manager characteristics, technology factors, organizational factors, and institutional influences as key issues affecting e-commerce adoption. Their study also recognized the impact that external pressure from industry, external suppliers, and the government could have on adoption (Wynn & Olayinka, 2021).

Agwu and Murray (2014) undertook contextual investigation research in six organizations in three unique locales of Nigeria, seeking to establish the factors impacting e-commerce adoption. The findings indicated that consumer readiness, IT skills shortage, and internet connectivity are key factors in determining e-business adoption and efficient website maintenance. Agwu and Murray (2015) also explored the barriers to e-commerce adoption in Nigeria focusing on three states—Lagos, Enugu, and Abuja. Their findings from the qualitative interview highlight a few inhibiting factors to e-commerce adoption which include lack of technical know-how, absence of an e-commerce regulatory security framework, poor internet access, and poor public infrastructure. Olatokun and Bankole (2011) also investigated e-business adoption in SMEs in Ibadan, southwestern Nigeria. Sixty SMEs were examined by means of questionnaires, and their findings proposed organization size was of little importance; however, the age of the organization was of more importance with the argument that younger organizations are more likely to progress to e-commerce systems and processes.

However, Singh and Hess (2017) contend that digitizing the selling, promoting, or procurement processes through technology alone will not likely benefit an organization, but rather a balanced interplay of technologies, individual up-skilling, and process re-designing is required. Additionally, Rodgers et al. (2002) assert that to enable organizations with expanding their customer base and increase their market share a clearly defined and adequately executed e-business strategy will deliver proficiency gains and other advantages for the organization.

Challenges in Nigeria's Business Environment

Studies have identified that micro and small businesses are faced with several challenges in doing business within the Nigerian business environment of which some are financial while others are not (Osotimehin et al., 2012). The financial limitation includes those factors that hinder SMEs from easily accessing finance which has been a major setback to the discovery and exploration of business ideas and the expansion of existing businesses (Gbandi and Amissah, 2014). The inability of small business owners to raise funds to expand their business has been linked to poor business history, high risks associated with starting a new business (which banks tend to avoid), insufficient collaterals, inadequate recordkeeping, and knowledge of the risks facing their business.

Conversely, the non-financial constraint impacting doing business in Nigeria are external influences. Previous research highlights these external influences as microeconomic insecurity and policy instability, high-interest rates and lack of access to financial institutions, inadequate infrastructure, trade restrictions and transportation, crime, theft, disorder, and corruption (Amank-wah-Amooah and Deborah, 2011; Fosu, 2003; Ochinanwata & Ezepue, 2016; Kimuyu, 2007).

Methodology

The researchers followed a procedure recommended by Saunders et al. (2012). The research strategy is "influenced by the researcher's philosophical approach and comprises the whole research approach and choosing of data collection, techniques and analysis processes" (Saunders et al., 2012, p. 126). The research adopts an exploratory research design to explore how entrepreneurs are using digital platforms to engage in developing businesses in Nigeria (Stebbins, 2001). This study adopts a qualitative research approach as its methodology, using primary evidence to explore the impact of digital platforms on micro and small business development, and performance in Nigeria.

The data for this research comprises primary data that consists of in-depth semi-structured interviews that were obtained from entrepreneurs using digital platforms to grow their businesses online in Nigeria. The interview sought to obtain descriptions of the lifeworld of the interviewee with respect to interpreting the meaning of the described phenomenon (Kvale, 2009, p. 51).

Firstly, online research is conducted to select businesses and examine their operations, their year of foundation, products, and services. Secondly, only firms that met the criterion of conducting their business activities and operation on a digital platform were identified and contacted. During the initial contact, the researcher inquired about the digital operation and services of the businesses. Only firms that identified themselves as wholly dependent on digital platforms were asked to participate in the study. Several firms that were contacted declined to participate, and only 15 firms accepted the invitation, and founders of those firms were selected to interview, and located in different cities in Nigeria. Hence, these firms and their founders have started adopting digital platforms in the last three years.

The interview was conducted, and each participant was informed of the aims, objectives, and purpose of the research. This helped to build trust and confidence among the participants. They were promised anonymity and confidentiality related to the discussion. All the interviews were recorded, but any information that might identify the participant's profile linked to their company was excluded. The interviews were conducted in English and lasted 40–60 minutes.

Analysis and Discussion

This chapter presents the findings from the interview transcripts related to the 15 SMEs and their founders, which were coded and then re-coded to identify the patterns and trends in the participants' views through thematic analysis. The analysis focuses on the key objectives of the research, which include how digital platform facilitates SME development and the challenges associated with small business adopting digital platforms in Nigeria to grow their business.

Physical, Online Presence, Customer Engagement

The below comments show how digital platforms have created enabling environment for individuals to develop a business which fosters entrepreneurial development in Nigeria.

> From the way I started, everybody can start that way. What do you need to have an online presence? As a small-scale business what you need is just a camera, most phones have a camera, in fact, all android phones have a camera, you snap your product, come online you post your product on any platform. (Participant 07)

> No, I'm working yeah, but I open the app like almost every 30 minutes, say 10 minutes, I usually have question that's coming from people, and I try as much as possible to respond to them as quickly as I can because if you waste time, the person might just go somewhere else. (Participant 02)

The data reveals that micro businesses that conduct their activities on digital platforms do not necessarily need capital which ordinarily would be used for renting shops and carrying out their business activities. All the participants cited the smartphone as a crucial mechanism for individuals and entrepreneurs building online micro businesses. Some micro businesses combine online and physical stores to meet customer needs and to serve different categories of customers. The finding reveals that the micro business started with having an online store where they learn about the nature of the business before establishing a physical presence.

> Because of the traffic being gathered from there. If you check, almost on a daily, most people don't know how to get some stuff. Like me, there was one time I wanted to search for a particular product what I did was I used hashtag, hashtag of the name of that particular product and I got people that were selling such products. (Participant 05)

> But our plan for social media was just to upload videos about our product and then write little description about the product. That's why we chose Instagram and Facebook, we just post and include our contact number and then customers contact us for items in stock and our price. (Participant 02)

Small businesses have different strategies for customer engagement and acquisition by providing educative insights about the product or service. Some firms solely engage customers purely online while others take a different approach by providing an accessible phone number those customers could easily reach to facilitate customer acquisition and transactions for those customers that do not have access to the internet.

> People are calling her for online delivery so the online presence and physical presence is clustering together, so we needs someone that can be replying to our online queries and taking online orders while someone is busy attending to our customers in store. (Participant 03)

The findings suggest that a hybrid approach of combining online and physical presence is crucial because in Nigeria's environment there is an inadequate power supply and unreliable internet access which hinder communication between customers and businesses on the internet (Osotimehin et al., 2012). The finding suggests that having a physical presence enables a micro business to reach and facilitate customer acquisitions. This hybrid approach is crucial because it helps to accommodate and align customers and micro businesses in Nigeria. Thus, the hybrid approach such as having digital and online presence activities benefits micro businesses.

The findings reveal that online micro businesses will benefit from adopting digital platforms because they will use them to engage, acquire customers, and transact business. Existing literature shows that micro business benefit from integrating e-commerce in their business (Chheda, 2014).

Challenges, Trust, and Authenticity

The findings suggest that there are many challenges facing online micro business in Nigeria. The most frequently cited challenges include digital skills required to handle and manage activities on digital platforms. This creates a barrier to small and micro businesses that want to adopt and use digital platforms to develop business. Online micro businesses face challenges such as customers cancelling orders as they do not have the money to pay for the goods when it is being delivered to them.

Sometimes some people even go as far as putting their phone off, after they have ordered the product, they will switch off their phone, I'll be on the road with the product hoping that I will get a customer meanwhile they have escaped. (Participant 10)

The data suggest different approaches to building trust and confidence in potential customers. One participant cited that review and feedback from previous customers are some of the approaches that build trust and confidence in potential customers.

The big external challenge we have is the poor internet accessibility, and we find it difficult to access customers everywhere due to the poor internet service.

Some of the challenges include infrastructural inadequacy, the epileptic state of the power supply, poor internet connectivity and paucity of data. (Participant 08)

Then another challenge she had was creating an online presence, because she didn't know how to do so … she is even still having that problem now, she said she didn't have someone that will be her ICT manager, she had to outsource the work to someone that would design her page and make it look like something up to standard and then will be marketing her, running ads on her page and it cost her some money but she is benefitting from that action. (Participant 01)

The finding shows that some of the owner-founders do not have adequate skills to handle and manage digital platform accounts. The previous finding indicates that inadequate in-house digital skills are some of the major barriers to adopting social media as a marketing tool in Nigeria (Ochinanwata, 2019).

Trust and authenticity are identified as another challenge facing online micro businesses in Nigeria. This is because there are many imposters and fake products that are selling on both e-commerce and social media platforms. The finding recommends review and feedback as a good approach to building trust and customers' confidence in the digital platform. This finding is in line with a study that shows that perception on online platforms creates a strong impact on brand awareness and brand trust, which results in a strong influence on customer acquisition and retention (McIntyre and Srinivasan, 2017).

Existing studies identified various challenges facing small and medium businesses in Nigeria such as access to finance, good road network, and insufficient power supply (Okpara & Koumbiadis, 2011). The finding from this research also shows that bad roads are another challenge facing micro and small businesses in Nigeria. For example, one of the participants cited that *"another one is a bad road when we gave food to dispatch rider and by the time the person got to the customer address, the food had spilt and was cold as a result of the bad road."* However, these challenges do not have a high impact on micro businesses that operate purely online.

Conclusion

To contribute to the theoretical knowledge on digital platforms and the research gaps in the Nigerian context, this paper explores the impact of digital platforms on SMEs' development and performance as well as the challenges associated with adopting digital platforms, where digital firms are still new and emergent businesses. The findings show that skills are a prerequisite for individuals and entrepreneurs operating online micro businesses as it is a fundamental attribute for those in Nigeria and similar developing countries. The study reveals that digital skills and information communication technology are crucial factors for adopting the digital platform for micro and small business development. The current research revealed that SMEs utilize digital technologies such as social media to market, identify, engage, and acquire customers to increase a firm's performance.

The findings highlighted that most challenges facing online micro businesses include trust because there are many fake products and imposters on the internet. Thus, making a video of oneself together with a product builds customer confidence. This challenge is different from challenges identified from previous literature such as lack of power supply and inadequate infrastructures that mainly associate with a physical business. The findings highlighted the importance of trust and building online customer confidence. The analysis showed that entrepreneurs developing small businesses need to ensure customer confidence through feedback and review on those platforms.

Considering the Nigerian education system, there is a need to incorporate various components of digital skills into the University curriculum in order to enable students to gain skills that enable them to start online small-scale businesses. Further research should focus on obtaining large-scale quantitative data to explore the independent and dependent variables on howdigital platforms enhance enterprise development in Nigeria.

References

Amankwah-Amoah, J., & Debrah, Y. A. (2011). The evolution of alliances in the global airline industry: A review of the African experience. *Thunderbird International Business Review, 53*(1), 37–40.

Amankwah-Amoah, J., Khan, Z., Wood, G., & Knight, G. (2021). COVID-19 and digitalization: The great acceleration. *Journal of Business Research, 136*, 602–611.

Agwu, E., & Murray, P. (2015). Empirical study of barriers to electronic commerce adoption by small and medium scale businesses in Nigeria. *International Journal of Innovation in the Digital Economy, 6*(2), 1–19.

Agwu, M. E., & Murray, J. P. (2014). Drivers and inhibitors to e-Commerce adoption among SMEs in Nigeria. *Journal of Emerging Trends in Computing and Information Sciences, 5*(3), 192–199.

Chaffey, D & Ellis-Chadwick, F. (2016). Digital marketing: Strategy, implementation and practice. (6th Ed), Pearson.

Chheda, S. H. (2014). *Impact of social media marketing on performance of micro and small businesses.* DY Patil University.

Cohen, S. S., Zysman, J., & DeLong, B. J. (2000). Tools for thought: What is new and important about the "E-conomy"?. *Berkeley Roundtable on the International Economy Working Paper 138.*

Emeti, C. I., & Onyeaghala, O. (2015). E-business adoption and consumer attitude in Nigeria. *European Journal of Business and Management, 7*(21), 76–87.

Evans, D. S. (2016). Multisided platforms, dynamic competition, and the assessment of market power for internet-based firms. *University of Chicago Coase-Sandor Institute for Law & Economics Research Paper, 753*.

Evans, P. C., & Gawer, A. (2016). *The rise of the platform enterprise: A global survey*. University of Surrey.

Fosu, A. K. (2003). Political instability and export performance in sub-Saharan Africa. *Journal of Development Studies, 39*(4), 68–83.

Gawer, A. (2014). Bridging differing perspectives on technological platforms: Toward an integrative framework. *Research Policy, 43*(7), 1239–1249.

Gbandi, E. C., & Amissah, G. (2014). Financing options for small and medium enterprises (SMEs) in Nigeria. *European Scientific Journal January*.

Giotopoulos, I., Kontolaimou, A., Korra, E., & Tsakanikas, A. (2017). What drives ICT adoption by SMEs? Evidence from a large-scale survey in Greece. *Journal of Business Research, 81*, 60–69.

Hagiu, A., & Wright, J. (2015). Multi-sided platforms. *International Journal of Industrial Organization, 43*, 162–174.

Huy, L. V., & Filiatrault, P. (2006). The adoption of e-commerce in SMEs in Vietnam: A study of users and prospectors. *PACIS 2006 proceedings*, pp. 1333–1344.

Janita, I., & Chong, W. K. (2013). Barriers of b2b e-business adoption in Indonesian SMEs: A Literature Analysis. *Procedia Computer Science, 17*, 571–578.

Jin, H., & Hurd, F. (2018). Exploring the impact of digital platforms on SME internationalization: New Zealand SMEs use of the Alibaba platform for Chinese market entry. *Journal of Asia-Pacific Business, 19*(2), 72–95.

Keisha, C. T. (2020). *Digital platforms and entrepreneurship in Trinidad and Tobago: An examination of their relationships using technology affordances and constraints*. Thesis, University of Southampton, Faculty of Social Sciences Business School, pp. 25–27.

Kvale, S (2009). *Doing interviews*. London, Sage.

Lai, L. S., & Turban, E. (2008). Groups formation and operations in the Web 2.0 environment and social networks. *Group Decision and negotiation, 17*, 387–402.

Laudon, J. P., Laudon, K. C. (2017). *Management information systems: Managing the digital firm*. Pearson Education Limited. Retrieved June 14, 2021, from https://paginas.fe.up.pt/~acbrito/laudon/ch1/chpt1-1main.htm

Li, W., Liu, K., Belitski, M., Ghobadian, A., & O'Regan, N. (2016). E-leadership through strategic alignment: An empirical study of small- and medium-sized enterprises in the digital age. *Journal of Information Technology, 31*(2), 185–206.

Kimuyu, P. (2007). Corruption, firm growth and export propensity in Kenya. *International Journal of Social Economics, 34*(3), 197–217.

McIntyre, D.P. and Srinivasan, A., (2017). Networks, platforms, and strategy: Emerging views and next steps. *Strategic management journal, 38*(1), pp.141–160.

Molla, A., & Licker, P. S. (2005). Perceived e-readiness factors in e-commerce adoption: An empirical investigation in a developing country. *International Journal of Electronic Commerce, 10*(1), 83–110.

Ochinanwata, N., & Ezepue, P. O. (2016). Platform business model constructs: Fostering innovative born-global firms in Sub-Sahara Africa. Proceeding of the Applied Business and Entrepreneurship International Conference, 9–11 November 2016, Las Vegas, USA: ISBN 978-1-963010-81-7.

Ochinanwata, N. H. (2019). *Integrated business modelling for developing digital internationalising firms in Nigeria*. Doctoral dissertation, Sheffield Hallam University.

Okpara, J. O., & Koumbiadis, N. (2011). Strategic export orientation and internationalisation barriers: Evidence from a developing economy. *Journal of International Business and Cultural Studies, 4*, 71–79.

Olatokun, W., & Bankole, B. (2011). Factors influencing electronic business technologies adoption and use by small and medium scale enterprises (SMEs) in a Nigerian municipality. *Journal of Internet banking and Commerce, 16*(3).

Osotimehin, K. O., Jegede, C. A., Akinlabi, B. H., & Olajide, O. T. (2012). An evaluation of the challenges and prospects of micro and small scale enterprises development in Nigeria. *American international journal of contemporary research, 2*(4), 174–185.

Parker, G., Alstyne, M. V., & Choudary, S. P. (2017). *Platform revolution: How networked markets are transforming the economy and how to make them work for you*. W. W. Norton and Company.

Parker, G. G., Van Alstyne, M. W., & Choudary, S. P. (2016). *Platform revolution: How networked markets are transforming the economy and how to make them work for you*. WW Norton and Company.

Raghavan, V., Wani, M., & Abraham, D. M. (2018). Exploring E-business in Indian SMEs: Adoption, trends and the way forward. In *Emerging markets from a multidisciplinary perspective* (pp. 95–106). Springer.

Rodgers, J. A., Yen, D. C., & Chou, D. C. (2002). Developing e-business; A strategic approach. *Information Management and Computer Security, 10*, 184–192.

Saunders, M., Lewis, P., & Thornhill, A. (2012). Research methods for business students. Pearson Education Ltd., Harlow.

Singh, A., & Hess, T. (2017). How chief digital officers promote the digital transformation of their companies. *MIS Quarterly Executive, 16*(1), 1–17.

Soto Setzke, D., Riasanow, T., Boehm, M., & Krcmar, H. (2023). Pathways to digital service innovation: The role of digital transformation strategies in established organizations. Information Systems Frontiers, 25(3), 1017–1037.

Spagnoletti, P., Resca, A., & Lee, G. (2015). A design theory for digital platforms supporting online communities: A multiple case study. *Journal of Information Technology, 30*(4), 364–380.

Stebbins, R. A. (2001). New directions in the theory and research of serious leisure.

Wynn, M., & Olayinka, O. (2021). E-business strategy in developing countries: A framework and checklist for the small business sector. *Sustainability, 13*(13), 7356.

Part V

Conclusion

9

Theoretical, Policy, and Managerial Implications for Entrepreneurial Practice in Africa

Eric Kwame Adae, Patience Rambe, Kojo Kakra Twum, Doreen Anyamesem Odame, and Robert E. Hinson

Introduction

The contributions of businesses and entrepreneurship to improved well-being, enhanced socioeconomic status, and the promotion of economic growth and development in general cannot be overemphasised. Entrepreneurial development is one of the most promising strategies to effectively overcome the current global economic crisis while securing future economic systems as it optimises production and distribution processes (Kapinga et al., 2018). Entrepreneurial activities provide income through decent and well-paying jobs for both skilled and unskilled labour and, in effect, increase household income. Entrepreneurship provides a wealth of opportunities for all parties in the business lifecycle, including suppliers, distributors, retailers, and consumers. At the macro level,

E. K. Adae (✉)
Drake University School of Journalism and Mass Communication, Des Moines, IA, USA
e-mail: eric.adae@drake.edu

entrepreneurial activities, especially manufacturing, improve a country's external account by decreasing imports and diversifying exports.

Although the broad field of entrepreneurship has been examined from historical, temporal, institutional, spatial, and social contexts (Welter, 2011), the appreciation of contemporary dynamics is essential to prevent the generalisation of patterns of specific entrepreneurial behaviours (Welter et al., 2016). As such, the proper conception, operationalisation, and application of the modern context of entrepreneurship are important for the development and sustenance of entrepreneurship, particularly in the understudied present-day African contexts.

This focus is fundamental in the emerging market context of Africa, where individuals of different backgrounds, experiences, and dynamics are called upon to overcome resource constraints and institutional hurdles to pursue entrepreneurship (Lim et al., 2016; Scott, Sinha, Gibb, & Akoorie, 2020). For women entrepreneurs, for instance, there is a wide configuration of factors that coalesce in explaining their success and failure in the institution and thriving of entrepreneurial ventures. These include the dominance of patriarchal norms (Simba et al. 2023), social stereotypes that project women as inferior to their male counterparts (Bobrowska and Conrad, 2017) and whose roles are reduced to procreation and consumption in domestic circles, the prevalence of social norms that undermine the social autonomy of women to pursue

---

P. Rambe
University of the Free State, Free State, South Africa
e-mail: prambe@cut.ac.za

K. K. Twum
Presbyterian University, Abetifi-Kwahu, Ghana
e-mail: twumkojo@presbyuniversity.edu.gh

D. A. Odame
Ghana Communication Technology University, Tesano – Accra, Ghana
e-mail: dodame@gctu.edu.gh

R. E. Hinson
Ghana Communication Technology University, Accra, Ghana

University of the Free State Business School, Bloemfontein, South Africa
e-mail: rehinson@gctu.edu.gh

entrepreneurship due to burdensome family responsibilities, and social norms that shape the demand for maintaining a good balance between work and family unit (Nxopo & Iwu, 2015). Moreover, female entrepreneurs are confronted with culturally imposed constraints that psychologically and physically impede their autonomy, aspirations, and priorities (Siba, 2019).

There is therefore an increased recognition of the urgent need for effective and tailored entrepreneurial behaviour and activities in Africa as a potent strategy for spurring economic growth and stability. Particularly, the private sector has a pivotal role to play in advancing this course. As explained in the introductory section, there are records of persistent challenges on the continent that hinder the establishment and growth of well-structured and well-performing businesses, compared to Western and Asian countries. A huge majority of entrepreneurs and business firms in Africa tend to be small-scale and informal in nature and structure. Unleashing the transformative potential of the private sector in Africa cannot be possible without the contributions of these small and medium-sized enterprises (SMEs) and social enterprises.

Industrialisation and entrepreneurship are particularly important for Africa's socioeconomic transformation because the continent's population is young and fast-growing. Lack of jobs for a population with this characteristic means the fight for poverty will be difficult, given that the most important determinant for the non-poor in Africa is employment and access to income (Oluwatayo & Babalola, 2020). When Western and Asian countries experienced similar challenges with their populations in decades past, entrepreneurship and job creation formed part of the critical drivers that helped turn the situation around (Wu & Si, 2018).

Theoretical and Policy Frameworks to Advance Entrepreneurship in Africa

International business and entrepreneurship have always been popular topics in economic and development discussions. Hammond (2013) identified entrepreneurship as a strong driving force for addressing

China's urban poverty, while Hajikhani (2020) explains that entrepreneurship is vital in building smart cities and dealing with the challenges of urbanisation. The concept of entrepreneurship has gained overwhelming contemporary interest because of the upsurge of the global economic crisis, especially following massive challenges to the global order such as the COVID-19 pandemic, the Russian invasion of Ukraine, and the many other natural disasters in several parts of the world. Entrepreneurship is thus widely considered a driver of sustainable socioeconomic development (Hammond, 2013).

Globalisation has caused many nations to integrate with each other, causing geographical boundaries to be erased (Witt, 2019). This integration has also globalised entrepreneurship, as entrepreneurial structures are no longer restricted within the boundaries of particular nation-states. National economies have expanded and have become interdependent with other economies (Witt, 2019). It is noteworthy, however, that globalisation has had a two-way effect on entrepreneurship: while globalisation has increased entrepreneurial and business possibilities, it has also created stiff competition that requires a relentless fight for resources, investments, and capital in order to remain competitive (Ordeñana et al., 2020).

While many challenges confront entrepreneurial development in Africa, there are many opportunities for driving the growth of SMEs across the continent. Among the theoretical and policy frameworks and recommendations for advancing entrepreneurship in Africa are several perspectives and levers of growth, including the entrepreneurial ecosystem perspective, the institutional void perspective, the financial constraints perspective, the business incubation perspective, skill segmentation, entrepreneurial visioning, innovation, business performance and action, and the African Union's Agenda 63 framework.

Entrepreneurial Ecosystem Perspective

Hagin and Caesar (2021) examined the major antecedents of success among SMEs in Ghana, focusing on the impact of several internal factors, including the nature of entrepreneurial orientation, managerial competence, and technological capabilities. Their all-round analysis also considered the impact on the growth and success of SMEs of such external factors as finance and capital, human resources, government policies, and related regulatory practices.

Managerial competence, access to external capital or finance, and government policies and practices were found to be significantly associated with the success (as indicated by the effectiveness and efficiency of business systems) of SMEs, while technological capabilities, human resource capabilities, and entrepreneurial orientation were not significantly related to the success of SMEs. The study therefore recommends that SMEs in Ghana exploit non-traditional avenues to raise funds to reduce their over-reliance on traditional financial institutions. Further, measures to reduce institutional bottlenecks, including understaffed national regulatory bodies, and provide adequate market information to SMEs are crucial.

Guéneau et al. (2022) wondered what made one type of entrepreneurial ecosystem (EE) more conducive to entrepreneurial dynamics than another. In this study, these scholars introduce the entrepreneurial ecosystem (EE) perspective and propose an unexplored inter-organisational ties analysis among all EE actors at a country-level scale. Based on the network theory perspective, Guéneau et al. (2022) conducted exploratory research in five low-income African countries using innovative research methods, namely quantitative graph theory, web scraping, and fuzzy-set qualitative comparative analysis, to understand the organisational patterns in these EEs and their impact on entrepreneurial outcomes. This research underlines the importance of EE network attributes to facilitate the easy distribution of entrepreneurial nurturing components to entrepreneurs.

Ondiba and Matsui (2019) were interested in examining the social attributes and factors influencing entrepreneurial behaviours among rural women in Kakamega County, Kenya. These researchers reported that at the marketplace, about 77% of the respondents participated in various social activities. Some 97% of the respondents attributed their business success to the help and inspiration from social networking groups and were inspired and motivated to pursue entrepreneurship because of these social activities at the market. An overwhelming majority (98%) of participants agreed that they started businesses to support their families financially. Reflecting on these findings, Ondiba and Matsui (2019) recommend further research on business behaviours, perceptions, and factors that influence the business performance and sustainability of rural women entrepreneurs.

Bate (2021) offered a comparative analysis of the entrepreneurial ecosystem, which has received little attention, of the BRICS club countries, with an especial focus on South Africa, Brazil, and India. Various entrepreneurship-economic growth-related measures, including the Global Entrepreneurship Index (GEI), Global Competitiveness Index (GCI), Index Economic Freedom (IEF), and Legatum Prosperity Index (LPI), were used in this study to compare the countries' entrepreneurial ecosystems. According to the GEI and GCI of 2018, China is leading the BRICS club in terms of growth and entrepreneurial ecosystem. LPI, IEF, and GEI put South Africa's entrepreneurial ecosystem in a favourable position as compared to Brazil and India.

This study illustrates that South Africa's tertiary education, coupled with low skill perception, was less effective in equipping the population to be entrepreneurs as compared to India and Brazil. Whereas Brazil and India were at their worst in internationalising their entrepreneurs and technological absorption, respectively. South Africa was found to be more like India in terms of product innovation and risk acceptance. Further, it was more like Brazil in terms of risk capital, technological absorption, opportunity perception, and sluggish economic growth. South Africa (57th out of 140 as of 2018) was categorised among those poorly performing countries in terms of start-up skills, networking, technology absorption, human capital, and risk capital pillars. To increase GEI by 5%, it should invest 77% of its extra resources on start-up skills, 18% on risk capital, and 5% on technology absorption.

Government Policies and Entrepreneurship Phases in Emerging Economies

Akinyemi and Adejumo (2018) examine entrepreneurship phases and study the impact of some government policies on entrepreneurial activities. Globally, it is well known that government policies can have far-reaching effects on entrepreneurial activities, whether directly or indirectly (Acs & Szerb, 2007). Research has shown that government policies relating to taxes and business regulations often affect entrepreneurial activities (Bygrave & Hunt, 2004; Kreft & Sobel, 2005). In recognition of the need for entrepreneurship policies, many countries have implemented both general and specific policies to promote entrepreneurial activities (Acs & Szerb, 2007). In many developing nations, policies have been implemented to promote entrepreneurial activities. For instance, in Nigeria, structures and programmes such as the Small and Medium Enterprises Development Agency (SMEDAN), the N-Power programme, the Government Enterprise and Empowerment Programme (GEEP), and the You-Win programme were designed to promote entrepreneurial activities by facilitating access to funds and other resources needed for SMEs (see, e.g., Oliyide, 2012).

Numerous studies have shown that government policies affect entrepreneurial activities, but there is a need to examine government policies across entrepreneurship phases. The heart of the matter for Akinyemi and Adejumo (2018) is whether these governmental policies equally impact every entrepreneurship phase. Particularly, their study sought to examine some policy factors that enhanced entrepreneurial activities in two of Africa's emerging economies, precisely to identify the most favourable government policy in each entrepreneurship phase.

They employed principal component analysis (PCA) to identify the most favourable government policy in each entrepreneurship phase. The findings show that the impact of government policies on entrepreneurial phases differs in both countries. Thus, their study concluded that some policies are more favourable than others in some phases, leading these scholars to make a clarion call for more studies on government policies across entrepreneurship phases.

Institutional Void Perspective

The institutional void perspective suggests that the presence of weak and underdeveloped institutions or the absence of institutional arrangements altogether does not support the effective and efficient functioning of the market (Khanna & Palepu, 1997). Emerging economies such as the African entrepreneurial landscape are confronted with an intricate mix of challenges that include a lack of adequate disclosure, a weak contract enforcement regime, a weak governance regime, a lack of uniformity of legal systems, rampant power outages due to poor power infrastructure, abundant red tape, a shortage of skilled workers, and a lack of financial credit availability, which curtails entrepreneurial development (Amankwah-Amoah et al., 2023).

Relative to Western businesses, entrepreneurs in Africa are often less likely to access banks due to their lack of collateral, lack of a strong and credible credit record, short banking history, and lack of business experience (Simba et al. 2023). Younger entrepreneurs are especially confronted with institutional challenges (Ojong, Simba, & Dana, 2021), which are further complicated by the paucity of laws and criminal sanctions that explicitly address harassment in business (World Bank, 2013; Ogundana et al., 2022). These institutional voids may negatively impact the capacity of entrepreneurs to negotiate and operate in a complex business environment.

Financial Constraints from a Perspective

Most small-scale businesses often operate in low-capital-intensive and low-growth-oriented sectors, such as the food processing, retail, and apparel sectors (Okunade, 2007). There is evidence to suggest that SMEs often struggle to access support from family members, business associations or networks, and the government (Ogundana et al., 2018). On the contrary, other studies have established that family members, especially spouses and children, are also the main benefactors through whom entrepreneurs may access start-up and working capital for their businesses.

Due to challenges such as lack of financial management, poor record keeping, and the newness and smallness of their firms (Stinchcombe, 1965), SME entrepreneurs often lack the required credibility to access finance from financial institutions such as banks. Generally, depleted financial resources, lack of access to grants (Burger & Owens, 2013), and lack of connections to other organisations (Amankwah-Amoah, 2016) are often cited as common reasons for SME organisational failure (Hager et al., 2004). This is especially true for female-owned businesses.

The literature on access to capital needs to be integrated with access to human capital to ensure the effective use of acquired and accumulated financial resources. Achieving the economic and developmental goals in Africa requires collaborative efforts from all stakeholders within the economy: the government, civil society groups, the private sector, individuals, and communities.

Evidence across Africa suggests that entrepreneurship displays a palpable gender divide that tells the story of the many disadvantages facing women-owned SMEs. For instance, Boateng and Poku (2019) examined the main constraints to accessing finance among women-owned small businesses in the Lower Manya Krobo Municipality in the Eastern Region of Ghana. The study revealed that there are major constraints facing women entrepreneurs, notably poor market demand and a lack of capital and credit. While many of these entrepreneurs meet the main requirements for being granted loans, there is a great deal of discrimination against women micro-entrepreneurs due to the institutionalised patrilineal inheritance system.

Boateng and Poku (2019) recommend a more inclusive small-business landscape that formally recognises the activities of women-run microbusinesses not only in the private sector of the economy but also within the lending models and structures, as these economic actors constitute a valuable area of economic growth. For instance, key national business promotion agencies in Ghana, such as the National Board for Small Scale Industries (NBSSI) through the Business Advisory Centre (BAC), should organise educational and training seminars regularly to educate women micro-entrepreneurs on business management to be able to negotiate effectively on the various landed properties in such a patriarchal system to reduce the high start-up mortality of women-run micro-businesses. Also, the study recommends to the National Identification Authority that it take actionable steps to fast-track the identification system of citizens, as it remains one of the major factors in reducing loan risks and interest rates.

Women and their lack of access to credit and capital are not the major challenge to entrepreneurial development in Africa. Youth entrepreneurs also face significant challenges. Seeing that youth entrepreneurship has been regarded as a tool for employment creation in Ethiopia, Ahmed and Ahmed (2021) investigated the major potential constraints of youth entrepreneurs in small and micro-enterprises in this African country.

Featuring a descriptive research design and a quantitative research (factor analysis) approach, the study focused on a target population of 5000 youth entrepreneurs between the ages of 18 and 29. It was found that a slew of factors militated against youth entrepreneurs in Ethiopia. These included unfavourable government policy, limited access to finance, limited access to the market, limited access to information and infrastructure, limited access to business assistance and support, limited access to entrepreneurship training and education, a lack of social support, unfavourable administrative conditions, and weak institutional linkage, which were the major potential constraints for youth entrepreneurs in the study area. The study draws implications for policymakers, the Ministry of Youth Development, the Chamber of Commerce and Industry, and the government to adopt multifaceted, multitargeted, and multitiered approaches in order to facilitate and encourage youth entrepreneurship.

The Business Incubation Perspective

Business incubation is crucial to the development of women entrepreneurs' businesses (Marlow & McAdam, 2015). Ideally, business incubators provide women entrepreneurs, as well as all entrepreneurs, with work premises, technical advice, access to information through ICT facilities, financial support through loans, and other business development services on demand in order to enable a smooth start, growth, competitiveness, and sustainability of enterprises (Chijoriga, 2003).

Business incubation also enables women entrepreneurs to identify potential customers and new markets where they could sell their products at high prices (Shahzad et al., 2012). Business incubators are meant to provide women entrepreneurs with infrastructural facilities such as flexible, affordable working space as well as shared office services (Ndabeni, 2008). Business incubators deliver training-related services to women entrepreneurs for capacity-building skills. Training could enable women entrepreneurs to acquire relevant skills for production, packaging, and marketing their businesses (Kimambo, 2005).

Given the significant role of women entrepreneurs in Africa's socioeconomic development, Kapinga et al. (2018) set out to explore and highlight the present status of the contribution of business and technology incubators to women entrepreneurs' businesses. These scholars observed that, overall, business and technology incubators offer insufficient support to their enterprises.

Kapinga and co-workers (2018) found that there is a serious lack of contextualisation in the services offered to incubatees by business and technology incubators, such that these services fall miserably short of addressing the felt needs of entrepreneurs, making their support less impactful. Thus, these scholars recommend the provision of incubators' services tailored to the real needs of women's businesses through the contextualisation of the incubators' services tailored to the incubatees' real needs, including appropriate training beyond business management.

Skills Segmentation and SME Innovativeness

For SMEs to thrive, they must be highly innovative (Njiraini et al., 2018). Njiraini et al. (2018) note that in Kenya, micro and small enterprises' (MSEs) propensity to innovate is still nascent despite the pivotal role played by these enterprises in the national economy.

Results from the analysis show that the average number of years of education for a production worker, physical capital intensity, age of an MSE, access to finance, and size of an MSE are important factors influencing MSEs innovation decisions (Njiraini et al., 2018). These scholars argue that human capital skills and an MSE's resource endowment positively influence an MSE's innovativeness. From a theoretical standpoint, they advocate for skills segmentation to isolate human capital skills that are most relevant for stimulating MSEs innovative activities. Also, they made a strong argument for physical capital and financial services for MSEs to be used to promote these enterprises' innovativeness.

Entrepreneurial Visioning, Innovation, and Performance

Kamuri (2022) observes that while entrepreneurial orientation's role in determining the performance of businesses has been empirically established, studies from Africa or an industry-ecosystem perspective have been scarce. Seeking to deepen current understandings of psychological perspectives of entrepreneurship, especially the vision for growth construct and its significance to firms in an industry ecosystem, Kamuri's (2022) study explored vision for growth as an individual entrepreneurial disposition and its relationship with innovation and performance outcomes among industry actors.

This study makes some recommendations in terms of training, policy, and practise interventions aimed at enhancing entrepreneurial vision and innovation from an industry-ecosystem perspective for the realisation of economic benefits in the wake of globalised competition.

Fatma et al. (2021) set out to empirically study the extent to which entrepreneurs' psychology affected their business venture success in North Africa. Using a sample of Tunisian entrepreneurs and the cognitive mapping technique, it emerged that psychology does affect business venture success and that entrepreneurial overconfidence and optimism biases can greatly affect the new venture's success.

The study further found that behavioural factors, especially overconfidence, optimism, and hope, had a profound impact on new ventures launched by female entrepreneurs compared to male entrepreneurs. The success of new ventures launched by male entrepreneurs was found to be less affected by behavioural factors; only the overconfidence bias could have an influence, and their new venture success remained dependent on their age, experience, and education.

Mainstream rational entrepreneurship theory assumes that new venture success can be explained by some traditional factors, such as entrepreneurial social capital and the availability of financial support. However, these findings suggest that beyond this rational theory, a wave of research papers, such as this work by Fatma et al. (2021), are making a valid case that entrepreneurial psychology is a fundamental dimension that can affect the entrepreneurial process and thus holds significant explanatory power for (new) venture success.

From a policy perspective, these findings suggest that entrepreneurial psychology is a vital factor that influences new venture success. Entrepreneurs' overconfidence bias and optimism level appeared to have explanatory power and consequently could explain why new ventures sometimes failed, even when they had sufficient financial support and a large social network. Policymakers should be aware that entrepreneur psychology is an important factor that can lead to the success or failure of new ventures.

Thus, the psychology of entrepreneurs emerged as one of the most relevant factors governing SME success. According to Fatma et al. (2021), it was time to create new strategies and support structures to integrate the psychology of entrepreneurs into plans to reduce venture failure while addressing the important question of how to govern entrepreneurs' psychology in such a manner as to increase new venture success.

Visioning and related psychological factors are one thing, but entrepreneurial behaviours that produce SME performance are quite a different thing. In the literature, some scholars have been interested in examining the key factors influencing entrepreneurial behaviour, particularly in the public sector. Tundui and Shiganza (2021) considered what constituted the key entrepreneurial behavioural factors in Tanzania's public sector.

Data on the antecedents of entrepreneurial behaviour involved a survey of employees of Tabora Urban Water Supply and Sanitation Authority (TUWASA) using a one-shot cross-sectional survey. Results showed that entrepreneurial behaviour was influenced by four main factors, of which goal clarity and the education level of the employee had the most significant and positive effect. Of the organisations investigated, only one variable emerged as having a significant influence on employees' entrepreneurial behaviour.

These results suggest that the management of the studied organisation must adopt a strategic management approach to motivate employees to unleash their entrepreneurial behaviour. This finding possibly presents a probing avenue for further research into the factors that contribute to the demonstration of entrepreneurial behaviour in the public sector.

The African Union's Agenda 63 Framework and Entrepreneurial Development in Africa

The African Union's Agenda 63 is a framework that attempts to achieve this collaboration through the mobilisation of manpower and the enhancement of human capital to facilitate resilience, business ownership, and economic ventures on the continent of Africa. Through its framework, the AU's Agenda 63 seeks to develop capable, inclusive, and accountable economic institutions at all levels and in all spheres—formal, informal, large, and small scale. There are roadmaps that attempt to address challenges that hold member nations back from achieving this aim, including purposefully nurturing transformative leadership and embracing a prosperous, peaceful, and all-inclusive African continent. This book contributes to the Agenda's aim of leveraging on past experiences to recommend key drivers that could catalyse the realisation of this goal (Ndzendze & Monyae, 2019).

The aftermath of the COVID-19 pandemic caused a severe contraction in Africa. For the first time in 20 years, Africa's growth rate declined by 1.9% in 2020 (IMF, 2021), and fiscal deficits also increased to 4.7%. In the face of these challenges, the Africa Continental Free Trade Area (AfCFTA) presents pooling and innovative solutions in the form of regional integration to help Africa recover from the effects of the pandemic and meet the goals of Agenda 2063 of the African Union. This is expected to be achieved through export diversification of locally produced goods, increased industrialisation, and coordination of Africa's trade policy (Pasara, 2020). It is estimated that if the well-conceived initiatives by AfCFTA are well implemented with optimum representation of all variables, Africa could record about a 0.5% increase in overall GDP, which may be equivalent to some $55 billion. About two-thirds of this amount is projected to come from the manufacturing sector (Geda & Yimer, 2019). Though these projections may seem a bit too modest compared to the context of the entire continent, the emphasis is on the structural transformation that will be recorded.

The United Nations Sustainable Development Goals (SDGs) were developed at a time of immense global poverty, youth unemployment, and systemic political and governance challenges. The SDGs, therefore, represent an unprecedented global consensus to address these global challenges (Willis, 2018). There are specific goals outlined in the SDGs, notably SDG 8, that also focus on actions and strategies that foster economic growth and development (Vaidya & Chatterji, 2020). Entrepreneurial activities indeed have the potential to impact not just one of the SDGs but several of them at once. This is because the SDGs are interdependent and indivisible (Collste, 2021). This explains the urgency of addressing factors that influence entrepreneurial activities and eventual growth.

Entrepreneurship in all its forms (informal, formal, large scale, and small scale) has the capability of contributing to achieving the SDGs through improved economic and social outcomes (Vaidya & Chatterji, 2020). The momentum and commitment to start a new business propel one to exploit limited resources for productivity (Muldoon et al., 2018), even in the face of institutional constraints and limitations, COVID-19, and other humanitarian crises (Willis, 2018). In this regard, there is high confidence that entrepreneurship can maximise the impact of the SDGs. This is possible because of the capability of entrepreneurship to create long-term and sustainable gains for individuals, communities, sections of the population, and the nation (Vaidya & Chatterji, 2020).

This book makes three main contributions to sustainable entrepreneurship in Africa. First, it offers some contemporary perspectives on the study of entrepreneurship by not only pointing out the circumstances that African entrepreneurs are confronted with but also demonstrating the specific traits that they possess that make them well-positioned to compete with their Western counterparts. This is particularly critical given the paucity of context-specific theoretical perspectives explaining the growth factors of businesses in the developing world. This undertheorisation is worsened by an apparent lack of scholarship on African entrepreneurship (Ogundana, Simba, Dana, & Liguori, 2022). This theoretical vacuum has contributed to a lack of knowledge about the activities of African entrepreneurs (Wiklund et al., 2009) and, broadly, of the developing world.

Second, this book suggests that, particularly in Africa, entrepreneurship cannot be treated independently but coalesces with a constellation of other factors such as access to funding and human capital. As the literature in this field suggests, grasping the resources, strategies, and institutions that entrepreneurs in Africa grapple with necessitates a multilevel and multipronged approach that accommodates institutional, political, economic, social, and cultural contexts and their implications for entrepreneurial activities and outcomes (Ojong, Simba, & Dana, 2021). Given the subtle and nubilous connection between context, institutions, and the entrepreneurial activities of entrepreneurs in emerging African economies, appreciating the complexity of entrepreneurship requires a synergetic approach that accommodates institutional arrangements, financial resource bases, sociocultural factors such as social networks, and the psychological disposition of the entrepreneur.

Third, given the potential of small-scale entrepreneurs to contribute directly to the growth and development of their industries, emphasises the need to challenge outmoded beliefs and practices that perpetuate subordination and unequal participation. For instance, as more females engage in entrepreneurship, their contribution has positively impacted economic productivity, thus affirming their economic value. For instance, across many African countries such as Nigeria, Ghana, Kenya, and Zimbabwe, most entrepreneurs who engage in informal and survivalist entrepreneurship are women.

Managerial Direction for Entrepreneurial Advancements in Africa

Undoubtedly, entrepreneurship can be an effective transformational force, not only for delivering but also for attaining the SDGs and sustainable economic transformation in Africa. This can be made possible through the attainment of economic growth and development through entrepreneurial activities. The concept of sustainability is embedded within the confines of entrepreneurship and demonstrated through empowerment, which enables economic development, poverty alleviation, and improvements in social value and social capital.

The notion of the continent of Africa as a theoretical concept continues to intrigue many scholars (Mbembe, 2017), with some scholars, including Nachum et al. (2022), calling for further research in and about Africa by scholars of international business and entrepreneurship, particularly through a careful consideration of the role of emergent indigenous Afrocentric philosophies, concepts, worldviews, folkways, and mores, such as Ubuntu and Africapitalism.

Kamoche et al. (2015) observed that Africa remained proportionately less represented in the fields of management, organisation studies, HR, and IB, with significantly more attention focused on economics and foreign trade, and work at one level infrequently compared to work at the other, other than in the most general terms. Kolk and Rivera-Santos (2018) argue that three dominant sets of theory have been deployed in Africa-related research: (orthodox) economic theory; institutional theory (of diverse hues and flavours); and stakeholder theory.

Within this context, we perceive several theoretical tensions and puzzles. As contend, few African firms have emerged as global players, which, in a sense, is reflective of the institutional and geographical diversity across the continent of Africa's 54 countries, with none having anywhere near the economic gravitas or domestic markets of Asian emerging economies such as India or China and without the strong regulatory commonalities and depth of ties of, say, the European Union.

Improvisation appears particularly pertinent in African organisational contexts that are prone to institutional turbulence and uncertainty owing to historical legacies and primary commodity dependence and pose significant challenges to strategic planning (see, e.g., Kamoche et al., 2015; Kiggundu, 1989; Munene, 1991). Other more recent accounts explore how firms in Africa build internal capabilities (e.g., better managerial capacity or employee skills) or engage in enabling activities (e.g., new market entry strategies) to cope with challenging circumstances in a manner that may indeed leave them much better off than before (see, e.g., George et al., 2016).

Some scholars believe that indigenous theorising about business in Africa involves Ubuntu as a theory, together with similar Afrocentric theoretical extensions. However, it has been suggested that such a theoretical trajectory may raise broader questions around the relative embeddedness of firms in societies, whether and how they seek compatibility in their activities with the needs of local communities, and the role of indigenous theory in better understanding the same (Amaeshi et al., 2018).

In formulating new theoretical pathways informed by Ubuntu, researchers might also pay attention to other emergent ideas informed by indigenous knowledge and the African socioeconomic context that speak to distinctly African social realities, on which Nachum and others (2022) are silent. In this regard, Africapitalism has also emerged as a promising avenue for further research that goes beyond economic theorising to raise new questions about how entrepreneurship can promote sustainable value creation, job creation, poverty alleviation, intra-African trade, and investments while taking into account the social impact of business (Amaeshi et al., 2018). A scrutiny of such work highlights the vibrant nature of theorising on Africa, for example, in terms of Ubuntu, Africapitalism, and more nuanced understandings of institutions than simply stories of voids or failure.

From the discussions throughout this book, the role of entrepreneurship in a sustainable and innovative industrial economy cannot be overemphasised. The Global Entrepreneurship Monitor (GEM) in Jeon (2018) hypothesises that a direct link between favourable conditions, entrepreneurial activities, and economic transformation stimulates income-generation activities that can further yield economic growth.

Arguably, entrepreneurship is emerging as an unavoidable option for both local and international economic development, even in turbulent times. Halabisky (2018) advises that entrepreneurship is the most important element in reducing not only national poverty but also that of vulnerable groups. This is because entrepreneurship has the greatest potential for creating jobs, reducing unemployment, and generating income. Consequently, entrepreneurship has taken centre stage in the public agenda of most countries.

Empirical findings and business experiences also establish a direct nexus between entrepreneurship, technology, and innovation (Gaynor et al., 2009). Bubou et al. (2014) also stress the point that a major driver for contemporary entrepreneurship is the transformation of scientific discovery into commercialised products. Unfortunately, there is poor commercialisation or inadequate application of technology and innovation in entrepreneurship in Africa, resulting in poor productive capacity.

The chapters in this book have outlined some brilliant opportunities that technology provides as an enabler for entrepreneurship across the continent of Africa. To support entrepreneurial growth in Africa, governments must focus on enlarging the pool of finance for new technological ventures that foster entrepreneurial advancement. Technological advancement in entrepreneurship is creating a new narrative and opening up opportunities for economic growth and transformation in Africa. Key technologies in the 4IR demonstrate the decentralisation and decentralization of entrepreneurship, making entrepreneurial activities less complex, even for indigenous businesses.

Technological adoption may present some challenges, such as mass unemployment (due to automation), cybercrime, increased vulnerability, and intrusion, among others. African leaders and stakeholders must put measures in place to deal with these challenges with basic and novel policies. As much as governments invest in building the entrepreneurial skills of citizens, there should also be measures to regulate the digital space to ensure data protection, internet access, and freedom. This coordination will require appropriate and holistic industrial policies. Just like most western countries, African countries must come up with tailored strategies that will protect and secure their digital space.

References

Acs, Z. J., & Szerb, L. (2007). Entrepreneurship, economic growth and public policy. *Small Business Economics, 28*, 109–122. https://doi.org/10.1007/s11187-006-9012-3

Ahmed, H. M. S., & Ahmed, Y. A. (2021). Constraints of youth entrepreneurs in Ethiopia. *Journal of Global Entrepreneurship Research, 11*, 337–346. https://doi.org/10.1007/s40497-021-00292-z

Akinyemi, F. O., & Adejumo, O. O. (2018). Government policies and entrepreneurship phases in emerging economies: Nigeria and South Africa. *J Glob Entrepr Res, 8*, 35. https://doi.org/10.1186/s40497-018-0131-5

Amaeshi, K., Okupe, A., & Idemudia, U. (2018). Introduction. In U. Idemudia, K. Amaeshi, & A. Okupe (Eds.), *Africapitalism: Rethinking the role of business in Africa* (pp. 1–18). Cambridge University Press.

Amankwah-Amoah, J. (2016). An integrative process model of organisational failure. *Journal of Business Research*, *69*(9), 3388–3397. https://doi.org/10.1016/j.jbusres.2016.02.005

Amankwah-Amoah, J., Nyuur, R. B., Hinson, R., Kosiba, J. P., Al-Tabbaa, O., & Cunningham, J. A. (2023). Entrepreneurial strategic posture and new technology ventures in an emerging economy. *International Journal of Entrepreneurial Behavior & Research*, *29*(2), 385–407. https://doi.org/10.1108/IJEBR-10-2021-0816

Bate, A. F. (2021). A comparative analysis on the entrepreneurial ecosystem of BRICS club countries: Practical emphasis on South Africa. *SN Business & Economics*, *1*, 121. https://doi.org/10.1007/s43546-021-00120-2

Boateng, S., & Poku, K. O. (2019). Accessing finance among women-owned small businesses: Evidence from lower Manya Krobo municipality, Ghana. *Journal of Global Entrepreneurship Research*, *9*, 5. https://doi.org/10.1186/s40497-018-0128-0

Bobrowska, S. & Conrad, H. (2017). Discourses of Female Entrepreneurship in the Japanese Business Press – 25 Years and Little Progress. *Japanese Studies*, *37*(1), 1–22, https://doi.org/10.1080/10371397.2017.1293474

Bubou, G. M., Siyanbola, W. O., Ekperiware, M. C., & Gumus, S. (2014). Science and technology entrepreneurship for economic development in Africa (SEEDA). *International Journal of Scientific and Engineering Research*, *5*(3), 921–927.

Bygrave, W., & Hunt, S. (2004). *Global entrepreneurship monitor: 2004 financing report*. Babson College and London Business School.

Chijoriga, M. M. (2003). *Report on the assessment of feasibility of a women business incubator*. United Republic of Tanzania, Ministry of Community Development, Gender and Children. https://www.empowerwomen.org/en/resources/documents/2015/1/report-on-the-assessment-of-feasibility-of-a-women-business-incubator?lang=en

Collste, D. (2021). *The Indivisible 2030 Agenda: Systems analysis for sustainability*. Doctoral dissertation, Stockholm Resilience Centre, Stockholm University.

Fatma, E. B., Mohamed, E. B., Dana, L. P., et al. (2021). Does entrepreneurs' psychology affect their business venture success? Empirical findings from North Africa. *International Entrepreneurship and Management Journal*, *17*, 921–962. https://doi.org/10.1007/s11365-020-00644-3

Gaynor, J., Mackiewicz, A., & Ramaswami, R. (2009). *Entrepreneurship and innovation: The leys to global economic recovery*. Ernst & Yang.

Geda, A., & Yimer, A. (2019). *The trade effects of the African Continental Free Trade Area (AfCFTA): An empirical analysis*. Addis Ababa University, Department of Economics.

George, G., Corbishley, C., Khayesi, J. N., Haas, M. R., & Tihanyi, L. (2016). Bringing Africa in: Promising directions for management research. *Academy of Management Journal, 59*(2), 377–393. https://doi.org/10.5465/amj.2016.4002

Guéneau, G., Chabaud, D., & Sauvannet, M. C. C. (2022). Opening entrepreneurial ecosystem's black box: The power of networks in African low-income countries. *International Entrepreneurship and Management Journal, 18*, 753–772. https://doi.org/10.1007/s11365-021-00775-1

Hager, M. A., Galaskiewicz, J., & Larson, J. A. (2004). Structural embeddedness and the liability of newness among nonprofit organizations. *Public Management Review, 6*(2), 159–188. https://doi.org/10.1080/1471903042000189083

Hagin, C., & Caesar, L. D. (2021). The antecedents of success among small- and medium-sized enterprises: evidence from Ghana. *Journal of Global Entrepreneurship Research, 11*, 279–297. https://doi.org/10.1007/s40497-021-00285-y

Hajikhani, A. (2020). Impact of Entrepreneurial Ecosystem Discussions in Smart Cities: Comprehensive Assessment of Social Media Data. *Smart Cities, 3*(1), 112–137. https://doi.org/10.3390/smartcities3010007

Halabisky, D. (2018). *Policy brief on women's entrepreneurship*. OECD Publishing.

Hammond, D. R. (2013). China's Response to Urban Poverty. *Policy Study Journal, 41*, 119–146. https://doi.org/10.1111/psj.12005

International Monetary Fund (IMF). (2021, April). Regional Economic Outlook - Sub-Saharan Africa: Navigating a Long Pandemic. https://www.imf.org/en/Publications/REO/SSA/Issues/2021/04/15/regional-economic-outlook-for-sub-saharan-africa-april-2021

Jeon, S. (2018). What influences entrepreneurial intentions? An empirical study using data from the global entrepreneurship monitor. *Academy of Entrepreneurship Journal, 24*(3), 1–15.

Kamoche, K., Siebers, L. Q., Mamman, A., & Newenham-Kahindi, A. (2015). The dynamics of managing people in the diverse cultural and institutional context of Africa. *Personnel Review, 44*(3), 330–345. https://doi.org/10.1108/PR-01-2015-0002

Kamuri, S. (2022). Understanding entrepreneurial vision for growth, innovation and performance in Kenya's leather industry. *Journal of Global Entrepreneurship Research, 12*, 119–130. https://doi.org/10.1007/s40497-022-00308-2

Kapinga, A. F., Suero Montero, C., Mwandosya, G. I., et al. (2018). Exploring the contribution of business and technology incubators to women entrepreneurs' business development in Dar es Salaam, Tanzania. *Journal of Global Entrepreneurship Research, 8*, 23. https://doi.org/10.1186/s40497-018-0111-9

Khanna, T., & Palepu, K. (1997). Why focused strategies may be wrong for emerging markets. *Harvard business review, 75*(4), 41–51.

Kiggundu, M. M. (1989). Managing organizations in developing countries. Boulder: Kumarian Press.

Kimambo, C. Z. (2005). Stimulating small and medium enterprises development for poverty reduction through business and technology incubation. In *Proceeding of the discourse on engineering contribution in poverty reduction* (pp. 109–124). University of Dar es Salaam Research Repository. http://repository.businessinsightz.org/bitstream/handle/20.500.12018/3010/Stimulating%20Small%20and%20Medium%20Enterprises%20 Development%20for%20Poverty%20Reduction%20through%20 Business%20and%20Technology%20Incubation.pdf?sequence=1 &isAllowed=y

Kolk, A., & Rivera-Santos, M. (2018). The state of research on Africa in business and management: Insights from a systematic review of key international journals. *Business & Society, 57*(3), 415–436. https://doi.org/10.1177/0007650316629129

Kreft, S. F., & Sobel, R. S. (2005). Public policy, entrepreneurship, and economic freedom. *Cato Journal, 25*, 595.

Lim, D. S., Oh, C. H., & De Clercq, D. (2016). Engagement in entrepreneurship in emerging economies: Interactive effects of individual-level factors and institutional conditions. *International Business Review, 25*(4), 933–945. https://doi.org/10.1016/j.ibusrev.2015.12.001

Marlow, S., & McAdam, M. (2015). Incubation or induction? Gendered identity work in the context of technology business incubation. *Journal of Entrepreneurship Theory and Practice, 39*(4), 791–816. https://doi.org/10.1111/etap.12062

Mbembe, A. (2017). Africa in theory. In B. Goldstone & J. Obarrio (Eds.), *African futures: Essays on crisis, emergence, and possibility* (Chicago, IL, 2017; Online ed., Chicago Scholarship Online, 21 September 2017). https://doi.org/10.7208/chicago/9780226402413.003.0015

Muldoon, J., Bauman, A., & Lucy, C. (2018). Entrepreneurial ecosystem: Do you trust or distrust? *Journal of Enterprising Communities: People and Places in the Global Economy, 12*(2), 158–177.

Munene, J. C. (1991). Organizational environment in Africa: A factor analysis of critical incidents. *Human Relations, 44*(5), 439–458. https://doi.org/10.1177/001872679104400502

Nachum, L., Stevens, C., Newenham-Kahindi, A., Lundan, S., Rose, E., & Wantchekon, L. (2022). Africa rising: Opportunities for advancing theory on people, institutions, and the nation state in international business. *Journal of International Business Studies 54*, 938–955. https://doi.org/10.1057/s41267-022-00581-z

Ndabeni, L. L. (2008). The contribution of business incubators and technology stations to small Enterprise development in South Africa. *Development Southern Africa, 25*(3), 258–268. https://doi.org/10.1080/03768350802212022

Ndzendze, B., & Monyae, D. (2019). China's belt and road initiative: linkages with the African Union's Agenda 2063 in historical perspective. *Transnational Corporations Review, 11*(1), 38–49, https://doi.org/10.1080/19186444.2019.1578160

Njiraini, P., Gachanja, P., & Omolo, J. (2018). Factors influencing micro and small enterprise's decision to innovate in Kenya. *Journal of Global Entrepreneurship Research, 8*, 34. https://doi.org/10.1186/s40497-018-0132-4

Nxopo, Z., & Iwu, C. G. (2015). The unique obstacles of female entrepreneurship in the tourism industry in Western Cape, South Africa. *Commonwealth Youth and Development, 13*(2), 55–71. https://doi.org/10.25159/1727-7140/1146

Ogundana, O., Simba, A., Dana, L-P., & Liguori, E. (2022). A growth model for understanding female-owned enterprises. *Journal of the International Council for Small Business*, https://doi.org/10.1080/26437015.2022.2100296

Ojong, N., Simba, A., & Dana, L. (2021). Female entrepreneurship in Africa: A review, trends, and future research directions. *Journal of Business Research, 132*, 233–248. https://doi.org/10.1016/j.jbusres.2021.04.032

Okunade, E. O. (2007). Influence of Leadership on Women Activities in Women-based Rural Development in Osun State. *Research Journal of Social Sciences, 2*, 22–24.

Oliyide, O. (2012). Law, credit risk management and Bank lending to SMEs in Nigeria. *Commonwealth Law Bulletin, 38*(4), 673–695. https://doi.org/10.1080/03050718.2012.707350

Oluwatayo, I. B., & Babalola, M. A. (2020). Asset ownership and income as drivers of household poverty in South Africa. *The Journal of Developing Areas, 54*(3).

Ondiba, H. A., & Matsui, K. (2019). Social attributes and factors influencing entrepreneurial behaviors among rural women in Kakamega County, Kenya. *Journal of Global Entrepreneurship Research, 9*, 2. https://doi.org/10.1186/s40497-018-0123-5

Ordeñana, X., Vera-Gilces, P., Zambrano-Vera, J., & Amaya, A. (2020). "Does all entrepreneurship matter? The contribution of entrepreneurial activity to economic growth". *Academia Revista Latinoamericana de Administración, 33*(1), 25–48. https://doi.org/10.1108/ARLA-11-2018-0256

Pasara, M. T. (2020). An overview of the obstacles to the African economic integration process in view of the African continental free trade area. *Africa Review, 12*(1), 1–17.

Scott, J. M., Sinha, P., Gibb, J., & Akoorie, M. (2020). "Introduction to the Research Handbook on Entrepreneurship in Emerging Economies," in: Paresha Sinha, Jenny Gibb, MichÂ"le Akoorie, & Jonathan M. Scott (eds.), Research Handbook on Entrepreneurship in Emerging Economies, Chapter 1, pages 1–25, Edward Elgar Publishing.

Shahzad, K., Bajwa, S. U., & Ali, Q. (2012). Role of incubation in women entrepreneurship development in Pakistan. *Asian Journal of Business Management, 200–208*. https://doi.org/10.2139/ssrn.2048316

Siba, E. (2019). Empowering women entrepreneurs in developing countries: Why current programs fall short. Available at: https://www.brookings.edu/wp-content/uploads/2019/02/Empowering-women-entreprenuers-in-developing-countries-190215.pdf

Simba, A., Tajeddin, M., Dana, L. P. et al. (2023). Deconstructing involuntary financial exclusion: a focus on African SMEs. *Small Bus Econ*. https://doi.org/10.1007/s11187-023-00767-1

Stinchcombe, A. L. (1965). Social Structure and Organizations. In *The Handbook of Organizations*, James G. March (Ed.). Chicago: Rand McNally & Co.

Tundui, C. S., & Shiganza, C. (2021). Determinants of entrepreneurial behaviour in the public sector in Tanzania: A case of water services provision. *Journal of Global Entrepreneurship Research, 11*, 189–199. https://doi.org/10.1007/s40497-021-00266-1

Vaidya, H., & Chatterji, T. (2020). SDG 11 sustainable cities and communities. In *Actioning the global goals for local impact* (pp. 173–185). Springer.

Welter, F. (2011). Contextualizing Entrepreneurship—Conceptual Challenges and Ways Forward. *Entrepreneurship Theory and Practice, 35*(1), 165–184. https://doi.org/10.1111/j.1540-6520.2010.00427.x

Welter, F., Gartner, W. B., & Wright, M. (2016). "The context of contextualizing contexts", In a Research Agenda for Entrepreneurship and Context, Edward Elgar Publishing.

Wiklund, J., Patzelt, H., & Shepherd, D. A. (2009). Building an integrative model of small business growth. *Small business economics, 32*, 351–374.

Willis, K. (2018). The sustainable development goals. In *The Routledge handbook of Latin American development* (pp. 121–131). Routledge.

Witt, M. A. (2019). De-globalization: Theories, predictions, and opportunities for international business research. *Journal of International Business Studies, 50*, 1053–1077. https://doi.org/10.1057/s41267-019-00219-7

World Bank. (2013). Ghana Enterprise Survey 2013, Available at: https://microdata.worldbank.org/index.php/catalog/2181/pdf-documentation

Wu, J., & Si, S. (2018). Poverty reduction through entrepreneurship: Incentives, social networks, and sustainability. *Asian Business & Management, 17*(4), 243–259.

Index

A

Academic curriculum, 12, 30, 31, 33–36, 39, 42, 44
Academic discourse, 81, 98, 128
Academic research, 108
Accelerators, 6, 100
Achievement attributes, 20
African-centered, 5
African social entrepreneur ecosystem, 113
African Society Entrepreneurs Network (ASEN), 114
African Union (AU), 8–10, 200, 210–212
Agenda 2063, 8–10, 210
Artificial Intelligence (AI), 155, 157, 158, 162–163
Autocorrelation, 34, 36, 37, 39–41

B

Base of the Pyramid (BOP), 79
BDA phenomenon, 160
Big data analytics (BDA), 160–162, 169
Bitcoin, 164
Blockchain, 155, 164
Blockchain technology, 158, 164–165, 169
Boundaries, 22, 56, 78, 114, 183, 200
Business, 3, 6, 8, 10, 12, 13, 21, 24–26, 28, 33, 37, 41, 53–68, 76, 78–87, 89–99, 107, 109–112, 115, 120, 125, 126, 128–131, 135, 136, 139, 140, 150, 151, 153–156, 158, 160–163, 165, 179–191, 197, 199–208, 210, 211, 213–215

Index

Business growth, 7, 8, 10, 11, 80–81, 84, 87, 95–97, 99, 100, 126
Business objective, 94, 161
Business sectors, 63, 80, 113
Business start-up, 10–12
Business-To-Business (B2B), 57, 181
Business-To-Customer (B2C), 57, 165, 181

C

Capital, 6, 9, 20, 24, 28, 29, 42, 55, 84, 93, 100, 109, 113, 131, 141, 153–155, 169, 187, 200–202, 204, 205, 207, 208, 210–212
Career path, 29
Catalyst, 4, 13, 107, 130
Categorization, 181, 182
Centralized, 9
Clean Team, 116
Coding errors, 32
Colonialism-centred economic, 112
Commercialisation, 149–170, 214
Competitiveness, 109, 132, 180, 183, 206
Computer vision (CV), 163
Continuity, 10, 11
Corruption, 9, 112, 185
Credibility, 13, 133–136, 140, 151, 204
Critical Success Factors, 81–82, 99, 101
Cronbach's alpha, 32, 33
Cross-sectional survey, 29, 209
Culture natural resources, 9

Customer-centric, 12
Customer misunderstandings, 81
Customer-To-Customer (C2C), 181

D

Data collection, 31–32, 84, 163, 185
Decentralization, 215
Descriptive statistics, 32, 34
Digital, 149, 151, 152, 154, 155, 159, 162, 165–167, 179–183, 185–191, 215
Digitalization, 179, 180
Digital platforms, 13, 165, 179–191
Diversification, 12, 94–96, 98–101, 210
Domestic, 7, 57, 76, 198, 213

E

E-business, 183, 184
E-commerce, 182–184, 188
Economic, 4, 5, 7, 20–22, 24–27, 30–31, 33, 55, 76–79, 81, 84, 101, 110, 112, 113, 115, 117, 131, 150, 151, 153, 182, 197, 199, 200, 205, 208, 210–214
Economic development, 4, 5, 21, 22, 57, 76, 80, 153, 180, 183, 212, 214
Economic growth, 4–6, 8–12, 14, 21, 54, 57, 115, 197, 199, 202, 205, 211, 212, 214, 215
Economic institutions, 9, 210
Economic sectors, 94
Ecosystems, 114, 151, 153, 154, 159, 165, 179, 208

Education, 9, 11, 19, 24, 26, 80, 83, 84, 112, 113, 115–119, 166, 191, 202, 206–209
Educational curriculum, 20, 25, 26
Employee pilfering, 81
Employment, 21, 41, 54, 80, 82, 84, 86, 117, 199, 206
Engine, 4, 22, 54, 55
Entrepreneurial ecosystems (EE), 13, 152–154, 168, 169, 200–202
Entrepreneurial inclination, 12, 19–42
Entrepreneurs' growth, 94, 100
Entrepreneurship, 3–8, 10–14, 19–45, 78, 85, 86, 107–120, 125, 152, 153, 155, 182, 197–209, 211–215
Entrepreneurship Development in Higher Education (EDHE), 150
Environmental, 7, 11, 20, 27, 83, 108, 114, 115, 168
Environmental changes, 83
Environmental values, 115
Equity, 9, 117
Excellent customer service, 53, 58, 60, 61, 63, 64, 66–68, 81, 99
Expansion, 12, 87, 94, 95, 98, 99, 101, 162, 185
Explanatory research design, 29

Facebook, 64, 90, 161, 182, 187
Family capital, 28, 29
Family influence, 31

Finance, 7, 9, 23, 62, 80, 81, 99, 113, 129, 152, 153, 184, 190, 201, 204–207, 215
Financial incentives, 100
Financial returns, 109, 118
Financial support, 12, 94, 96, 98, 101, 134–135, 206, 208, 209
Forward-looking approach, 87
Fourth Industrial Revolution (4IR), 13, 149–170, 215

Geographical distance, 12, 33
Geographical location, 20, 25, 30, 31, 36–37, 39, 42, 44
Geopolitical position, 9
Gilbert's law, 99
Global Entrepreneurship Monitor (GEM), 214
Global Entrepreneurship Report, 20
Globalised, 200, 208
Globalization, 9, 130
Green sustainability management, 82
Gross Domestic Product (GDP), 54, 79, 82, 114, 154, 210

Head-Up Displays (HUDs), 167
Higher Education Research Development in the Central Region (HERDIC), 150
High tech start-ups, 151, 156
History, 9, 108, 165, 185, 204
Holistic, 11, 37–39, 161
Human activity recognition (HAR), 163

Human well-being and human capital, 115
Hybrid approach, 188

Incentives, 9, 10, 152, 169
Incubators, 6, 76, 153, 167, 206, 207
Industrialisation, 199, 210
Inequalities and conflicts, 9
Inferential statistics, 32
Informal economy, 12, 75–101
Informal sector, 22, 27, 57, 77–79
Information, 25, 28, 31, 41, 65, 66, 91, 128, 130, 159–162, 164, 179, 181–183, 186, 190, 201, 206
Information technology (IT), 119, 134, 154, 183, 184
INNOVA DDB, 136
Innovation, 4, 5, 9, 10, 13, 23, 62, 63, 76, 80, 99, 118, 151, 152, 157, 158, 160, 162, 163, 166, 167, 180, 182, 200, 202, 207–209, 214
Institution, 9, 19, 24, 27, 28, 30, 54, 78, 96, 128, 150, 157, 167, 185, 198, 201, 203, 204, 210, 212, 214
Inter-American Development Bank Report, 157
International markets, 7, 76, 130
Internet, 55, 61, 90, 151, 154, 155, 158, 183, 184, 188–190, 215
Internet of Things (IoT), 155, 158–160, 169

Investments, 7, 9, 10, 78, 111, 126–128, 134, 135, 141, 200, 214

Job creation, 4, 5, 7, 19, 54, 119, 199, 214
Justice, 9, 81

Labour, 21, 57, 78–81, 83, 99, 131, 154, 197
Leadership skills, 20
Local, 5, 12, 13, 58, 63, 113, 115, 116, 120, 125, 130–133, 136, 139, 150, 152–154, 167, 214
Long-term, 87, 119, 211
Loyal Customer promotion, 89, 93

Managerial, 7, 8, 13, 54, 131, 132, 197–215
Marketing strategy, 59, 80, 81, 87–94, 98, 99, 159
Maslow's love and belongingness needs theory, 27
Mathematically methods, 29
Maza, 116
Means, 11, 19, 30, 32, 33, 44, 65, 66, 86, 90, 96, 110, 112, 127, 128, 132, 140, 141, 163, 182, 184, 199, 206
Micro businesses, 56, 187–190, 205
Migration, 23, 27

Millennium Development
    Goal, 6, 10
Mpedigree, 118
Multi-collinearity, 34, 36, 37, 39–41
Multiple regression, 32, 37, 41

N

Neoliberal perspective, 78
Networking, 28, 160, 201, 202
Networks, 21, 23, 28, 109, 116,
    128, 132, 135, 137, 151,
    153–155, 157, 158, 160, 181,
    182, 190, 201, 204, 209, 212
Norms, 21, 23, 63, 77, 198, 199
N-Power program, 7, 203

O

Omissions, 32
Online exchange, 179
Online marketing, 90
Operationalization, 77, 78
Organisational, 59, 152, 167, 201,
    205, 213

P

Parental influence, 39, 41
Parental views, 33
Parents influence, 30, 31, 42
Parent views, 12, 20, 29
Peer association, 12, 27, 28, 30, 31,
    33, 39–41
Peer networks, 113
Platform, 5, 13, 63, 64, 66, 90, 94,
    158, 160, 179–191
Playpump, 113

Ploughing back profit, 12
Policy, 4, 6, 7, 11, 13, 56, 81, 83,
    99, 100, 153, 154,
    185, 197–215
Political, 6, 7, 9, 79, 112, 130,
    211, 212
Poor governance, 9
Poor health care, 112
Predictors, 8, 21, 24, 34, 36,
    37, 39–42
Private, 11, 24, 45, 109
Private sector, 19, 54, 78, 114,
    199, 205
Promotion of gender equity, 117
Prosperity, 9
Public, 9, 11, 12, 19, 24, 42, 44, 45,
    99, 100, 108, 115, 116,
    184, 214
Public goods, 112
Public-private partnership, 120
Public sector, 78, 209

Q

Q-Drum inventions, 113
Quality brand, 89

R

Rapid urbanization, 27
Referrals, 89, 91, 98, 101
Regression analysis, 32, 33, 37
Researchers, 20, 22, 29–32, 60, 86,
    87, 126, 130, 132, 133, 185,
    186, 201, 214
Resource, 3, 4, 7, 9, 12, 13, 22, 23,
    26, 28, 44, 57, 58, 62, 80, 97,
    100, 108–110, 112, 113, 115,

118, 120, 126–141, 151–157, 161, 163, 169, 182, 198, 200–205, 207, 211, 212
Risk-taking attitude, 20
R-square, 40

S
Savings, 9
Science, 9, 150, 161, 162
Security issues, 81, 91
Self-efficacy, 23, 26
Skilled human resources, 81, 99
Small and Medium Enterprises Development Agency (SMEDAN), 7, 203
Small Medium Enterprise (SMEs), 12, 13, 28, 55, 56, 64, 68, 179–191, 199–201, 203–205, 207, 209
Small, micro and medium enterprises (SMMEs), 157
Smartphone, 65, 66, 162, 166, 187
Social, 5, 20, 77, 107, 126, 154, 198
Social attitudes, 23
Social capital, 28, 126–128, 138, 140, 141, 208, 212
Social capital theory, 28, 126–128
Social change, 107
Social Enterprise Academy Africa (SEAA), 114
Social entrepreneurs (SE), 108–115, 117, 119, 120
Social entrepreneurship, 107–120
Social factors, 20, 27, 31, 33
Social forces, 23
Socialized perspective, 22

Social media, 13, 66, 90, 98, 187, 189, 190
Social mission, 109, 110
Sociological perspective, 21–23
Sociological perspective entrepreneurship, 23
Sociological variables, 23
Soronko Solutions, 118, 119
Standard deviations, 32, 33
Standards of living and wellbeing, 9
Startup, 10, 11
Students Records and Management Information Section (SRMIS), 30
Sub-Saharan Africa, 21, 75–101, 112–114
Surveys, 29, 30, 32, 33, 209
Sustainability, 6, 11, 12, 62, 64, 82, 118, 202, 206, 212
Sustainable Development Goals (SDGs), 6, 10–11, 13–14, 210–212

T
Task performance attitude, 20
Teaching agendas, 108
Technology, 5, 13, 56, 63, 80, 81, 115, 132, 149–170, 179, 180, 182–184, 190, 202, 207, 215
Technology and innovation, 9, 214
Technology social venture (TSV), 118–119
Theory of Critical Success Factors, 81–82
Theory of Planned Behaviour (TPB), 21, 23–24

Index

Tonaton, 90
Traditional, 11, 63, 90, 109, 113, 118, 164, 183, 201, 208
Traditional marketing, 66, 94
Traditional methods, 109
Transformation, 8, 9, 150, 155, 156, 179, 180, 199, 210, 212, 214, 215
Transmitted, 28

V

Values, 3, 21, 23, 32, 33, 40, 55, 56, 62, 63, 67, 76, 110, 113, 115, 131, 149, 153, 156, 161, 164, 180, 182, 212, 214

Variations, 41, 84, 181
Venture capitalists, 153
VIF scores, 34, 36, 41
VIF values, 37
Virtual and augmented reality (VR/AR), 155, 165–167
Virtual reality (VR), 165, 166, 169

W

Word-of-mouth, 91

Y

You-Win programme, 7, 203